UNDER-STANDING AUSTEN

KEY CONCEPTS IN THE SIX NOVELS

MAGGIE LANE

ROBERT HALE · LONDON

ISBN 978-0-7090-9078-6

Robert Hale Limited
Clerkenwell House
Clerkenwell Green
London EC1R 0HT

www.halebooks.com

A catalogue record for this book is available from the British Library

2 4 6 8 10 9 7 5 3 1

Typeset by e-type, Liverpool
Printed in Great Britain by the MPG Books Group,
Bodmin and King's Lynn

To my husband, John, who has waited
a long time for this

Contents

Introduction

WHEN, AS A child, Jane Austen wrote her spoof *History of England* to amuse her family, having insisted on the title page that it was by 'a partial, prejudiced and ignorant historian', she added, 'N.B. There will be very few dates in this work.' As a mature writer, she might with equal truth have promised that there would be very few concrete terms in her novels. Descriptions of clothes, faces, meals, houses and journeys are scanty. The few such details that she does vouchsafe are endowed consequently with a huge significance, and are pored over and committed to memory by her avid readership. The world seems full of people who can tell you exactly what Henry Crawford and William Price ate for breakfast on the day of their journey to London, or which heroine's best gown was white with glossy spots. (In fact *Mastermind* soon learnt to forbid the life and work of Jane Austen as a specialist subject, too many potential contenders being too well versed in its minutiae.)

Unlike her contemporary Walter Scott or the great Victorian novelists like Dickens and George Eliot, Jane Austen does not attempt to conjure up a visual world, leaving most of that to our own imagination (or to the filmmakers who would recreate it so beguilingly). But this minimalistic approach betrays no failure of imagination on Jane Austen's part. Her creed was consistent from youth to maturity. In a letter of 9 September 1814, at the height of her own success, she advised her niece Anna, who was attempting to write a novel and had sent the opening chapters for criticism, 'You describe a sweet place, but your descriptions are often more minute than will be liked. You give too many particulars of right hand & left'.

Reliance on a vocabulary of abstract nouns and their related adjectives was her preferred mode, and it served her well. Her subject is the relationships between men and women, and their struggles to identify and live a good life. Physical details are largely superfluous to this purpose, but the finer points of character and behaviour require a generally accepted lexicon of moral and humane values. As a consequence her stories have a timeless quality, while yet being rooted in a very specific and long-since disappeared society – a curious paradox, and part of her unique magic. While other novelists of the eighteenth and nineteenth centuries may seem longwinded to the modern mind, their treasures having to be hunted down among the verbiage, Jane Austen's sentences spring as freshly and succinctly off the page for us as they did for their first delighted readers. That is why she appeals to a general readership as much as to an academic one; the pleasures of reading Jane Austen and the levels on which she may be read and reread are inexhaustible.

Nevertheless, there is a danger, as years pass and manners and morals subtly change, of our losing both the certainties and the nuances she conveyed to her own generation and those which followed. There has, perhaps, been a greater change in mindset in the last fifty years than in the one hundred and fifty years preceding. The purpose of the present study is to illuminate Jane Austen's meaning when the passage of time might have partially obscured it and to demonstrate the spectrum of values she attaches to important abstract nouns. Her philosophy and deepest-held convictions are embedded in this group of words and we get most out of her books if we grasp their full meaning. For all her lightness of touch, Jane Austen is a didactic writer, setting out not only to entertain but to show in action and recommend the values she had absorbed from the Christian tradition and from the Enlightenment. More than anything, she is concerned with balance – the balance between reason and feeling; the balance between excess and insufficiency. 'Like all other qualities of the mind, it should have its proportions and limits', reflects Anne Elliot, thinking in this instance of firmness of character.

Each chapter of the present book focuses on a specific concept or group of related concepts, quoting liberally across the range of the six novels. These concepts are the colours on her palette, the threads in her workbasket, out of which each one of her novels is fashioned, and the same important words recur again and again. In deciding which of the many possible quotations to use, my aim has been to select not only those which pin down the meaning of the term with precision, or ally it with other words which reflect helpfully back upon it, but those which best illustrate Jane Austen's awareness of the subtlety or contradictions inherent in the concept.

The juvenilia, unfinished fragments and letters have not been quarried for examples, partly because the result would have been unwieldy, and partly because their different tone of voice might confuse the discussion. And I have always tried to keep in mind the dire example of Mr Collins, who in showing the view from his humble abode, points out every feature 'with a minuteness which left beauty entirely behind'. It is hoped that a secondary pleasure of reading (as indeed of writing) the present work is the chance to revisit familiar passages in a different context and in revealing juxtapositions. All Jane Austen's admirers must lament that there are only six novels; but by dwelling among the actual words she wrote, encountering them afresh, we can extend our enjoyment and return to her novels with enhanced admiration for the perceptiveness, humour and economy of her prose.

This book is aimed at the general reader, albeit one familiar with the novels, and its methods have been adopted for ease of reading. In a work so full of quotations it seems desirable to avoid the ugliness of multiple quotation marks, so all phrases containing the terms under examination are printed in a different typeface to the main text, with only characters' speech retaining quotation marks. All other quotations have the conventional marks. Similarly, page references for every quotation would litter the page and spoil the reader's enjoyment, so sufficient context has been given to make each one intelligible, but the easiest way for those who wish to check further is to use the wordsearch facility of an electronic concordance to Jane Austen's novels, which may easily be found online. In the few instances where other writers' work is alluded to, these can be traced under the word concerned in the Oxford English Dictionary, which has been used to provide the history and earliest literary usages of each term.

There are now two scholarly editions of Jane Austen's work, published respectively by Oxford and Cambridge University Presses – the former in the twentieth century and the latter in the first decade of the present century, both equally useful when a definitive text, and full notes, are required. Each includes a short but highly pertinent introduction to Jane Austen's English usage. Full details are given in the Bibliography.

Although many, if not most, of Jane Austen's critics touch on the beauties and idiosyncrasies of her language, only three, to my knowledge, make this their main focus, and two of these were written some forty years ago. *Jane Austen's English* by K.C. Phillipps (Andre Deutsch, 1970) ranges across vocabulary, sentence structure and modes of address. *Some Words of Jane Austen* by Stuart M. Tave (University of Chicago Press, 1973) takes each heroine and examines the particular words which define her virtues and her mistakes. *The Language of Jane Austen* by Myra Stokes (Macmillan, 1991) adopts a linguistic approach to the terms used by the novelist, dividing them into the four areas on which characters are judged: manners, spirits, head and heart. All three books are illuminating, but it seemed to me that it was time for a new study, one which looks in greater depth at a limited number of essential concepts key to Jane Austen's world view.

'We must not be nice, and ask for all the virtues into the bargain,' says one of Jane Austen's most articulate heroines, Emma Woodhouse – using the word *nice* in its correct sense of choosy, or fastidious. But 'all the virtues' are precisely what Jane Austen is concerned to identify, illustrate, dissect and promulgate in her dramas of domestic and social interaction. Like the Bible, she teaches by telling stories, by breathing life into erring and striving characters whose struggles and achievements have resonance for us today. In a less homogenous age, we may envy or we may deplore the very idea of an agreed set of rules, but it is certain that if they had not been there for her to draw upon, or had she found herself essentially at variance with those to which she was expected to subscribe, her novels would be very different – or would not have been written at all.

Jane Austen's was an age of abstract nouns. We need only look at her gravestone in Winchester Cathedral, the inscription of which is thought to have been composed by her brother Henry, to register their preponderance:

In Memory of
JANE AUSTEN
youngest daughter of the late
Revd GEORGE AUSTEN,
formerly Rector of Steventon in this County
she departed this Life on the 18th of July 1817,
aged 41, after a long illness supported with
the patience and the hopes of a Christian.

The benevolence of her heart,
the sweetness of her temper, and
the extraordinary endowments of her mind
obtained the regard of all who knew her, and
the warmest love of her intimate connections.

Their grief is in proportion to their affection
they know their loss to be irreparable,
but in their deepest affliction they are consoled
by a firm though humble hope that her charity,
devotion, faith and purity, have rendered
her soul acceptable in the sight of her
REDEEMER.

1

Genius, Wit and Taste

I N HER FAMOUS defence of the novel in Chapter Five of *Northanger Abbey*, Jane Austen suggests that many readers, trying to appear highbrow, are guilty of **undervaluing the labour of the novelist, and of slighting the performances which have only genius, wit and taste to recommend them.**

This is a generous assessment on her part. The novels which occupy the leisure hours of Catherine Morland and Isabella Thorpe do not seem to have much of *genius, wit* or *taste* about them to us today; the passage of time has rendered them almost unreadable, except out of curiosity. It is Jane Austen's own novels, of course, which are so gloriously endowed with these qualities. They are what help to make her novels so 'light and bright and sparkling' for all time.

Genius, wit and *taste* are attributes which she undoubtedly possessed herself, as a person, and which the most delightful characters of her imagination display. Elizabeth Bennet, Emma Woodhouse and Henry Tilney – even Mary Crawford – bewitch us by the intelligence and playfulness of their mental processes. However, as with even the most attractive quality, there are inherent dangers: in particular, wit may turn to cruelty, taste may be used snobbishly to put down others. In so many of her plots, Jane Austen teaches that the lucky possessors of these gifts must use them generously in their social interactions.

Of the three words, *genius* is the most problematic for the modern reader. The word originally meant the predominant characteristic of a person, place or age. Marianne Dashwood uses it in this sense when she enquires of the bemused Sir John Middleton about the exciting new acquaintance Willoughby, '**What are his pursuits, his talents and genius?**' Today we use the term genius almost exclusively to denote someone with inborn ability and creativity of the highest order. In Jane Austen's time, too, it sometimes carries this more exalted meaning, although in her novels only negatively when Sir Thomas Bertram is aware that **he must not expect a genius in Mr Rushworth** or mockingly when Henry Tilney pretends to quote from Catherine's journal entry about himself: '**seems a most extraordinary genius**'.

Genius is much more often used as an abstract noun than a personal one by Jane Austen. Sometimes it is virtually a synonym for cleverness. The young Fanny Price, at first slow in her lessons, '**shows a great want of genius and emulation**' according to her Aunt Norris. Modest Edward Ferrars, resisting his mother's ambition for him to cut a fine figure in the world, claims '**I cannot be forced into genius and eloquence.**' The very different hero Frederick Wentworth has plenty of ambition and confidence in his own abilities. As Anne discovers from the navy lists in the years after she has broken off her engagement, **his genius and ardour had seemed to foresee and to command his prosperous path.**

Flair and aptitude – real or imaginary – are often all that is meant by *genius*. Mr Knightley says drily, '**I do not pretend to Emma's genius for foretelling and guessing.**' He is being sarcastic of course, as foretelling and guessing are hardly skills of much worth. Neither is knowing a thing or two about muslins, but when Mrs Allen hears Henry Tilney pronounce on the subject she is **quite struck by his genius.** Jane Austen's comedy includes using a grandiose word for a banal subject.

On other occasions the connection to the word ingenuity is apparent, as when Catherine Morland, visiting her future home, sees among its attractions **a meadow on which Henry's genius had begun to act.** Similarly General Tilney shows off the kitchen arrangements at Northanger masterminded by himself: **when the genius of others had failed, his own had often produced the perfection wanted.**

This association with improvements of landscape or buildings brings to mind that other Henry, Henry Crawford of *Mansfield Park*. As his sister Mary says, looking back on the visit to Sotherton, '**Only think what grand things were produced there by our all going with him one hot day in August to drive about the grounds, and see his genius take fire!**' Of course she is alluding to Henry's flirting skills as much as his flair for garden design. Mary herself is acknowledged by Edmund to have **the mind of genius** when he excuses her eagerness to act. Though he deprecates the rage for theatricals sweeping through Mansfield, he understands that a woman of superior abilities like Mary might be forgiven for welcoming the opportunity to try her powers in something new.

The two heroines with the highest opinion of themselves, Emma Woodhouse and Elizabeth Bennet, both use the word *genius* of themselves, albeit in moments of self-reproach. Emma, meditating on her faults and comparing herself to others around her, is **really for the time convinced that Harriet was the superior creature of the two – and that to resemble her would be more for her own welfare and happiness than all that genius or intelligence could do.** Elizabeth, castigating herself for her prejudice against Darcy, tells Jane, '**And yet I meant to be uncommonly clever in taking so decided a dislike to him, without any reason. It is such a spur to one's genius, such an opening for wit to have a dislike of that kind.**'

Elizabeth Bennet must be the wittiest heroine not only in Jane Austen but in all English literature, with the possible exception of Shakespeare's Beatrice. Readers delight in Elizabeth's spirited repartee, and her creator was moved to call her 'the most delightful creature ever to appear in print'. Oddly, the only character in the novel itself to use the word *wit* in connection with Elizabeth is Mr Collins. Dense as he is, it has not escaped him that Elizabeth is livelier and funnier than most women. This is not what he wants in a wife, but he barges ahead with his proposal of marriage, confident that his patroness Lady Catherine will do his work for him and repress Elizabeth's personality: '**your wit and vivacity I think must be acceptable to her, especially when tempered with the silence and respect which her rank will inevitably excite**'.

It is notable that at no point during his own growing admiration for Elizabeth does Mr Darcy call her verbal dexterity by the name of *wit*, won over as he quickly is by that 'mixture of sweetness and archness in her manner which made it difficult for her to affront anybody'. In this sentence – one of the few in which the narrative does not proceed through Elizabeth's eyes – Jane Austen takes care to assure her readers that her heroine, for all her freedom of speech, is in no danger of turning into a termagant. In creating Elizabeth, Jane Austen was aware that in her society the quality of wit, in a woman, may be a little suspect, if not sweetened by natural charm. (The clergyman Dr John Gregory, in his popular conduct book *A Father's Legacy to his Daughters* of 1774 warns young women: 'Wit is the most dangerous talent you can possess. It must be guarded with great discretion and good nature, otherwise it will create you many enemies.') So when Elizabeth refers to her past behaviour to Darcy as 'impudence', he softens it into 'the liveliness of your mind'. Not that all contemporary readers were convinced: the writer Mary Russell Mitford in a letter of 1814 deplored 'so pert, so worldly a heroine as the beloved of such a man as Darcy'.

Elizabeth might be unjust to Darcy in the early stages of their acquaintance, but she never sets out to wound him or anybody else by her wit, only to defend herself against those who, like Bingley's sisters, Mr Collins and Lady Catherine de Bourgh – sometimes even her own mother – would, in their various ways, like to crush the spirit out of her. Wit for Elizabeth is both a defence mechanism against the pressures of her society and a means of attracting those who know how to value intelligence and true feeling above social status and money.

The character in *Pride and Prejudice* who does misuse his wit is the person from whom Elizabeth has inherited hers – her father. He may have the best lines in the book (with power to make us laugh every time we read them), but he is not the best person. Guilty of many a put-down to his wife and daughters, he is an object lesson to Elizabeth in the dangers of using her verbal skills cruelly. Elizabeth has long acknowledged the impropriety of her father's attitude, even while sharing his tendency to laugh at the follies of others; but when he mocks the man she loves, unaware of the great change in Darcy, she feels what it is like to be hurt by his words: **never had his wit been directed in a manner so little agreeable to her.**

Another male character whose wit occasionally gets the better of him is Henry Tilney, whose sister sometimes has to remonstrate with him for appearing rude. There is no malice in Henry, but his mind cannot help delighting in its own superiority. Even Catherine, doting on him as she does, and not understanding half he says, suspects that he allows himself too much liberty in teasing other people. Is there a danger that their marriage will resemble the Bennets', with one partner much quicker and cleverer than the other? Probably not, as Henry has more reason to respect Catherine's native intelligence than Mr Bennet does *his* wife's; but in both Mr Bennet and Henry Tilney, Jane Austen shows that men as well as women must learn to curb their tongues for the sake of other people's feelings. (It is a lesson that she probably felt she needed regular reminders of herself; certainly she asked for help in being tolerant of other people's shortcomings in two prayers she composed.)

Emma Woodhouse is in a different social space from Elizabeth, and she does not have Elizabeth's justification for asserting her wit. Superior in wealth and status as well as quickness of mind to almost all around her, Emma's duty is to be gracious and forbearing to all, a duty which is normally no hardship to her. When her playfulness of speech begins to confuse her father, she quickly leaves off. Though provoked by Mr Elton's foolishness during his wedding visit, she remains composed and afterwards **would not permit a hasty or a witty word from herself about his manners.** But on one occasion she cannot resist being amusing at someone else's expense. Her lapse occurs during the hot and bothered picnic at Box Hill, and it takes Mr Knightley to point out the hurtfulness of her witticism: '**How could you be so unfeeling to Miss Bates? How could you be so insolent in your wit to a woman of her character, age and situation? Emma, I had not thought it possible.**'

Earlier in the novel, seeds of confusion are sown by Mr Elton's apparently seeing **ready wit** in Harriet Smith (really in Emma herself), an instance in the novels where *wit* implies not wordplay (though the phrase occurs in a charade) so much as general intelligence and quickness of comprehension. The one meaning often shades into the other. *Emma* is more concerned with puzzles and word games of various sorts than any other Jane Austen novel, the whole plot in fact being a puzzle with clues that readers, like Emma herself, are invited to solve. Befitting a limited society where people have little to occupy their time, this obsession with wordplay culminates at Box Hill, where Mr Weston produces **a very indifferent piece of wit** and Mrs Elton boasts, '**I am not one of those who have witty things to say at everybody's service. I do not pretend to be a wit.**'

As with the false merriment that substitutes for rational conversation at Box Hill, wit can be the meanest form of social currency. Too often its tendency is to impress or oppress others. When Sir Walter Elliot makes a heavy joke, his agent, Mr Shepherd, **laughed, as he knew he must, at this wit.** Miss Bingley's **wit flowed long** on the subject of what a charming mother-in-law Mr Darcy will have in Mrs Bennet – while Darcy listens unmoved. The difference between Caroline Bingley's wit and Elizabeth Bennet's is that the former proceeds from ill-nature and meanness of spirit.

Marianne Dashwood deplores '**any common-place phrase by which wit is intended**' (an open rebuke to Sir John Middleton, who has joked about her 'setting her cap' at Willoughby) and she is equally indignant at his and Mrs Jennings' combined raillery towards Colonel Brandon, protesting '**When is a man to be safe from such wit, if age and infirmity will not protect him?**'

Subsequently **their attention and wit were drawn off to his more fortunate rival.** Willoughby's closeness to Marianne becomes the subject of their unwanted remarks. *Sense and Sensibility* seems to have more of these digs and jibes than any other novel, reflecting the uncongenial society in which the Dashwood sisters have their being. When Robert Ferrars is **recalled from wit to wisdom,** he has been indulging in great hilarity at the idea of his brother as a clergyman, 'reading prayers in a white surplice, and publishing the banns of marriage between John Smith and Mary Brown'. Elinor is forced to listen to this offensive nonsense with only a disapproving look to vent her feelings.

These are all examples of what passes for wit, but are anything but funny or original. Even the wit of a superior mind, however, arouses contrary emotions in different people. For nineteen-year-old Anne Elliot, her suitor's verbal fluency is one of his charms: **such confidence, powerful in its own warmth, and bewitching in the wit which often expressed it** inspires her with trust. But Frederick Wentworth's glib tongue creates only suspicion in Anne's prudent godmother: **Lady Russell had little taste for wit.** Perfectly good people can shy away from wit: Catherine Morland's parents **seldom aimed at wit of any kind.** With so many negative examples, we have to conclude that to Jane Austen herself, for all her sense of fun and delight in cleverness, the possession of wit was sometimes deeply suspect.

Mansfield Park is often seen as the least sparkling of Jane Austen's novels. Much is due to its distrust of wit, and the ultimate rejection of those characters who possess it. Edmund Bertram, the solid hero, has his creator's approval when he claims **'there is not the least wit in my nature',** and Fanny Price, who loves him but is being courted by a very different gentleman, **was not to be won by all that gallantry and wit and good-nature together could do; or, at least, she would not be won by them nearly so soon, without the assistance of sentiment and feeling, and seriousness on serious subjects.** Therein lies the value scheme of the book. In any other Jane Austen novel, a woman with the following attributes would surely be the heroine, or the heroine's true friend: **The harp arrived, and rather added to her beauty, wit, and good-humour; for she played with the greatest obligingness, with an expression and taste which were peculiarly becoming.** But this is Mary Crawford, one of those whose wit – and puns – are to be her downfall.

With Mary Crawford's harp we encounter the third of the words to be examined in this chapter, *taste,* in a musical context, a context in which it is often to be found in Jane Austen. In *Pride and Prejudice,* though Mary Bennet prides herself on her piano-playing, her performance sadly shows **neither genius nor taste.** Lady Catherine de Bourgh boasts, **'There are few people in England, I suppose, who have more true enjoyment of music than myself, or a better natural taste',** while in *Emma* Mrs Elton, on coming into the neighbourhood of Highbury, lets everyone know, **'I am doatingly fond of music – passionately fond; and my friends say I am not entirely devoid of taste.'**

Poor Harriet Smith, whose taste in many things is found wanting by Emma (**Emma felt the bad taste of her friend**) attempts to praise Emma's piano-playing after the Coles' party in the following exchange:

'Mr Cole said how much taste you had; and Mr Frank Churchill talked

a great deal about your taste, and that he valued taste much more than execution.'

'Ah! but Jane Fairfax has them both, Harriet.'

'Are you sure? I saw she had execution, but I did not know she had any taste. Nobody talked about it.'

But music is not the only context in which taste is measured. More broadly, it stands for good judgement in every area of life. Mr Elton's charade – the one in which he seems to find *ready wit* in Harriet – is to Emma **a jumble without taste or truth** and his gallantry towards herself an **error of judgment, of knowledge, of taste, as one proof among others that he had not always lived in the best society.**

Taste in a Jane Austen novel is about conduct, making the right choices, saying the right things, appreciating the best books, music, pictures, landscape. So many pitfalls! So much opportunity for one character to despise another! Elizabeth Bennet is pronounced by the Bingley sisters to **have no conversation, no stile, no taste, no beauty** – which says more about their snobbishness than Elizabeth's abilities, as Darcy soon recognizes; although, not realizing how he has changed his mind about her, Elizabeth accuses him of hoping for **'the pleasure of despising my taste'.**

A fastidious taste can sometimes act as an impediment to happiness: Darcy almost fails to discover Elizabeth, while Anne Elliot, having **gentleness, modesty, taste, and feeling** even at the age of nineteen, is prevented from forming a second attachment by **the nice tone of her mind, the fastidiousness of her taste.** (Her lover, Captain Wentworth, by contrast has **quick taste**, which almost leads him into committing himself to an impulsive, disastrous second choice.) Marianne Dashwood, so sure of her own opinions, is particularly scathing about the taste of everyone – except Willoughby – outside her own family. It is true that the family at Barton Park are characterized by **a shameless want of taste** which, among other offences, manifests itself by talking through Marianne's piano-playing. The narrator confirms that Sir John Middleton and his wife have very little in common beyond sharing **a total want of talent and taste.**

But Marianne finds even the two men who turn out to be the heroes sadly lacking: in her estimation Colonel Brandon has **'neither genius,** taste nor spirit' and Edward Ferrars 'no real taste'. Marianne has her own definition of taste: that rapturous delight, which, in her opinion, could alone be called taste. Her declaration that she could never fall in love with a man 'whose taste did not in every particular coincide with my own' seems fulfilled when Willoughby comes into her life. 'The same books, the same passages were idolised by each,' though Marianne fails to notice that Willoughby largely follows where she leads.

Elinor's defence of Edward, while stiff, is touching: 'Upon the whole, I venture to pronounce that his mind is well-informed, his enjoyment of books exceedingly great, his imagination lively, his observation just and correct, and his taste delicate and pure.' Elsewhere, defending his ignorance of drawing, Elinor speaks of Edward's 'propriety and simplicity of taste, which in general direct him perfectly right'. As the novel progresses, wearied by so many second-rate people around her, Elinor reflects on how much she values by comparison Edward's generous temper, simple taste and diffident feelings. Edward Ferrars is far from the dashing hero, he is not easy to warm to (many readers find him disappointing), but if we remember the nouns and adjectives that keep company with *taste* in Elinor's mind when she thinks of him – *propriety, simplicity, delicate, pure, generous, diffident* – we can be sure of his unshowy worth.

Edward himself, with disarming modesty, confesses to 'ignorance and want of taste,' though he is referring only to knowledge of the picturesque and is half-teasing Marianne. In another novel written during the 1790s rage for the picturesque, *Northanger Abbey*, Henry and Eleanor Tilney demonstrate their knowledge and taste. On a walk near Bath, they look at the landscape with the eyes of persons accustomed to drawing, and decided on its capability of being formed into pictures, with all the eagerness of real taste. But their companion, Catherine Morland, cannot contribute to the discourse. She knew nothing of drawing – nothing of taste. But no matter, she listens intently to what Henry says and he became perfectly satisfied of her having a great deal of natural taste. Catherine's *natural taste* marks her out to be worthy of Henry. Like young Susan Price's innate taste for the genteel and well-appointed, all worthy characters have at the very least a natural, inborn good taste.

Taste may refer to appreciation of the arts, to buildings and landscape, to morals, manners and a general attitude of sensibility. It is this last which is meant in *Persuasion* when the narrator speaks of autumn's **influence on the mind of taste and tenderness**. In *Mansfield Park*, Mary Crawford has **none of Fanny's delicacy of taste, of mind, of feeling** – all signs of sensibility. Mary is indifferent to the natural world that Fanny eagerly observes on the journey to Sotherton. Henry Crawford, though sharing many of his sister's values, differs from her insofar as he is sensitive enough to adapt his demeanour and even his interests to the person he is with. In Portsmouth, walking with Fanny along the ramparts on a fine spring day, **they often stopt with the same sentiment and taste, leaning against the wall, some minutes, to look and admire.**

Edmund Bertram, who in Fanny's childhood has **encouraged her taste, and corrected her judgement**, assures her when she protests that she and Henry **'have not one taste in common'** that in fact they have **'moral and literary tastes in common'**. And it is true that when Crawford is reading Shakespeare aloud – and doing it supremely well – Fanny cannot close her mind or her ears: **taste was too strong in her. She was forced to listen.** As an actor, Henry has demonstrated **more confidence than Edmund, more judgement than Tom, more talent and taste than Mr Yates.**

Taste is often associated with manners. Elizabeth Bennet glories in every sentence addresses by her uncle Mr Gardiner to Darcy **which marked his intelligence, his taste, or his good manners** – despite his living near his own warehouses in Cheapside! When Catherine Morland meets the conceited, flirtatious Captain Tilney, she quickly concludes that **his taste and manners were beyond a doubt decidedly inferior** to his brother's. Henry Crawford, in advising Edmund Bertram on how he may remodel the parsonage house at Thornton Lacey, asserts, **'From being a mere gentleman's residence, it becomes, by judicious improvement, the residence of a man of education, taste, modern manners, good connections.'**

A house – and its grounds – can express all this, and more. When Elizabeth Bennet first beholds Pemberley, **she had never seen a place for which nature had done more, or where natural beauty had been so little**

counteracted by an awkward taste. She is even more impressed when she goes inside Mr Darcy's house: **Elizabeth saw, with admiration of his taste, that it was neither gaudy nor uselessly fine.** No wonder she is struck by the idea that 'to be mistress of Pemberley would be something!'

Lack of gaudiness or show – in a word, simplicity – is almost always the key to good taste. As Fanny Price remarks of the shrubbery at Mansfield Parsonage: **'I must admire the taste Mrs Grant has shown in all this. There is such a quiet simplicity in the plan of the walk!'** Both Elizabeth and Fanny are, in fact, admiring their future homes, though they do not know it at the time.

Most important, perhaps, is taste in judging people – the ability to recognize true worth in character. All the heroes and heroines possess or learn to possess this ability. But they are not the only ones. For all his grievous faults and ultimate unworthiness to marry Fanny, Henry Crawford, we are told, **had moral taste enough to value** her probity. And Mary Crawford, having thrown away her chance of marrying Edmund, **was long in finding ... anyone who could satisfy the better taste she had acquired at Mansfield.** It is because the Crawfords, in their slightly different ways, have acquired that **moral taste** or **better taste** in their dealings with the family at Mansfield that (though entirely their own fault), their ultimate ejection from its paradise is so painful.

2

Elegance

IF ONE WORD sums up the world of Jane Austen, it is surely *elegance*. Deriving from the Latin *eligere* to elect, or choose, elegance is the result of choosing appropriately for the occasion and circumstances, whether what is being chosen is clothes or conduct.

With a few exceptions, Jane Austen's characters speak and behave with elegance, dress elegantly, and inhabit elegant houses. Like its close relations decorum, propriety and gentility, elegance is fundamentally a matter of mind and manners, but unlike them it is predominantly applied to the material and visual world.

For many people today, this is part of what makes her novels and their film and TV adaptations so enjoyable. For others, however, it is what puts them off Jane Austen. They find the world she depicts *too* polished, pretty and genteel. This was the nub of Charlotte Brontë's criticism when she likened her predecessor's novels to neat, well-fenced gardens, full of self-controlled ladies and gentlemen, with nothing of wild nature about them.

The interesting thing is that Jane Austen herself was ambivalent about *elegance*. Admiring and extolling it as a virtue most of the time, she was aware that it could be used as a cover for selfishness and lack of heart. It is a concept to which she gives many shades of meaning.

In *Sense and Sensibility*, for example, we see that Mrs Dashwood and her daughters possess an innate elegance which lifts them above their reduced social standing and cramped home. It takes only one visit to Barton Cottage by Willoughby **to assure him of the sense, elegance, mutual affection and domestic comfort of the family**. The qualities grouped with elegance here – sense and affection, i.e. head and heart – unambiguously attest to its good connotations. But the kind of elegance on display at the great house Barton Park is another matter. The narrator tells us that **the Middletons lived in a style of equal hospitality and elegance. The former was for Sir John's gratification, and the latter for that of his lady.** This sounds promising, but the Dashwoods soon discover that Lady Middleton is empty-headed and cold-hearted: she **piqued herself on the elegance of her table, and of all her domestic arrangements; and from this kind of vanity was her greatest enjoyment of any of their parties.** Elegance here springs not from any wish to make guests comfortable but from an immoderate love of display, from caring too much about the impression one makes.

In this early novel, Jane Austen is dealing not exactly in stereotypes – her characters are too full of life and individuality – but certainly in schematic contrasts designed to highlight the idiosyncrasies of her gallery of characters, a legacy from the eighteenth-century novel which was generally read for entertainment value rather than for psychological truth and power. Neither Lady Middleton's husband nor her mother, Mrs Jennings, nor her sister, Mrs Palmer, seem likely to belong to her. There is not an ounce of elegance in any of them. Mrs Palmer's **manners were by no means so elegant as her sister's, but they were much more prepossessing** in that she smiles all the time. All three are good-humoured; Sir John and Mrs Jennings enjoy a good joke, and do not care how much they embarrass their company. An elegant mind would strive to avoid causing embarrassment, out of care for others' feelings. There is not much more to Sir John than being sociable for his own gratification, another form of selfishness, and Charlotte Palmer is a nonentity; but as the novel progresses Mrs Jennings turns out to have a real warmth of heart that counteracts her lack of elegance. Even Marianne learns to value her sincerely. It is possible, therefore, to be entirely without elegance, yet to have the approval of the author.

Elegance in the novels is not a solely female attribute. On his first appearance in the Dashwoods' lives, Willoughby, whose person is immediately seen to be **uncommonly handsome** and his manner **frank and graceful**, impresses all four inhabitants of the cottage with his **youth, beauty and elegance.** This terminology might momentarily startle in connection with a man, but there is no suggestion of effeminacy about Willoughby, with his guns and his dogs about him. When the family ask Sir John about this interesting stranger and are told that one Christmas he danced from eight until four without once sitting down, **'Did he indeed?' cried Marianne with sparkling eyes, 'and with elegance, with spirit?'** Elsewhere on the spectrum of elegance in this novel are the Steele sisters: poor like the Dashwoods, but unlike them, on the make: **Lucy was certainly not so elegant and her sister not even genteel.** Lucy has learnt to cultivate **a smartness of air, which though it did not give actual elegance or grace, gave distinction to her person.** Some, like Lady Middleton, are taken in, but Elinor soon detects in her **a want of real elegance and artlessness.** It is the very artfulness of Lucy which makes the attempted elegance of her dress and conversation so distasteful to the discerning like Elinor. (Poor Lucy and Nancy, of course, have not had Elinor and Marianne's advantages in being brought up by a delightful mother in comfortable surroundings, and perhaps Lucy can be forgiven for doing the best she can for herself – at least she is clever enough to know that elegance is what she should be aiming for; Nancy has no idea.)

So in this first published novel of Jane Austen's it is possible to identify various sorts of elegance and pseudo-elegance carrying widely different degrees of authorial approval and disapproval. Similar ambivalences can be traced in her other novels. In *Pride and Prejudice*, elegance is shown as a good quality in the character of Mrs Gardiner, for example, who behaves faultlessly on all occasions (unlike her two sisters-in-law, Mrs Bennet and Mrs Phillips) and who is introduced as **an amiable, intelligent, elegant woman and a great favourite** with her nieces: like the Dashwoods, her elegance is associated with right qualities of head and heart.

Unlike some of the heroines of Jane Austen's other books, Elizabeth Bennet is not especially noted for elegance, being too natural and spirited; her swift walk through three miles of country, 'jumping over stiles and springing over puddles' and arriving at Netherfield with 'weary ankles, dirty stockings and a face glowing with the warmth of exercise' is hardly the behaviour of a woman who places elegance above other considerations, such as anxiety to see her sick sister. In fact both Elizabeth and Jane are infinitely more elegant than their hoydenish younger sisters – Elizabeth rarely, and Jane never, behave less than impeccably; and Elizabeth certainly knows how to recognize true elegance. When she first sees the interior of Pemberley she is struck with admiration of Mr Darcy's taste in furniture, which has **less of splendour, and more real elegance, than the furniture of Rosings.** Here, *elegance* is pitted not against the vulgarity of poverty, but the vulgarity of show. The novel ends happily with Elizabeth enjoying **all the comfort and elegance of their family party at Pemberley.** *Elegance* alone might have implied an over-correct formality, but *comfort* rescues it from any such meaning. For the first time in her life Elizabeth can dwell in a home that is harmonious and orderly.

More often in this novel, *elegance* is a cold, heartless thing. Bingley's sisters have it in spades; their dresses and their evening entertainments are alike described as *elegant*, they write letters on **elegant, little, hot-pressed paper** and even their personal maids appear as **the two elegant ladies who waited on his sisters.** Mr Collins boasts that he dreams up **little elegant compliments** to please his patron, Lady Catherine; and unable to believe that Elizabeth could turn down his marriage proposal, he brushes off her refusal as **the usual practice of elegant females,** who first refuse the man they intend to accept. Elizabeth protests against having **that kind of elegance which consists in tormenting a respectable man.** If Mr Collins persists in disbelieving her, she determines to apply to her father, **whose behaviour at least could not be mistaken for the affectation and coquetry of an elegant female.**

True elegance oils the wheels of social intercourse and encourages pleasing behaviour, but false elegance concerns itself with the superficial things of life. When Lydia elopes with Wickham, what her mother regrets most is not Lydia's loss of virtue but her own disappointment in not being able to arrange those usual **attendants of elegant nuptials, fine muslins, new carriages and servants.**

Persuasion carries a similar dichotomy between what might be called 'good' and 'bad' elegance. Anne Elliot is perhaps the most thoroughly elegant of any of Jane Austen's heroines. She is introduced to us as having **an elegance of mind and sweetness of character, which must have placed her high with any people of real understanding.** When her old school friend Mrs Smith meets her again after the lapse of many years, she finds Anne to be an **elegant little woman of seven and twenty:** and a new acquaintance, Captain Benwick, lists Anne's attractions as '**elegance, sweetness, beauty'.** Her cousin, Mr Elliot, commends her translation of an Italian song as being in '**clear, comprehensible, elegant English**' and even Anne herself, reflecting somewhat enviously on the happy family life of the Musgrove sisters, acknowledges that she **would not have given up her own more elegant and cultivated mind** for all their advantages.

This is very different from **the heartless elegance of her father and sister.** Elizabeth Elliot **was certainly very handsome, with well-bred, elegant manners** but she lacks the higher virtues of Anne's sweetness of character or cultivation of mind. In a small country neighbourhood, years have gone by with little to **vary the sameness and the elegance, the prosperity and the nothingness** of Sir Walter and Elizabeth's way of life, while in Bath they pass their evenings in **the elegant stupidity of private parties** and even worse, display **anxious elegance** when encountering social superiors. When Elizabeth plans an evening party – being too ashamed of the contraction of their means which a dinner invitation would betray – she determines that **it shall be a regular party, small but most elegant** and her satisfaction lies not in giving hospitality to her near relations but in **the continually improving detail of all the embellishments which were to make it the most completely elegant of its kind in Bath.** Elizabeth's values are reminiscent of Lady Middleton's. Jane Austen had met her share of this type of female, especially in London and Bath.

As with Mrs Jennings in *Sense and Sensibility, Persuasion* contains characters who are **not at all elegant** but are nevertheless 'very good sort of people, friendly and hospitable,' in the elder Musgroves. Perhaps Jane Austen is able to forgive lack of elegance in the older generation more than in younger people, who have had the benefit of a better education. Their son Charles Musgrove has not the strength of character to regulate his own life well, but would have been improved by a better wife (he had wanted to marry Anne, but has settled for her sister Mary): a woman of real understanding might have given more consequence to his character, and more usefulness, rationality and elegance to his habits and pursuits. Elegance may seem a strange noun to attach to male pursuits, but again, it carries with it the meaning of well-chosen.

In *Mansfield Park, elegance* is a catch-all commendation between and about a set of characters living in material comfort and style. The Bertram sisters and Mary Crawford are all distinguished for elegance and accomplishments; the former are very elegant, agreeable girls and the latter is a sweet, pretty, lively, elegant girl, with a harp as elegant as herself and even Mrs Grant, wife of the Rector, is an elegant lady. At Mansfield Parsonage the dinner itself was plentiful and elegant while at Sotherton the midday meal has been prepared with abundance and elegance.

A more morally weighty use of the word comes when, staying at her parents' noisy, dirty, home in Portsmouth, Fanny Price realizes how much she values the elegance, propriety, regularity and harmony of life in Mansfield Park, despite all the suffering she has undergone there. Fanny herself has a modest and elegant mind and dances with quiet, light elegance, and in admirable time. Modesty and quietness mark out the nature of Fanny's elegance as quite different from that of her cousins. At the ball given for her by her uncle, she is abashed rather than gratified at having to lead off the dancing and to be placed above so many elegant young women!

In *Northanger Abbey* the concept of elegance is almost wholly confined to the material wealth of the Abbey itself, which is furnished in all the profusion and elegance of modern taste, and where the costliness or elegance of the décor is of no interest to Catherine, who nevertheless has the elegance of the breakfast set forced on her notice by General Tilney. Catherine herself is too natural and artless to be elegant; like Elizabeth Bennet she can run when occasion requires (in Catherine's case through the streets of Bath, concerned only to vindicate herself to the Tilneys). When elegance is applied to a person in this novel it is to the admirable Eleanor Tilney, whose manners have more real elegance though 'less stylishness' than those of Catherine's other female acquaintance in Bath, Isabella Thorpe.

But it is the novel *Emma* which discusses elegance most overtly and insistently, because the rather snobbish heroine herself has **the highest value for elegance: and elegance, whether of person or of mind, she saw so little of in Highbury.** Emma routinely assesses her acquaintance for their degree of elegance. On first meeting Harriet she considers the girl needs only **a little more knowledge and elegance to be quite perfect,** and when Emma comes to sketch her, she gives Harriet **a little more height, and considerably more elegance.** One wonders quite how she does this. Her sketch of her sister Isabella captures **quite her own little elegant figure** and in this instance Emma has not had to improve her subject, as the narrator later informs us that **Mrs John Knightley was a pretty, elegant little woman, of gentle, quiet manners.**

Prettiness is not a prerequisite of elegance, however, as Miss Bates describes Miss Campbell as '**plain – but extremely elegant and amiable**'. Miss Campbell has been brought up by sensible parents in good society, so she has every advantage except the face she was born with. Augusta Elton, on the other hand, despite 'a face not unpretty' has the drawback of coming from 'the very heart of Bristol', and Emma soon concludes that '**neither feature, nor air, nor voice, nor manner were elegant**'. A dreadful litany! There is **ease but not elegance** in her demeanour. This does not prevent her setting herself up as the most elegant person in Highbury: at one gathering Mrs Elton is **as elegant as lace and pearls could make her** and on another, **the studied elegance of her dress, and her smiles of graciousness,** disgust Emma. As for Mrs Elton's vulgar habit of referring to 'Mr E' or 'Knightley', Emma calls this ironically '**elegant terseness**'.

Emma is equally critical of Mr Elton, even before she is disillusioned with him, **there being a want of elegance of feature which she could not dispense with,** though she considers him good enough for Harriet. Emma finds that **with all the gentleness of his address, true elegance was sometimes wanting.** That is, he does not always choose his line of conduct judiciously, a character fault that shows itself with increasing severity as the novel progresses. Even the gentlemanlike and charming Frank Churchill, in his eagerness to collect enough people together for a dance, is indifferent to what Emma calls 'confusion of rank', an indifference which for her **bordered too much on inelegance of mind.** As with the other male examples, this brings out the sense inherent in the word of choice and judgement.

Amusingly, the book which is read aloud in the evenings by the young farmer Robert Martin at Abbey Mill Farm, during Harriet Smith's summer visit, is *Elegant Extracts* – a strange choice, possibly, for a man whom Emma on first sight calls 'so very clownish, so totally without air'. But Emma is wholly mistaken about this man, and his choice of reading matter might have been one hint among many that he is worthier than she gives him credit for. In fact, the two volumes of this work by Vicesimus Knox, *Elegant Extracts; or, useful and entertaining passages in prose (1770)* and *Elegant Extracts; or, useful and entertaining pieces of poetry (1784)*, are ideally chosen as the reading matter for leisure moments at Abbey Mill Farm, where the hard-working, honest family, without being too pretentious, are in the process of improving themselves in education and social polish.

The person from whom Emma finds it impossible to withold her admiration is Jane Fairfax. **Jane Fairfax was very elegant, remarkably elegant.** She has **a style of beauty, of which elegance was the reigning characteristic** and her pale skin gives **peculiar elegance to her face.** Emma, while failing to befriend her, admits: **'She is the sort of elegant creature that one cannot keep one's eyes from'.** Emma is astonished when Frank Churchill only hesitatingly agrees with her praise of Jane, and she muses that **there must be a very distinct sort of elegance for the fashionable world, if Jane Fairfax could be thought only ordinarily gifted with it.** Of course, as we later learn, Frank is not expressing his true opinion, and subsequently he raves about Jane's beauty.

Emma finds it hard to like Jane, but **when she considered what all this elegance was destined to** (Jane is to be a governess) she cannot but feel sorry for her. Even for Emma, however, elegance can be too much of a good thing, if it is used to conceal feelings; and when towards the end of the novel Jane speaks out from the heart, Emma finds it **infinitely more becoming to her than all the elegance of her usual composure.**

Emma herself is not described as *elegant*, perhaps she does not need to be: she is 'handsome' and 'clever' and for all her follies we cannot doubt that everything she does is done *elegantly*. Her father praises her handwriting; Mr Knightley loves to look at her, Harriet loves to listen to her, the Coles and Bateses defer to her; as a hostess, she is 'never indifferent to the credit of doing everything well and attentively' – which could be considered one definition of *elegance*. When she imagines herself refusing a marriage proposal from Frank Churchill her brain gets busy **fancying interesting dialogues, and inventing elegant letters**; and her original plan for the excursion to Box Hill, before Mr Weston interferes, is for all **to be done in a quiet, unpretending, elegant way, infinitely superior to the bustle and preparation, the regular eating and drinking, and picnic parade of the Eltons and the Sucklings.** The elegance of Jane Fairfax is easy to account for: like her friend Miss Campbell, she has been brought up in London amid **the rational pleasures of an elegant society and a judicious mixture of home and amusement**; but how and where has Emma learnt *her* ideas of elegance? Mixing with hardly any social equals, never leaving home, she can only have imbibed them from her governess, now Mrs Weston. Frank Churchill, who has spent time in the fashionable world, commends Mrs Weston's **'elegant, agreeable manners'** as well as her youthful looks. When Mrs Elton presumes to praise her, however, with a patronising attitude and an expression of surprise considering she has formerly been a governess, she deeply offends Emma. **'Mrs. Weston's manners'**, says Emma reprovingly, **'were always particularly good. Their propriety, simplicity, and elegance, would make them the safest model for any young woman.'** This could be a circular argument, but we feel that though Emma is wrong about many things during the course of the novel, this assertion is endorsed by Jane Austen herself. The association of elegance with propriety and simplicity marks her own personal ideal, the one that all her novels are concerned to promote.

3

Openness and Reserve

WHILE JANE AUSTEN consistently upholds the moral values of her religion and society, some values are dearer to her heart than others, and her own personality shines through in the warmth and frequency with which she recommends them. *Openness*, or *open-heartedness*, is one of the qualities frequently praised by her just as its opposite, *reserve*, is usually regarded with suspicion.

A key passage occurs in *Persuasion*, the late novel that seems to embody all that the mature Jane has thought and learnt about life: **Mr Elliot was rational, discreet, polished, but he was not open. There was never any burst of feeling, any warmth of indignation or delight, at the evil or good of others. This, to Anne, was a decided imperfection ... She prized the frank, the open-hearted, the eager character beyond all others. Warmth and enthusiasm did captivate her still. She felt that she could so much more depend upon the sincerity of those who sometimes looked or said a careless or a hasty thing, than of those whose presence of mind never varied, whose tongue never slipped.**

Although these thoughts are Anne's, coloured by her enduring love for Captain Wentworth, they do seem to be endorsed by the author. And when Louisa Musgrove, in her impetuous way, enters into even wilder praise for the men of the navy, we feel Jane Austen smiling indulgently at Louisa's enthusiasm for **their friendliness, their brotherliness, their openness, their uprightness; protesting that she was convinced of sailors having more worth and warmth than any other set of men in England; that they only knew how to live, and they only deserved to be respected and loved.**

Anne shares all these opinions, in a less exaggerated way, though she does not express them. Indeed, Anne rarely gives voice to her thoughts and feelings. She could herself be accused of being reserved: not by *Persuasion*'s readers, for her mind is fully open to us; but by the novel's other characters. How astonished they all must be when the engagement of Captain Wentworth and Miss Anne Elliot is announced! It must seem to have come out of nowhere. Anne herself is one of whom it could be said that her 'presence of mind never varied' (at least as far as her outward behaviour is concerned) and her 'tongue never slipped'. However, the delicate emotional situation in which she finds herself, the mores of her day regarding what women may say, and her innate good manners all amply excuse her and account for this apparent contradiction in the novel's value scheme.

It is fitting that Anne, the more thoughtful character, brackets *openness* not with *friendliness*, like Louisa, but with *sincerity*: a more important virtue, in that it enables people to read other people's characters more accurately, to be confident that they are not concealing guilty secrets or ulterior motives (Mr Elliot is in fact concealing both).

That is why, although *openness* can be a charming quality in either sex, in the world of Jane Austen it is particularly desirable in men. The marriageable young woman in an Austen novel desperately needs all the help she can get in assessing the worth of any man who approaches her. Her future happiness depends on how well she can make out his character in the limited encounters available to her.

Thus in *Pride and Prejudice*, Elizabeth Bennet, despite the acuteness of her intelligence, goes spectacularly wrong when she judges Darcy and Wickham, because on first meeting Darcy is *haughty, reserved, and fastidious*. Elizabeth is at fault in jumping to conclusions – but Darcy is not blameless. Later, visiting Pemberley with the Gardiners, Elizabeth finds Darcy altered: she has never seen him *so free from self-consequence, or unbending reserve as now*. His character improves as the result of his love for her; but Elizabeth also comes to recognize not only that reserve may conceal a really valuable character, but that a measure of reserve may be right and proper among new acquaintance.

For she has been misled not only by Darcy's reserve, but by

the opposite quality in Wickham. 'Poor Wickham; there is such an expression of goodness in his countenance! such an openness and gentleness in his manner', as Jane Bennet laments when the truth comes out; but Elizabeth's more penetrating intelligence leads her to realize that it was improper of Wickham to make such communications to a stranger as he made to her, at almost their first meeting, on the subject of the Darcy family affairs.

Another young man whose apparent openness from the beginning of acquaintance brings heartache to those it deceives is Willoughby in *Sense and Sensibility*. Willoughby enters the story as a young man of good abilities, quick imagination, lively spirits and open, affectionate manners. Just the sort of man to fall in love with, then – as Marianne, and to some extent her mother, duly do. Only Elinor remains slightly cautious, but even she is beguiled by his manner, in proof of which is the scene towards the end of the novel when Willoughby turns up at Cleveland in the middle of the night, believing Marianne to be dying. Despite all the torment his unfaithful behaviour has caused her sister, bringing her almost to death's door, in listening to his excuses and regrets, Elinor finds herself worked on by that open, affectionate and lively manner which it was no merit to possess.

Why does Jane Austen deny him merit? Not because openness is not meritorious, but because Willoughby cannot help but be that way – it is just a manner, the gift of nature. As Elinor by this time knows, Willoughby's openness extends only as far as his social persona, while his fundamental selfishness lurks beneath.

What about the other men in *Sense and Sensibility?* Readers have often found the two 'heroes' dull, and deplored the fate of the two heroines in ending up with them. In contrast to Willoughby's openness, both Edward Ferrars and Colonel Brandon are apt to be reserved. Marianne throws this accusation at Edward when he first arrives at Barton Cottage (coming, as we later discover, directly from having visited Lucy Steele, to whom he is secretly and regretfully betrothed), and he begins by claiming to be shy:

'If I could persuade myself that my manners were perfectly easy and graceful, I should not be shy.'

'But you would still be reserved', said Marianne, 'and that is worse.'

Edward stared. 'Reserved! Am I reserved, Marianne?'

'Yes, very.'

'I do not understand you', replied he, colouring. 'Reserved! – how, in what manner? What am I to tell you? What can you suppose?'

Another man with a guilty secret to hide. But in Edward's case, of course, he is trying to do the right thing by everybody, and Elinor has already fallen in love with him at a time when (forgetting about Lucy) **his behaviour gave every indication of an open, affectionate heart.**

Elinor is also the one to make allowances for Colonel Brandon in the first days of their acquaintance. **In spite of his gravity and reserve she beheld in him an object of interest. His manners, though serious, were mild; and his reserve appeared rather the result of some oppression of spirits than from any natural gloominess of temper.** Amusingly, by the end of the novel Mrs Dashwood, having transferred her maternal approval from Willoughby to Brandon, can even claim for him the precious quality: **'Such openness! Such sincerity! No-one can be deceived in *him*.'**

Almost as appropriate a title (if not nearly as euphonious a one) as *Sense and Sensibility* for this novel might be *Openness and Reserve*, for not only do the male characters take positions on this scale, but the two sisters exemplify these characteristics. Marianne, of course, is all openness, acknowledging – or perhaps boasting – **'I have been open and sincere where I ought to have been reserved, spiritless, dull and deceitful,'** while her letters to the errant Willoughby remain injudiciously **affectionate, open, honest, confiding.** Meanwhile Elinor, with better understanding of how to conduct herself in public, and with other people's secrets to protect, is accused by her sister of not communicating. Misunderstood, Elinor is **distressed by this charge of reserve in herself, which she was not at liberty to do away.** In all three cases, then, Elinor, Edward and Brandon, reserve is caused by circumstances rather than being natural to their characters. Happier times allow them to throw it off.

A worse kind of reserve is that of Lady Middleton, because it is habitual and conceals no depth of feeling: **though well-bred, she was reserved, cold, and had nothing to say.** At first her silence is a relief after the garrulity of her husband and mother, but it does not denote sound judgement: **Elinor needed little observation to perceive that her reserve was mere calmness of manner with which sense had little to do.**

Worse still is the reserve which is adopted in order to gloat over those not admitted to a secret; this is the case with Isabella Thorpe in *Northanger Abbey*, when she confides news of her engagement to James Morland to *his* sister, Catherine, but not to *her own* sisters, Anne and Maria, though they are all present together. Whispering and hinting, Isabella's behaviour is self-important and intended to be hurtful, and it is one of the first occasions when Catherine finds something to censure in her friend. **To Catherine's simple feelings, this odd sort of reserve seemed neither kindly meant, nor consistently supported.** Catherine herself has **a disposition cheerful and open, without conceit or affectation of any kind**, the precise opposite of Isabella. Henry Tilney plays on the contrast when there seems a danger of his brother Frederick's marrying Isabella. **'Prepare for your sister-in-law, Eleanor'**, he tells his sister, **'and such a sister-in-law as you must delight in! Open, candid, artless, guileless, with affections strong but simple, forming no pretensions, and knowing no disguise.'**

'Such a sister-in-law, Henry, I should delight in', replies Eleanor with a smile. She is, of course, as both brother and sister know – and as the reader knows – referring to Catherine, and her readiness to welcome her into the family should Henry choose her as his wife. Only Catherine, who is with them, fails to understand that this affectionate picture applies to herself.

If Catherine's disposition is **open ... without affectation of any kind**, Isabella emerges from the events of the story as a woman full of guile and artfulness, only affecting to be open in order to impress. In this she is contrasted not only with Catherine but with Eleanor, the true friend, whose manners on first acquaintance **showed good sense and good breeding; they were neither shy nor affectedly open; and she seemed capable of being young, attractive, and at a ball without trying to fix the attention of every man near her, and without exaggerated feelings.**

Mary Crawford in *Mansfield Park* is said to possess **openness of heart**, but as the words are Edmund Bertram's, spoken at the height of his infatuation with Mary, they are a perhaps a better picture of *his* heart than Mary's. '**I had not been in the room five minutes**', Edmund tells Fanny, '**before she began introducing it** [the subject of Henry Crawford's proposal to Fanny] **with all that openness of heart and sweet peculiarity of manner, that spirit and ingenuousness, which are so much a part of herself.**' Edmund's purpose in this conversation with Fanny is to persuade her into acceptance of Crawford, but his own passion leads him into praise of another woman that Fanny finds hard to bear – and almost certainly impossible to agree with.

Fanny herself suffers too much from **shyness and reserve** to be called *open* – though nobody could be more honest than she. (Henry Crawford calls her 'a very honest reckoner'.) Two of her siblings, however, have more fearless temperaments, and they are both described as *open*. William is **a young man of an open, pleasant countenance, and frank, unstudied, but feeling and respectful manners,** just what a young man in his position should be. Susan has **an open, sensible countenance; she was like William.** Nevertheless, not until she has been in Portsmouth for at least a fortnight does Fanny begin to see promising material in Susan, so different is she in demeanour from herself, being argumentative and assertive. But the saving grace: Susan's **temper was open.** Having acted in a way she fears Fanny cannot approve, Susan 'acknowledged her fears, blamed herself for having contended so warmly, and from that hour Fanny, understanding the worth of her disposition' forms a real friendship with her sister and is able to guide her into better behaviour.

Fanny's reserve stems from shyness and timidity, from natural modesty and a mental self-sufficiency that has been encouraged by the circumstances of her uprooting to Mansfield, but is actually innate: 'her own thoughts were habitually her best companions'. Her uncle's reserve is made of sterner stuff. While his daughters are growing up, **the reserve of his manners repressed all the flow of their spirits before him,** with the disastrous outcome that he does not understand *them*, and they do not confide in *him*. Towards the end of the novel he reflects on 'his own severity' as playing a part in their ultimate downfall. Before this access of self-knowledge, however, the besotted Edmund wonders what Mary Crawford thinks of his father, who has just returned from Antigua, telling Fanny, '**She must admire him as a fine-looking man, with** most gentlemanlike, dignified, consistent manners; but perhaps having seen him so seldom, his reserve may be a little repulsive.' (*Repulsive* in Jane Austen's terminology means not what we mean by it, disgusting or revolting, but merely liable to repel.)

Perhaps the character most associated with reserve in any of Jane Austen's novels is Jane Fairfax, in *Emma*. In their earlier acquaintance Emma has always been repelled by such coldness and reserve – such apparent indifference whether she pleased or not. Now, on Jane's return to Highbury, Emma finds her again so cold, so cautious! There was no getting at her real opinion. Wrapt up in a cloak of politeness, she seemed determined to hazard nothing. She was disgustingly, she was suspiciously reserved. Jane's reserve, justified to some extent by circumstances (as is later revealed) leaves her open to Emma's powers of invention. While Emma is wrong to circulate the suspicions which dart so easily into her brain, had Jane not been suspiciously reserved they would not have arisen. Both women share some part of the blame for what goes wrong between them.

Mr Knightley, trying to encourage their friendship, assures Emma, 'you will soon overcome all that part of her reserve which ought to be overcome, all that has its foundation in diffidence. What arises from discretion must be honoured'. But a few weeks later, when Emma suggests he might be in love with Jane himself, he admits, 'Her temper [is] excellent in its power of forbearance, patience, self-control; but it wants openness. She is reserved, more reserved, I think, than she used to be – And I love an open temper.'

The open temper which he loves without yet realizing it is, of course, Emma's own. Emma also discusses Jane's major fault with her new acquaintance, Frank Churchill. 'It is a most repulsive quality, indeed', said he. 'Oftentimes very convenient, no doubt, but never pleasing. There is safety in reserve, but no attraction. One cannot love a reserved person.' Unbeknown to Emma, this is exactly the opposite of the real state of Frank's heart; but she speaks greater truth than she knows when she replies, 'Not till the reserve ceases towards oneself; and then the attraction may be the greater.'

Jane and Frank have a mutual secret to keep; Jane's strategy is *reserve* (though she has always been fairly reserved) and Frank's quite

41

the reverse: he adopts a spurious *openness* that takes everyone in. Emma's first assessment of him is that **he appeared to have a very open temper – certainly a very lively and cheerful one.** She finds **nothing of the pride or reserve** she expected in one of his privileged upbringing. But when the secret engagement is finally revealed, she looks back and finds it hard to forgive the way he came among them with deceptive **profusions of openness and simplicity** which misled them all, and which led *her*, in particular, into injudicious confidences. Like Willoughby and Wickham, Frank Churchill has deployed **profusions of openness** to play a double game.

When Mr Knightley praises his tenant farmer, Robert Martin, as being **'open, straightforward and very well-judging'**, this represents authorial approval both for Mr Knightley and for Robert Martin himself. We can be assured that Mr Martin is a worthy young man because Mr Knightley thinks so; and his thinking so proves that he too is **open, straightforward and very well-judging**, with none of the snobbery that gets in the way of Emma's own judgements. What Emma and Mr Knightley do have in common is a love of openness. **'I love an open temper'** as Mr Knightley has said and **'If you knew how I love everything that is decided and open'**, Emma says to Jane – to a Jane released from secrecy. Emma also acknowledges that it is **an affectionate, open manner** that makes Harriet, her sister and father universally liked. And while she begins by deploring the most *open*, least *reserved* character in the novel, Miss Bates: 'so undistinguishing, and unfastidious, and so apt to tell everything to everybody', Emma learns to see beyond the prattle to the real goodness within.

On different occasions early in the book both Emma and Mr Knightley describe the friendly, hospitable Mr Weston as 'open-hearted'. But later, Emma revises her opinion somewhat: **She liked his open manners, but a little less of open-heartedness would have made him a higher character.** He is indiscriminatingly friendly with everybody, and Emma comes to understand that 'general benevolence, but not general friendship, made a man what he ought to be' – a portrait of Mr Knightley himself, of course. The lesson of *Emma*, as of all Jane Austen's writing, is that opposing qualities need to be balanced, and that while *openness* is usually preferable to *reserve*, and certainly more attractive, *reserve* is sometimes necessary and *openness* can go too far.

4

Exertion and Composure

'YOU HAVE DRAWN two pretty pictures', says Emma to Mr
Knightley at the beginning of their story, when he is berating
her about her match-making, 'but I think there may be a
third – a something between the do-nothing and the do-all'. Jane
Austen's characters have continually to make choices between activity
and inaction – between trying to make events go in the direction they
desire, and standing back to let life unfold. On a scale of which the
extremes are officiousness (Mrs Norris being the best example) and
indolence (her sister Lady Bertram), or heroism (William Price) and
selfish indulgence (Henry Crawford, who is momentarily ashamed
of the contrast) Jane Austen commonly settles at mid-point and
advocates *exertion* on one side and *composure* on the other.

The two qualities are complementary and have several things in
common. Most importantly, they usually have to be struggled for.
If they were easy to attain, they would be less meritorious. They are
most necessary at times of great emotion. The object of both is to
shield other people from unnecessary suffering and to protect the
individual concerned from unpleasant notice.

The more difficult kind of exertion comprehends self-command and
is a mental effort, but exertion also exists in the more straightforward
sense of action, of getting things done, which is usually associated
with men. As Anne Elliot says somewhat enviously but certainly
admiringly of the opposite sex, 'You are forced on exertion. You
have always a profession, pursuits, business of some sort or other....'
Young William Price has tasted the glory of heroism, of usefulness, of
exertion, of endurance in his naval career. Used to the same sort of

44

life, Captain Wentworth helps Anne's friend, the widow Mrs Smith, out of her tangled financial affairs by exercising **the activity and exertion of a fearless man**. It is because he is so accustomed to activity that Wentworth finds it difficult to do nothing when constrained by convention. **'I could exert myself, I could do something'**, is how he expresses his relief on finding himself freed from involvement with Louisa Musgrove. Now again his destiny is in his own hands, just as he likes it.

Edmund Bertram's exertions on behalf of his sick brother Tom take place in their home, but are probably rather more related to his profession of clergyman and confessor than to a nursing role: **trying to bury his own feelings in exertions for the relief of his brother's**. But even the domestic life of women offers opportunities for proper exertion. When Anne is staying with the young Musgrove family, **in the children she had an object of interest, amusement and exertion**, taking her out of herself and enabling her to be of use to others, which gives purpose to her life. A greater call upon her strength of mind is made during the crisis at Lyme. Afterwards, she hears that Captain Wentworth **had expressed his hope of Miss Elliot's not being the worse for her exertions, and had spoken of those exertions as great. This was handsome, and gave her more pleasure than almost anything else could have done**. Anne does not yet realize quite how much Captain Wentworth has been impressed by the way she alone preserves her presence of mind at the time of the accident. He has begun to see in her again the woman he would wish as his life's partner, and we can be sure that if they become parents of a family, any crises it faces will be shouldered together.

Jane and Elizabeth Bennet are particularly unfortunate in that neither of their parents is in the habit of exerting themselves for the good of the family as a whole. Mr Bennet **would never exert himself to restrain the wild giddiness** of his younger daughters and on the one occasion when he shakes himself out of his usual inertia, travelling to London in his rage against the runaway Lydia, he fails to write to the anxious family remaining at home: they know him to be **on all common occasions a most negligent and dilatory correspondent, but at such a time, they had hoped for exertion**.

Under ordinary circumstances, Mrs Bennet's faults are rather those of hyperactivity and interference than indolence like her husband – but during the same crisis over Lydia, she too fails utterly to exert herself for the sake of other members of the household. She becomes an added burden to Jane and Elizabeth at this trying time: **a mother incapable of exertion and requiring constant attendance.** Jane, the most charitable of souls, knows how her mother ought to behave but excuses her conduct when she writes to Elizabeth: '**My poor mother is really ill and keeps her room. Could she exert herself it would be better, but this is not to be expected.**' On Elizabeth's arrival home Jane admits that her mother has frequently been in hysterics. Soon Elizabeth witnesses for herself the utter self-centredness of their mother's response to family crisis: tears and lamentations of regret; complaints of her own sufferings and ill-usage; blaming everybody except herself and venting her feelings on the servant who attends her upstairs. Just when Jane has other worries to contend with, she has been forced to become the mother to her own mother – not because Mrs Bennet is ill, but because she is as immature and selfish as a small child.

Another mother who fails to exert herself, this time habitually and not only in moments of crisis, is the slatternly Mrs Price of *Mansfield Park*, whose Portsmouth home is consequently the abode of noise, disorder and impropriety, and whose large family is brought up, as Fanny sees, in the midst of negligence and error. **Her disposition was naturally easy and indolent, like Lady Bertram's; and a situation of similar affluence and do-nothingness would have been much more suited to her capacity than the exertions and self-denials of the one which her imprudent marriage had placed her in.** Mrs Price has only herself to blame for marrying without sufficient income, but the suffering of her innocent children is without extenuation.

Jane Austen often seems to specialize in inadequate mothers, though each fails her daughters in her own particular fashion. A more delightful mother who also needs a lesson in exertion is Mrs Dashwood, whose grief on the death of her husband, though more warranted and more worthy in itself than the tantrums of Mrs Bennet, is encouraged and renewed by herself and her second daughter, Marianne. They give themselves up wholly to their sorrow. **Elinor too** was deeply afflicted, but still she could struggle, she could exert herself. These exertions consist partly of making the necessary arrangements to receive her rather unpleasant brother and sister-in-law into what is now their home. In a reversal of roles, nineteen-year-old Elinor strives to rouse her mother to similar exertion, although it is some time before Mrs Dashwood's mind became capable of some other exertion than that of heightening its affliction by melancholy remembrances; exertion wrongly exercised can be worse than no exertion at all.

Later, afflicted by an equal or greater grief in the defection of Willoughby, Marianne's tears and lamentations again stream forth unchecked by any consideration of those around her. 'Exert yourself, dear Marianne', begs her sister and, to strengthen her plea, 'Think of your mother – for her sake you must exert yourself.' But Marianne scorns to conceal or attempt to subdue her misery, even though those who love her must suffer from her lack of self-command. 'Oh how easy for those who have no sorrows of their own to talk of exertion', she throws back at Elinor. Of course, she is wrong; her sister has had quite as hard a struggle for exertion under similar circumstances when she first hears that the man she loves, Edward Ferrars, is secretly engaged to another women. As the story is unfolded to Elinor, she makes her replies with an exertion of spirits, which increased with her increase of emotion. When she can no longer doubt the truth of what Lucy Steele is, exultingly, telling her, for a few moments, she was almost overcome – her heart sank within her, and she could hardly stand; but exertion was indispensably necessary, and she struggled so resolutely against the oppression of her feelings, that her success was speedy, and for the time complete. She will not give Lucy the satisfaction of seeing her hurt and disappointment, nor will she spread the hurt and disappointment to her mother and sisters by any self-indulgent wallowing in her grief. Besides, Lucy has told her of the secret engagement in confidence, and Elinor's strong sense of honour forbids her to break a confidence. Preserving Lucy's secret and her own self-respect obliged her to unceasing exertion for many months to come, at the same time as she is trying to cope with Marianne's flagrant misery.

Unfortunately, when Marianne does come to understand and to acknowledge the constant and painful exertion Elinor has been silently practising, it does not have the effect that Elinor had hoped in making the revelation, **to urge her to exertion now;** Marianne is so completely dispirited by the comparison between herself and her sister that though regretting **most bitterly that she had never exerted herself before ... she still fancied present exertion impossible.** It is only after her narrow escape from death and the reflections brought on by a long convalescence that she begins to evince **a mind awakened to reasonable exertion,** much to Elinor's satisfaction. Elinor herself has one last – and most difficult – call on her exertion. The Dashwoods have every reason to believe Edward now married to Lucy, when he calls at their cottage. Conversation is stilted, and then dries up altogether. **Elinor, resolving to exert herself, though fearing the sound of her own voice,** asks politely after Mrs Ferrars – and she is rewarded by the discovery that Lucy has married Edward's brother.

Amongst all her failings and her high opinion of herself, it is one of the redeeming virtues of Emma Woodhouse that she understands the necessity of, and practises, exertion towards those who look to her for comfort. Despite the fact that Harriet's unexpected meeting with the Martins, and their unexpectedly good behaviour on the occasion, causes some uncomfortable feelings of her own, she **exerted herself** to make Harriet comfortable by talking her out of her distress. The novel is book-ended by two evenings that see Emma alone with her fidgety father and only the backgammon board to amuse away the long hours. In the very first chapter, as Emma grieves on her own account for the loss of Miss Taylor's companionship, she nevertheless smiles and chats as cheerfully as possible and **spared no exertions to ... get her father tolerably through the evening, and be attacked by no regrets but her own.** The months pass as other characters come and go from Highbury, until another evening of trying solitude arises, one that circumstance suggests will be the pattern of all Emma's evenings to come. With Mr Woodhouse affected by the stormy weather **he could only be kept tolerably comfortable by almost ceaseless attention on his daughter's side, and by exertions which had never cost her half so much before.** Emma's own mind is in turmoil at this, the lowest point in her story, but she still puts her father's comfort first, when it would be so easy to become impatient with his foolish ways. She shields him from knowledge of her own distress, just as Elinor shields her parent.

Mr Knightley observes this quality consistently at work in Emma; he loves her for it; at a time of crisis, he places his confidence in it. Thinking that Emma is upset by the revelation about Frank Churchill, he draws her arm within his, pressing it to his heart, and says, **in a tone of great sensibility, speaking low: 'Time, my dearest Emma, time will heal the wound. Your own excellent sense; your exertions for your father's sake...'.**

We see Emma practising exertion in action, and we also hear her promoting it in speech. Unable, despite many patient conversations, to persuade Harriet to cease being restless and anxious about the Eltons, Emma changes tack, appealing not to Harriet's reason but to her affection for herself: **'I have not said, exert yourself, Harriet, for my sake; think less, talk less of Mr Elton for my sake; because, for your own sake rather, I would wish it to be done, for the sake of what is more important than my comfort – a habit of self-command in you, a consideration of what is your duty, an attention to propriety, an endeavour to avoid the suspicions of others, to save your health and credit, and restore your tranquillity. These are the motives that I have been pressing on you. They are very important, and sorry I am that you cannot feel them sufficiently to act upon them. My being saved from pain is a very secondary consideration. I want you to save yourself from greater pain. Perhaps I may sometimes have felt that Harriet would not forget what was due – or rather, what would be kind by me.'**

For all Emma's foolishnesses, as this speech shows, she has an excellent understanding of her society's mores and a strict personal code of morality. Of all the ways she had ever planned for Harriet's improvement, from finding her a husband to getting her to read more, this speech is possibly the greatest service she ever does, in fact, render her. The effect on tender-hearted Harriet is immediate. If it proves lasting, if the lesson sinks in, it will strengthen her mind for the rest of her life.

A young Fanny Price grows into a similar maturity unaided by anything but experience and her own reflections. Fanny has always struggled to do the right thing, and to submit uncomplainingly to whatever treatment is meted out to her; she has never forced knowledge of her sufferings on anybody else, even the sympathetic Edmund. But the term *exertion* is not used in connection with her until more than halfway through *Mansfield Park*, when crisis comes in the form of a proposal of marriage from Henry Crawford and her uncle's grave displeasure at her refusal. After a long and distressing interview, Sir Thomas leaves her crying bitterly, but returns in a quarter of an hour to recommend exertion, for her own sake and his, and as a way of shielding herself from the notice of her aunts – all the same reasons which Emma has urged on Harriet, in effect. **She walked out directly as her uncle recommended, and followed his advice throughout as far as she could; did check her tears, did earnestly try to compose her spirits and strengthen her mind. She wished to prove to him that she did desire his comfort, and sought to regain his favour; and he had given her another strong motive for exertion, in keeping the whole affair from the knowledge of her aunts.**

Fanny again has to exert herself when attacked on the same subject, albeit fondly, by the man she secretly loves, her cousin Edmund, requiring **a pause of recollection and exertion** before she can counter his hurtful yet well-meaning arguments in favour of Henry Crawford's suit. This habit of exertion stands Fanny in good stead later when, incarcerated in Portsmouth, she is cut off from knowledge of the events unfolding in Mansfield and London concerning those in whom she has most interest. After the arrival of a letter from Mary Crawford revealing that Edmund has arrived in London – a fact which, Fanny hardly doubts, will be followed very soon by their engagement – she is in dreadful suspense awaiting a letter from Edmund himself, to the point of neglecting her usual employments, especially reading and conversation with her younger sister Susan. Just like Harriet Smith, for three or four days Fanny is in a most restless, anxious state of mind, as no letter arrives to confirm or allay her fears. But Fanny is better equipped than Harriet with understanding, especially with understanding her duty: **At length, a something like composure succeeded. Suspense must be submitted to, and must not be allowed to wear her out, and make her useless. Time did something, her own exertions something** more, and she resumed her attentions to Susan, and again awakened the same interest in them.

Like any other quality, *exertion* can be misplaced, overdone, or practised for the wrong reasons. Mrs Elton's rallying cry to Emma on behalf of Jane Fairfax: '**We must exert ourselves and endeavour to do something for her**', sounds kind enough but is in fact interfering, patronizing and, insofar as she is trying to ally herself with the first lady of Highbury, Emma, a symptom of pretension and self-importance. Self-importance is also the root of Mrs Norris's vaunted **much exertion and many sacrifices** during Sir Thomas's absence from Mansfield. The result of her efforts is the disastrous marriage between her niece and Mr Rushworth, and the result of *that* is the destruction of the peace and reputation of the family. Misconceived exertion indeed. Henry Crawford also owes his loss of peace and happiness to exertion applied to the wrong object. While it all should have gone towards trying to win Fanny's love (Edmund considers her worth **every effort of patience, every exertion of mind** that Crawford can bring to bear – and for a while Henry does make that effort), in the end he cannot resist another game, **he must exert himself to subdue** Mrs Rushworth's resentment, and thus becomes entangled by his own vanity.

We have seen in Fanny's struggles how composure is linked with exertion. For her, and for many of Jane Austen's characters, they are two sides of the same coin. As she walks in the shrubbery at Mansfield after the painful interview with Sir Thomas, Fanny **did earnestly try to compose her spirits**; and, left in ignorance day after day in Portsmouth, **something like composure** is arrived at. *Composure* – the idea of bringing things properly into relationship – manifests itself both as the outward appearance of normal social demeanour, and the inward calming of emotion. Jane Austen approves of both. They save heartache for the individual, preserve privacy, and avoid spreading misery to other people. These aims might run counter to the prevailing wisdom and behaviour of our own time, but for Jane Austen they are both a religious and a social imperative.

Elizabeth Bennet, on the embarrassing occasion of Darcy's morning visit to Longbourn, in company with Bingley, **sat intently at work, striving to be composed**. She does not know what Darcy's arrival portends, whether it can possibly be that he still wishes to marry her after all that has happened between their two families. At first she speaks as little as civility allows, fearing that anything she ventures might be misconstrued. But after a while a rude remark of her mother's, levelled at Mr Darcy, draws from Elizabeth **the exertion of speaking, which nothing else had so effectually done before.** By striving for both *composure* and *exertion*, as the demands of the moment require, she avoids arousing the curiosity of her family and at the same time does her social duty by their visitor, whatever might be his intentions towards herself. Later, when she has accepted Mr Darcy's renewed proposals of marriage, and explained her reasons for loving him to her doubting father, **Elizabeth's mind was now relieved from a heavy weight; and after half an hour's quiet reflection in her own room, she was able to join the others with tolerable composure.** She reflects because she feels the momentousness of the occasion, and she composes herself to go back into company because she does not want to awaken curiosity in the rest of her family. Elizabeth will choose her own time for communication – a time when Darcy is not present to be embarrassed by the reaction it evokes.

Elinor Dashwood, committed as we have seen to *exertion*, is also an advocate of *composure*. When Lucy Steele is forcing her confidences on Elinor, she replies **with a composure of voice, under which was concealed an emotion and distress beyond anything she had ever felt before.** Her sister Marianne scorns such subterfuge, as she would consider it. She has already, early in the novel, expressed dismay for the way Elinor listens to Edward Ferrars' tame manner of reading poetry **with so much composure** and, when they come to leave Norland, exclaimed of the couple, **'How cold, how composed were their last adieus!'** Opportunity to show her own different response to a lovers' parting will come. When Willoughby leaves Devonshire abruptly, Marianne **would have been ashamed to look her family in the face next morning, had she not risen from her bed in more need of repose than when she lay down in it. But the feelings which made such composure a disgrace, left her in no danger of incurring it. She was awake the whole night, and she wept the greatest part of it. She got up with an headache, was unable to talk, and unwilling to take any nourishment;**

giving pain every moment to her mother and sisters, and forbidding all attempt at consolation from either. And at this point, Marianne has no suspicion that the parting from Willoughby is more than a temporary interruption to their love story.

'Pray, pray be composed', cries Elinor to Marianne, when they glimpse Willoughby at a party, the first sight of him since the sisters' arrival in London. But to be composed at such a moment was not only beyond the reach of Marianne, it was beyond her wish. As she greets and then – staggered by his cool reception – upbraids him, Marianne's face goes from crimson to white and she utters cries of wretchedness that all can hear, quite uncaring for her own reputation. Trying to shield her sister from general observation, Elinor endeavours but fails to persuade Marianne to check her agitation, to wait, at least, with the appearance of composure, till she might speak to him with more privacy. Willoughby manages the encounter better, in one sense at least. At first Elinor observes him struggling for composure until he is able to speak calmly; and then, his embarrassment returning with Marianne's appeals, as if, on catching the eye of the young lady to whom he had previously been talking, he felt the necessity of instant exertion, he recovered himself again. This combination of composure and exertion during a difficult encounter in a public place is behaviour which would be correct and admirable in an innocent heroine, the very behaviour Elinor herself is urging on Marianne – but in Willoughby it is coldly calculating, and confirms him as a cad. He does have residual feelings for Marianne, but in the cause of self-interest he is able to suppress them in front of the rich young woman to whom he is now engaged.

This is the problem with composure. Usually the sign of unselfish consideration for others, it can be used to mask evil propensities, double dealing, or simply coldness of heart and lack of feeling. (This is what Marianne, mistakenly, assumes composure *always* signifies.) In *Pride and Prejudice*, Mr Collins and Charlotte Lucas have no real feelings for each other. It is questionable whether Mr Collins is capable of feeling for anybody. When he proposes to Elizabeth, the idea of Mr Collins, with all his solemn composure, being run away with by his feelings, as he claims, makes Elizabeth almost laugh out loud. It is no laughing matter to her, however, when three days later

Mr Collins proposes more successfully to her friend Charlotte, meeting with open encouragement the very reverse of Elizabeth's disdain. Having gained her point – a home and husband, albeit such a husband – **Charlotte herself was tolerably composed.** She has to encounter Elizabeth's incredulity, but **as it was no more than she had expected, she soon regained her composure.** And when Elizabeth comes to visit the newly married couple, she observes and cannot help admiring Charlotte's **composure in bearing with her husband.** For Jane Austen, such composure is a virtue, for however wrong Charlotte was to marry Mr Collins, she now has a duty neither to disparage him nor to repine at her decision.

Elizabeth understands the desirability of composure, especially in women, who have so few means of fending off the ridicule of society. When her sister Jane begins to feel a preference for Mr Bingley, which seems to be reciprocated, Elizabeth **considered with pleasure that it was not likely to be discovered by the world in general, since Jane united with great strength of feeling, a composure of temper and a uniform cheerfulness of manner, which would guard her from the suspicions of the impertinent.** (Were Marianne Dashwood in this novel, she would never be able to believe that 'strength of feeling' and *composure* could exist at the same time in the same person, as it does in Jane.)

Composure may be a question of manners or of self-respect. When Mr Darcy makes his first, ungracious proposal of marriage to Elizabeth, **she tried, however, to compose herself to answer him with patience** and further into the encounter, as he offends her more and more, **she tried to the utmost to speak with composure.** On understanding that she means to reject him, Darcy also has a struggle for *composure*, though his seems less an effort of politeness than a determination not to let her see how much he is affronted. **He was struggling for the appearance of composure, and would not open his lips, till he believed himself to have attained it.** The following day, he hands her a letter of self-justification and explanation **with a look of haughty composure.** Later, however, when they meet by chance at Pemberley, **he absolutely started, and for a moment seemed immoveable from surprise; but shortly recovering himself, advanced towards the party, and spoke to Elizabeth, if not in terms of perfect composure, at** least of perfect civility. Darcy is a changed man, thanks to Elizabeth's rebukes, and now his deeper feelings make *composure* harder for him to attain. **Whether he had felt more of pain or pleasure in seeing her, she could not tell, but he certainly had not seen her with composure.** The difficulty is contagious, because so is the depth of feeling. About to be introduced to his sister Georgiana, the usually self-assured Elizabeth **is quite amazed at her own discomposure** and walks up and down the room **endeavouring to compose herself.** And when the Darcys and Mr Bingley arrive, **she wanted to ascertain the feelings of each of her visitors, she wanted to compose her own.** Composure is certainly not incompatible with feeling.

The negative connotations of the word are exemplified in two of the most overbearing, cold and correct older men in the novels, Sir Walter Elliot and General Tilney. When Sir Walter and Elizabeth Elliot enter the White Hart Inn in Bath, their presence ensures that **the comfort, the freedom, the gaiety of the room was over, hushed into cold composure, determined silence, or insipid talk.** As a house guest at Northanger Abbey, Catherine Morland is truly comfortable only when General Tilney is absent; he expects the household to conform to his every rule, and his hints of punctuality **did not advance her composure.** He signally fails in his duty of hospitality, of putting his visitors at their ease.

Jane Fairfax's composure is more amenable to different interpretation. She has a secret to keep, and on her arrival in Highbury, Emma finds her uncommunicative and undemonstrative: **her composure was odious.** Then, when the secret is out, Emma marvels at Jane's composure while Frank was flirting with herself: '**Composure with a witness!**' she calls it – or as we would say, composure with a vengeance – in which Emma finds 'a degree of placidity which I can neither comprehend nor respect'. And eventually, when the two young women meet on friendly terms, Jane betrays **a blush and a hesitation which Emma thought more becoming to her than all the elegance of her usual composure.**

However, it must be remembered that we are viewing these encounters through Emma's eyes, and that Jane's composure may be annoyingly inconvenient to Emma, who likes to see into everybody's heart, rather than wrong in itself. In similar circumstances of a hidden emotional attachment, composure almost always attracts authorial approval. Emma herself encourages it in Harriet, who is liable to **a flutter of spirits which Miss Woodhouse hoped very soon to compose,** or laments its want: despite the passage of months since Harriet's disappointment in Mr Elton, and all Emma's efforts to reason away the hopeless attachment, it is now evident that Harriet has still not attained such a state of composure as will carry her safely through the arrival of his bride in Highbury. It is strangely right for Harriet to conceal *her* feelings from the neighbourhood at large, but not for Jane Fairfax to do so.

Emma applies the same high standards to herself as to Harriet, or even more so in her own case, knowing there is no excuse for a woman of her intelligence and strength of mind to fall short. In the depth of her own unhappiness, when she thinks that Mr Knightley is lost to her, and that she has only herself and her own errors to blame, she struggles hard for composure, for acceptance of a necessary evil. **The only source whence anything like consolation or composure could be drawn, was in the resolution of her own better conduct, and the hope that, however inferior in spirit and gaiety might be the following and every future winter of her life to the past, it would yet find her more rational, more acquainted with herself, and leave her less to regret when it were gone.**

Anne Elliot too seeks composure at various painful junctures of her story. When Captain Wentworth sees her for the first time in eight years following the breaking of their engagement, he says in response to Henrietta Musgrove's enquiry that Anne is so altered he would not have known her again. If Anne had been harbouring even the remotest hopes that on seeing her his love would re-ignite, his words brutally quash them. Repeated to her by her sister, these words **were of a sobering tendency; they allayed agitation; they composed, and consequently must make her happier.** She considers that it is better to be without hope entirely than to be racked by alternating hopes and fears. At Lyme, Mary's jealous claims to be allowed to stay behind and look after Louisa mean that she is substituted for Anne at the last moment. Captain Wentworth, knowing that Anne would be much more useful, finds it hard to conceal his vexation. Anne hopes he does not think her reluctant to minister to Louisa, but politeness forbids her putting her own case in opposition to Mary. Forced back on silence, as Anne so often is, **she endeavoured to be composed, and to be just.**

In Bath, Anne is bewitched for a moment by the picture Lady Russell paints of Anne's succeeding to her mother's place at Kellynch by virtue of a possible marriage to her father's heir. So discomposed is the usually calm and collected Anne, that she has to rise from her seat and walk about to dispel the effect of such a suggestion on her imagination. It is when her imagination carries through the picture into Mr Elliot's actually proposing that the charm is broken. The **image of Mr Elliot speaking for himself brought Anne to composure again.** She does not love the man for himself, and could never marry him, though at this stage she knows no actual harm of him.

Subsequently, Mr Elliot's villainy is revealed by Anne's old school friend, Mrs Smith. Shocked and horrified, Anne resolves to tell Lady Russell what she has learnt, and then to wait **with as much composure as possible** for the discovery to be revealed to her father and sister. But by now Anne is beginning to have hopes of Captain Wentworth again, hopes that make every other concern trivial: **and after all, her greatest want of composure would be in that quarter of the mind which could not be opened to Lady Russell; in that flow of anxieties and fears which must be all to herself.**

The novel gathers to its climax in the White Hart Inn, where (in two rewritten chapters) Jane Austen brings the principal characters together on two successive mornings. At the beginning of her story, as Anne contemplated the past, she deplored the prudence she had been forced into and **that over-anxious caution which seems to insult exertion and distrust Providence!** Now, as 'all that this world could do for her' hangs in the balance, Anne needs to draw on all her reserves of both *exertion* and *composure*. The first morning, amid the company, there is opportunity for some highly interesting but inconclusive conversation with Captain Wentworth, in which she discerns (and tries to dispel) jealousy of Mr Elliot. That this costs the normally retiring Anne some exertion is shown when, on being begged to return and dine with the Musgroves, she must decline: **her spirits had been so long exerted that at present she felt unequal to more, and fit only for home, where she might be sure of being as silent as she chose.** Revived by a night's sleep, she expects to encounter Captain Wentworth some time during the following day, but finds him already at the White Hart when she arrives. **She had only to ... sit down, be outwardly composed, and feel herself plunged at once in all the agitations which she had merely laid her account of tasting a little before the morning closed. She was deep in the happiness of such misery, or the misery of such happiness, instantly.** But Anne remains **outwardly composed**, so that no one guesses she has a special interest in Captain Wentworth. Their engagement, entered into in the course of that morning, must take all their friends utterly by surprise when it is announced. As many critics have remarked, the achievement of these two rewritten chapters is that Anne wins through to her happy destiny by virtue of her own talk and actions at last – by the judicious blend of *exertion* and *composure* that has always marked this most admirable of heroines.

5

ℒiberality and Candour

THESE TWO QUALITIES are linked by the notion of generosity. *Liberality* might manifest itself as generosity either of purse or spirit. *Candour* (in its eighteenth-century meaning) is generosity in forming judgements of other people. Elizabeth Bennet speaks of her sister's **'generous candour'** and in Elinor Dashwood's mind **'candid allowances and generous qualifications'** are synonyms. Miss Bates, forgivingly, speaks with **candour and generosity** of Emma Woodhouse's cruel wit. Meanwhile liberality and generosity, being almost synonyms themselves, and therefore not often used in the same sentence by Jane Austen, are coupled once in the novels when George Wickham, amid all his criticism of Mr Darcy, has to admit that his pride **'has often led him to be liberal and generous – to give his money freely, to display hospitality, to assist his tenants, and relieve the poor'.**

This is liberality in money matters, and it occurs fairly frequently in the novels. It is usually men who have the wealth to dispense; but on occasion a woman might have the opportunity to be either generous or otherwise from her purse. Instinctive good nature and understanding of how to behave stand Catherine Morland in good stead during her enforced journey from Northanger Abbey to her home seventy miles away without the protection of a servant or gentleman: **her youth, civil manners and liberal pay procured her all the attention that a traveller like herself could require.**

When the surprise gift to Jane Fairfax of a pianoforte is under discussion, Emma (somewhat deviously) rejoices in **Colonel Campbell's being so rich and so liberal.** The illegitimate Harriet Smith's **allowance is very liberal; nothing has ever been grudged for her improvement or**

comfort. From this evidence alone, Emma deduces that Harriet's unknown father must be a gentleman – whereas he turns out to be 'a tradesman, rich enough to afford her the comfortable maintenance which had ever been hers'; and when Robert Martin seeks permission to marry her, the young man is **treated liberally** by the father. As well he might: Robert Martin has conveniently taken Harriet off her father's conscience – and balance sheet – for good.

In this liberal treatment, Robert Martin has his reward for not expecting Harriet to bring to the marriage anything but her own self; his first marriage proposal is made in writing, and as even Emma has to acknowledge, the letter **expressed good sense, warm attachment, liberality, propriety, even delicacy of feeling.** These are the qualities that should characterize any offer of marriage, but especially when the groom is in better worldly circumstances than the bride. Henry Crawford, too, has made his proposals for Fanny to her uncle in a very satisfactory manner: **he had done it all so well, so openly, so liberally, so properly** in Sir Thomas's eyes. Presumably by *liberally* Sir Thomas chiefly means that Mr Crawford offers all and asks little or nothing in financial terms. Both suitors, being thoroughly in love, are all generosity.

Some of the most hypocritical characters deceive themselves about their own liberality. At the beginning of *Sense and Sensibility*, when John Dashwood considers how he might fulfil his promise to his dying father to take care of his sisters, and with the prospect of his own inheritance making him feel 'capable of generosity', he resolves **'Yes, he would give them three thousand pounds: it would be liberal and handsome!'** In the event his wife persuades him, by degrees, to do nothing for them at all. Their mother finds that she has **firmly relied on the liberality of his intentions** in vain. Mrs John Dashwood, *née* Ferrars, has acquired her meanness from her mother; Elinor attributes Edward Ferrars's dejection to **some want of liberality in his mother.** The subsequent twists of the story show that Mrs Ferrars is liberal to her eldest son neither in financial terms nor in unselfish wishes for his happiness.

Another hypocrite is Mrs Norris in *Mansfield Park*. Having helped persuade Sir Thomas to relieve her impoverished sister, Mrs Price, of the upbringing of little Fanny, without having herself 'the least intention of being at any expense whatever in her maintenance', Mrs Norris walks home **in the happy belief of being the most liberal-minded sister and aunt in the world.** This is our introduction to Mrs Norris's character. **Nobody knew better how to dictate liberality to others; but her love of money was equal to her love of directing, and she knew quite as well how to save her own as to spend that of her friends.** Her subsequent assertion that she has been **'a liberal housekeeper'** is not to be trusted, nor is her claim to hate 'pitiful doings' – the antithesis of liberality.

Liberality, like liberty in deriving from the Latin word for freedom, can mean not only giving freely but treating oneself freely – a far less meritorious concept. Thus Tom Bertram has **all the liberal dispositions of the eldest son,** that is, spending his father's money recklessly and getting into debt. There is no suggestion that Frank Churchill runs up debts on his uncle's account, but still, he spends freely on pleasure (Weymouth; the pianoforte) and is **a very liberal thanker, with his thousands and tens of thousands** of thanks in a letter, a reflection of the lack of rigour of his mind. Both young men fit the definition of liberal as inclining to laxity and indulgence. Charles Musgrove is another young man with no profession, maintaining his home, wife and growing family on the money allowed to him by his father, who has many younger children of his own to support. Charles at least has the grace to acknowledge that the elder Mr Musgrove **'has always been a very kind, liberal father to me'** and, though united with his wife in wishing they had more money, does not begrudge his sisters' receiving their share of the family wealth on marriage.

One of the earliest uses of the concept of liberality was in relation to education: a liberal education comprised study 'worthy of a free man', that is, directed towards the intellectual enlargement and refinement of the mind, not restricted to the technical or mechanical training of one who must work for his living. There is an echo of this in *Emma*, where Jane Austen mocks the prospectuses of expensive, fashionable girls' schools:

Mrs Goddard was mistress of a school – not of a seminary, or an establishment, or anything which professed, in long sentences of refined nonsense, to combine liberal acquirements with elegant morality,

upon new principles and new systems – and where young ladies for enormous pay might be screwed out of health and into vanity – but a real, honest, old-fashioned boarding-school, where a reasonable quantity of accomplishments were sold at a reasonable price, and where girls might be sent to be out of the way, and scramble themselves into a little education, without any danger of coming back prodigies.

In the same novel, Mrs Elton, as with a pretentiousness to equal that of the prospectus-writers, employs the same two epithets – *liberal* and *elegant* – in another educational reference. With even more absurdity, she applies them to a mere nursery establishment in the family of one Mrs Smallridge, near Bristol, where the post of governess to three little girls is on offer. We hear the words not from Mrs Elton's own mouth, but repeated without irony or scepticism by the simple, easily impressed Miss Bates.

The concept of liberality is evoked particularly often in this novel. Mr and Mrs Coles, rising in prosperity, are said to be **very good sort of people, friendly, liberal and unpretending.** Their liberality, as far as we observe it, consists in giving dinner-parties (unlike the mean-minded Sir Walter and Elizabeth Elliot in *Persuasion*), and purchasing a piano for the occasional entertainment of their neighbours, but in more general terms they are well-disposed towards everybody, including those less fortunate than themselves, like the Bateses. Emma acknowledges that actual poverty, in those trying to keep up appearances, contracts the mind and sours the temper to the detriment of liberality. 'Those who **can barely live, and who live perforce in a very small, and generally very inferior society, may well be illiberal and cross**', she muses, although excepting the good-hearted Miss Bates from this rule.

Vulgarity, or lack of education, is also too apt to militate against liberality. So that Elinor Dashwood, in arriving at the London home of Mrs Jennings, where she and her sister are to be house-guests for several weeks, is all the more relieved to observe that **everything in her household arrangements was conducted on the most liberal plan.** Since the Dashwood sisters are indifferent to food – on the journey to London, they do not care whether they eat salmon or cod, boiled fowls or veal cutlets – this liberality probably extends to the number and conduct of her servants and the comfort of her furnishings as well as to her housekeeping: indeed, the house is handsome and handsomely fitted up, and everything runs smoothly and calmly. In her own home Mrs Jennings does not stint herself, but she is equally generous to her young visitors, as we discover when she fetches the last drop of Constantia wine to ease Marianne's heartache, or tries to tempt her appetite with sweetmeats and delicacies.

Often liberality with material things shades into liberality of mind – kindness and openheartedness – Mrs Jennings perhaps being a case in point. When Sir Thomas Bertram assists Mrs Price **liberally in the education and disposal of her sons** he is giving her not only money but the benefit of his time, thought and effort. Miss Bates is truly grateful for **Mr Knightley's most liberal supply** of apples from his orchard, but this is but a symptom of the prevailing liberality of his habitual conduct to everybody. So, when he speaks critically of Frank Churchill before he has even seen him, it is out of character, and Emma reflects that **to take a dislike to a young man, only because he appeared to be of a different disposition from himself, was unworthy of the real liberality of mind which she was used to acknowledge in him; for, with all the high opinion of himself which she had often laid to his charge, she had never before for a moment supposed that it could make him unjust to the merit of another.** This is liberality as breadth of mind, freedom from prejudice or bias towards the self and the self's concerns.

Charles Musgrove employs the negative form of the word in acknowledging the moral imperative of this quality of justice and magnanimity: **'I hope you do not think I am so illiberal as to want every man to have the same objects and pleasures as myself'**, he tells Anne. And Elinor Dashwood avers: **'I will not raise objections against anyone's conduct on so illiberal a foundation as a difference in judgement from myself, or a deviation from what I may think right and consistent.'**

The fastidious Marianne Dashwood deplores commonplace expressions and jokes: **'their tendency is gross and illiberal'** she reproves Sir John Middleton. Elizabeth Bennet herself is guilty of one lapse. Having told her aunt, with worldly unconcern, that the only charm of Miss King, who has supplanted her as the object of Wickham's attentions, is her sudden acquisition of ten thousand pounds, she later hears Lydia **'answer for it he never cared three straws about her. Who** could about such a nasty little freckled thing?' Elizabeth was shocked to think that, however incapable of such coarseness of *expression* herself, the coarseness of the *sentiment* was little other than her own breast had formerly harboured and fancied liberal! Recognizing her fault, Elizabeth (who has uttered a few coarse expressions, such as saving her breath to cool her porridge), refines herself to be worthy of her role as lady of Pemberley, consort of Mr Darcy.

Elizabeth admires from the heart the **forbearance and liberality** of Mr Darcy's behaviour towards the man he has every reason to detest, George Wickham. Darcy's *liberality*, a real part of his personality, extends even to those not in his patronage, as Wickham himself acknowledges: '**with the rich he is liberal-minded, just, sincere, rational**'. This consistent *liberality*, extended to equals and inferiors alike and as appropriate, characterizes both the landowning gentlemen among Jane Ausen's heroes, Mr Darcy and Mr Knightley, the two who have the most people's happiness in their power.

The true gentleman, of any profession or none, must number *liberality* among his attributes if he is to deserve the appellation. One of Lord Chesterfield's most important instructions to his son is, 'If you have not liberal and engaging manners, you will be nobody.' When we read that Mr Elliot, in Bath, **lived with the liberality of a man of fortune**, it is not clear whether he has been observed in acts of charity and neighbourliness or – more likely – is free and easy in his personal expenditure; either way, he has plenty of money at his disposal, and being grand and careless with it has a certain sort of merit in denoting the elevated mind of a gentleman – even if it by no means matches the merit of a Mr Knightley or a Mr Darcy. Aspiring gentlemen – from the farmer Robert Martin to the naval characters in *Persuasion* – fully deserve to be acknowledged as gentlemen if they behave with real liberality.

'**Gentlemen of the navy are well to deal with … they have very liberal notions**', says the lawyer Mr Shepherd when trying to recommend the profession as tenants to Sir Walter Elliot, and his daughter Mrs Clay adds, '**besides their liberality, they are so neat and careful in all their ways!**' Mary Crawford tells her brother that, even if he ceases to love Fanny Price after she becomes his wife as much as he loves her now,

'She would yet find in you the liberality and good-breeding of a gentleman'. (This is exactly what Lady Bertram finds in *her* husband, Sir Thomas, whom Mary considers the best husband of her acquaintance.) But to the more sensitive Fanny, good manners would be poor consolation for lack of true affection and confidence.

Mary Crawford's values are increasingly being seen as dubious as the novel works its way to conclusion. She is again the speaker in one of the few sentences in the novels which couple *liberality* with *candour*. Maria Rushworth has abandoned her marriage to run away with Henry Crawford, and Mary is wondering how she can recover her place in society: '**with good dinners, and large parties, there will always be those who will be glad of her acquaintance; and there is, undoubtedly, more liberality and candour on those points than formerly**'. Mary Crawford is wrong, the dupe of wishful thinking, perhaps. She is standing on the verge of the Victorian period, when there will be *less* **liberality** and **candour** on points of sexual misconduct than ever before in our history.

Candour is one of those words which have undergone a significant shift in meaning between Jane Austen's time and our own. Deriving from the Latin word for whiteness, by extension it can imply various human qualities, from sincerity to almost its opposite, mildness. Now, of course, we understand by a candid person one who is outspoken, frank, truthful almost to the point of rudeness. We would hardly recognize Dr Johnson's definition of *candid* as 'free from malice, not desiring to find fault'. But in *Pride and Prejudice*, this exactly describes the quality that astonishes Elizabeth Bennet in her sister Jane: 'You never see a fault in anybody. All the world are good and agreeable in your eyes. I never heard you speak ill of a human being in my life', she says and, when Jane protests that she always speaks what she thinks, Elizabeth continues, '**I know you do; and it is *that* which makes the wonder. With *your* good sense, to be so honestly blind to the follies and nonsense of others! Affectation of candour is common enough – one meets with it everywhere. But to be candid without ostentation or design belongs to you alone.**'

This quality is not just *ascribed* to Jane: we *see* it in almost every action or speech of hers, as she seeks to put the best gloss on everybody's conduct. When Meryton society takes against Mr Darcy, Jane is the only person to suppose there may be extenuating circumstances unknown to them: **her mild and steady candour always pleaded for allowances.** Elizabeth is right that this is no affectation in her sister – of course, it would be insufferable if it were, turning a sweet character into a priggish, self-satisfied one. Emma Woodhouse finds Jane Fairfax guilty on this count. The two young women entertain the company with music; Emma, aware that her performance is not to be compared with Jane's, is over-sensitive to the other woman's normal politeness: **the thanks and praise which necessarily followed appeared to her an affectation of candour, an air of greatness, meaning only to show off in higher style her own very superior performance.** Channelling her uncomfortable feelings of inferiority into criticism of Jane, Emma is certainly not being candid herself in this judgement.

Affectation of candour was common enough in polished eighteenth-century society to be pilloried by Sheridan in *School for Scandal*, one of whose characters is called Mrs Candour. Emma Woodhouse has something to say about **the candour and common sense of the world,** that is, the qualities the public bring to bear on general topics. Talking to Harriet Smith about the difference which a good income makes to the way a single woman is treated – a poor woman being viewed as a ridiculous, disagreeable old maid while a spinster of independent fortune may be as respectable, pleasant and sensible as anyone else, Emma says that '**the distinction is not quite so much against the candour and common sense of the world as it appears at first**' because there are rational reasons for the difference: a small income does often make a person mean-spirited, resentful or hypersensitive.

Jane Bennet is not stupid – but her intelligence does not match Elizabeth's. While honouring and valuing her sister's charitable outlook, Elizabeth prides herself on her own very different response to people around her – as she thinks of it, a more realistic, clear-sighted response. And even though Elizabeth's judgement of others turns out in two important instances to be badly wrong, it is Elizabeth's more critical mind that the reader delights in. Elizabeth is, in fact, when fortified by reason, no less generous of spirit than Jane. Forced by the evidence to confront her own misjudgements, Elizabeth berates herself: '**I, who have prided myself on my discernment! Who have often disdained the generous candour of my sister, and gratified my vanity, in useless or blameable distrust! How humiliating is this discovery!**' Yet the moral of the story is hardly that everybody should be as candid as Jane Bennet – who, after all, makes her own mistakes relative to the Bingley sisters, and whose saintly habit of making allowances for Mrs Bennet's bad behaviour convinces neither Elizabeth nor the author to do the same. Perhaps Jane Austen expects no more from herself or other people than is summed up by Alexander Pope in his 1732 *Essay on Man*: 'Laugh where we must, be candid where we can.'

The other character in the novels who shows *candour* in all her dealings with others must be Anne Elliot of *Persuasion*, a heroine whom Jane Austen called 'almost too good for me'. Ready though she is to make allowances for other people – her father and elder sister perhaps excepted – the term itself is never applied to Anne. Its only use in the novel is when describing Mr Elliot, who seems for a while to have all the virtues, as **steady, observant, moderate, candid**. Insofar as Anne cannot help distrusting this appearance of virtue, she is, perhaps, herself less candid than wise.

The problem is that *candour* is too often in opposition to *common sense*. '**It is my wish to be candid in my judgement of everybody**', says another heroine, Elinor Dashwood, struggling like Anne Elliot and Elizabeth Bennet to arrive at a just assessment of male worth when there are so very few clues to the real character of the men who enter their lives. Elinor's mother is urging her to make allowances for Willoughby's strange behaviour in so abruptly leaving Devonshire and Marianne, allowances which do not sit comfortably with Elinor's understanding. Not long afterwards, however, when puzzled by and displeased with some of the behaviour (equally unaccountable) of the man she loves herself, Edward Ferrars, Elinor is **very well disposed on the whole to regard his actions with all the candid allowances and generous qualifications, which had been rather more painfully extorted from her, for Willoughby's service, by her mother**. Even in her heroines, Jane Austen loves to point up inconsistencies in behaviour; and indeed, Elinor's inconsistency here, under the influence of love, endears her to us.

'His observations have stretched much farther than your candour', Elinor says to Willoughby and Marianne in defence of Colonel Brandon, whom they have been criticizing ungenerously, accusing the two careless young lovers, wrapped up only in each other, of being 'prejudiced and unjust'. To be just in judgement is to be correct; to be *candid* in judgement is to make allowances, perhaps to assume innocence unless proven guilty, and above all to take the self out of the equation, to see things from the other person's point of view. Fanny Price, whose moral code is strict (for herself and others) cannot help being judgemental when she sees so much dubious behaviour around her, but she is wary of allowing her dislike of what the Crawfords stand for, and in particular her jealousy of Mary, to colour her judgement: **Fanny was the only one of the party who found anything to dislike; but since the day at Sotherton, she could never see Mr Crawford with either sister without observation, and seldom without wonder or censure; and had her confidence in her own judgement been equal to her exercise of it in every other respect, had she been sure that she was seeing clearly, and judging candidly, she would probably have made some important communications to her usual confidant.**

When Frank Churchill arrives, after much anticipation, in Highbury, the simple folk there are not disposed to find fault: **In general, he was judged throughout the parishes of Donwell and Highbury with great candour; liberal allowances were made for the little excesses of such a handsome young man – one who smiled so often and bowed so well.** The only person not so *candid*, not distracted by smiles and bows from his 'powers of censure' is Mr Knightley; and that is because self intrudes: he is already jealous of Emma's liking for Frank – even if he does not yet realize it himself. Mr Knightley, usually unfailing to his neighbours in his *liberality* and *candour*, has this one weak spot.

'**I know it will be read with candour and indulgence**', Frank writes to his stepmother, when sending a long letter to explain away his bad behaviour in concealing his secret engagement. As it is: by Mrs Weston, by Emma, and even by Mr Knightley, now that he has secured Emma for his own.

Another character hoping his apologies will be met with candour, though in this instance the offence is not his own but his father's, is

Henry Tilney, calling on Mrs Morland to ascertain that Catherine has got safely home after being turned out so peremptorily from Northanger Abbey in his absence. **He did not address himself to an uncandid judge or a resentful heart. Far from comprehending him or his sister in their father's misconduct, Mrs Morland had always been kindly disposed towards each.** Her 'unaffected benevolence' and 'unlooked-for mildness' relieve his heart and show him, if he needed to be shown, where Catherine gets her own character, which he has already praised as **'open, candid, artless, guileless'**.

A willingness to put aside self as an essential part of *candour* occurs twice more in *Mansfield Park*. When Edmund discovers Fanny has a headache after doing errands for her two aunts on a hot day, Mrs Norris shifts the blame from herself to her sister, but the **more candid Lady Bertram** accepts her share. Of more moment is Henry Crawford's first proper conversation with Fanny, when he returns to Mansfield after the marriage of Maria Bertram, and starts to chat to the reluctant Fanny about the abandoned theatricals. Forced to answer, she reproves him in a speech that is, for her, both long and angry. **He was surprised; but after a few moments' silent consideration of her, replied in a calmer, graver tone, and as if the candid result of conviction,** 'I believe you are right. It was more pleasant than prudent.' Henry begins to think, speak and behave differently from this moment.

Though these last three examples fit with the eighteenth-century definition of *candour* as an unselfish generosity of spirit, they also shade towards the modern meaning of frankness and sincerity. It is possible to see and understand how the transition happened. Once, and once only, does Jane Austen use the term as we would do today. It is in the mouth of Mrs Elton, who says, **'You know I candidly told you I should form my own opinion ... I never compliment'**. Since Mrs Elton is full of vulgarities of speech, there seems a reasonable likelihood that Jane Austen had heard this new use for the word and found it vulgar.

6

Gentility

JANE AUSTEN FAMOUSLY concerns herself with only one class in society, the gentry – the class below the aristocracy but with education, manners, money and leisure sufficient to raise them above the labouring masses, and to give them scope to make life choices, both little and great, that were denied to the poor. It is these life choices that are Jane Austen's novelistic concern. Just as Shakespeare focuses often on kings and rulers, because they had the power and freedom to act out their impulses, so by the eighteenth century the diffusion of prosperity and education gave rise to the novel about middling people. Their dilemmas, both petty and important, inspired a new literary genre, to which Jane Austen was heir.

The words *gentility*, *gentry*, *gentleman* and so forth come from the same root as generation and genus, meaning originally simply 'born', or by extension family, race, peoples – the French *gens*. Developing into the sense of 'well-born', the concept of gentility became associated with ideas of courtesy, chivalry, graceful manners and noble conduct. From this the idea of gentleness itself derived, being held to be the characteristic demeanour of the gentry – people who are gently spoken, gently behaved, polished, not uncouth, with knowledge of the world beyond their own immediate experience. Shakespeare has his lower orders address their betters as 'gentles'. He also uses the word as a verb, meaning to raise to the rank of the gentry, as when Henry V promises that every rough soldier who fights with him at Agincourt, 'Be he ne'er so vile / This day shall gentle his condition.'

Many commentators over the centuries saw society divided into 'gentles and simples' or 'gentles and commons'. As late as 1788 Frances

Burney could write in her journal, describing a visit by George III, 'All Cheltenham was drawn into the High Street, the gentles on one side and the commons on the other'. When, in his 1874 novel *Far From the Madding Crowd*, Thomas Hardy writes of all the girls of the neighbourhood, both gentle and simple, falling in love with his hero, he is not describing their dispositions, as may be thought today, but their rank.

Within the gentry, of course, there were many gradations, the manifestations of which, in speech and behaviour, were immediately detectable to the well-tuned English mind, so that a new acquaintance could (probably still can, for we have not yet lost our detective skills or our fascination with class) be placed within five minutes of meeting. This furnishes Jane Austen, as her predecessors, with a great deal of material, to be treated both playfully and seriously.

In the early pages of *Northanger Abbey* the narrator, giving notice of the class of people her story concerns, asks archly, **What young lady of common gentility will reach the age of sixteen without altering her name as far as she can?** Alluding to a common happening in fiction, and suggesting therefore the yearnings of young-lady novel-readers to inhabit the world of romance, and thus render their lives more exciting, the question also instructs us, the readers, that while the preoccupations of comfortably circumstanced people can seem amusingly trivial, yet they are worth attending to as part of the fabric of everyday life.

It is no exaggeration to say that all Jane Austen's protagonists belong to the gentry at some level. Servants, shopkeepers and so forth are sometimes mentioned by name, occasionally even have a line to speak, but take no part in the great moral drama – not necessarily through want of sympathy or insight on her part, but because their opportunities were minimal. But though all her characters belong to the gentry, not all are gentlemen (or the female equivalent, which may be expressed as either gentlewomen or ladies). For while the word gentleman denotes a social rank, more is required if the term is to be fully deserved: a manner of behaving, thinking, speaking, relating to others. And here, for reasons of upbringing, intelligence or personality, some of those who have claims to the rank of gentry fall short when judged as gentlemen. How else can Elizabeth Bennet so justly upbraid Darcy, one of the highest-born characters in the novels (his mother actually belonging to the aristocracy) for his insulting proposal: **'It spared me the concern I might have felt in refusing you, had you behaved in a more gentlemanlike manner'**? These are the words that cut him to the quick and make him, once his angry resentment has died down, resolve to reform himself.

'He is a gentleman; I am a gentleman's daughter. So far we are equal', Elizabeth says boldly to Lady Catherine de Bourgh, who is trying to make out that the alliance with her nephew would be degrading to him. Elizabeth is right; for all Darcy's superiority in wealth and landholdings, and her own dubious assortment of relations, they belong to the same rank. She would not be stepping out of her sphere in marrying him. Darcy's mother remains Lady Anne Darcy, because she is the daughter of an earl. Women take their husband's rank on marriage, if it is superior to their own, but do not lose rank if it is inferior to that of their father. Lady Anne's sister, Lady Catherine, also retains her Christian name title when she marries a baronet, Sir Lewis de Bourgh. Had Sir Lewis married a woman with no pre-existing title, his wife and widow would be known as Lady de Bourgh – just as Sir Thomas Bertram's wife is Lady Bertram, not Lady Maria Bertram.

None of Jane Austen's heroines marries a title, though there is a hint at the end of *Persuasion* that Captain Frederick Wentworth may be made a baronet for his services to the Royal Navy, in which case his wife will become Lady Wentworth. Of course, had a title been her object, Anne Elliot could have married her cousin Mr Elliot, and after her own father's death have become Lady Elliot: 'the idea of becoming what her mother had been; of having the precious name of "Lady Elliot" first revived in herself ... was a charm which she could not immediately resist'. But she does resist. Unlike her father and eldest sister, title *per se* is nothing to Anne. Elizabeth Elliot, by contrast, will look on nobody without one: she hopes 'to be solicited by baronet-blood within the next twelvemonth or two', though in setting her heart on her cousin, 'there was not a baronet from A to Z whom her feelings could have so willingly acknowledged as an equal'.

The late Lady Elliot – Anne and Elizabeth's mother – was not herself the daughter of a baronet, but of a gentleman: James Stevenson, Esq. of South Park in the county of Gloucester, according to Sir Walter's favourite book, the *Baronetage*. Snob though he is, just as much as his eldest daughter, Sir Walter evidently married a little beneath him, while susceptibility to *his* title, together with his handsome appearance, are the only things, the narrator tells us, for which the late Lady Elliot requires pardon. Thereafter, she led a blameless life. *Esquire*, these days either meaningless or a term of mockery, was the courtesy title awarded to a gentleman without other title in written address or description. It occurs again in *Persuasion* in the letter addressed by Mr Elliot to his friend **Charles Smith, Esq.** There is no female equivalent, Mrs being the counterpart of the less elevated Mr, the correct term to use in speech. Fanny Price protests that the appellation Mr Bertram **'just stands for a gentleman, and that's all'** whereas Mr Edmund Bertram – the customary way to refer to a younger son – has character. Likewise, all of Highbury refer to Mr Frank Churchill, to distinguish him from his uncle Mr Churchill. The same applied to unmarried sisters: Miss Bennet, Miss Elizabeth Bennet, Miss Austen, Miss Jane Austen, etc. It is worth mentioning that unlike our practice today, Mrs was often given as a courtesy title to an older unmarried woman, usually one who was head of her household or a high-ranking servant. Mrs Goddard, mistress of the school in *Emma*, and Mrs Reynolds, housekeeper at Pemberley, are not necessarily widows. Jane Austen's own sister, after their mother's death the only remaining inhabitant of Chawton Cottage, was sometimes addressed as Mrs Austen.

Sir Walter refers to himself as a **private gentleman: 'To live no longer with the decencies even of a private gentleman!'** he protests when faced with economies necessary to pay off his debts. The phrase signifies a gentleman of means and leisure, not holding public office or required to entertain dignitaries of state, but living self-sufficiently on his own property. His friend Lady Russell is sympathetic to his distress but adamant that there is something even more important than rank: **'A great deal is due to the feelings of a gentleman,'** she says, but **'there is still more due to the character of an honest man.'** This is a consideration conveniently overlooked by Sir Walter, or he would not have spent more than he receives in the first place: his inability to pay tradesmen's bills is damaging to men of much slighter means than his own.

For all his own deficiencies as an honourable gentleman, Sir Walter sets the bar high in admitting other men to gentry status. **'You misled me by the term gentleman'**, he says of a country curate who has been so described. **'I thought you were speaking of some man of property: Mr Wentworth was nobody, I remember; quite unconnected; nothing to do with the Strafford family. One wonders how the names of many of our nobility become so common.'** Sir Walter, who also inveighs against the navy for 'bringing persons of obscure birth into undue distinction, and raising men to honours which their fathers and grandfathers never dreamt of' is wrong about the navy, as it is the purpose of the novel to demonstrate: **Captain Harville, though not equalling Captain Wentworth in manners, was a perfect gentleman;** and he is certainly wrong about the curate, with his university education, whatever may be his background (and as it happens, he is brother to the well-mannered Captain Wentworth and the **well-spoken, genteel Mrs Croft**). We see the effect of university education also in Charles Hayter, the eldest son of a farming family, who would, **from their parents' inferior, retired, and unpolished way of living, and their own defective education, have been hardly in any class at all ... this eldest son of course excepted, who had chosen to be a scholar and a gentleman** by going to university and becoming ordained and who is consequently 'very superior in cultivation and manners to all the rest'.

Anne, who judges people on their merit, not on their wealth or rank, could not deplore her father's attitude more; yet even she is gratified to discover, from two very brief encounters with her cousin before they realize each other's identity, **that the future owner of Kellynch was undoubtedly a gentleman.** Since there is no doubt of his lineage, belonging as he does to her own family, it can only be his manners that she might before have doubted. All that Mr Elliot has done at this point is to stand aside politely at the head of some steps leading up from the beach at Lyme, and to apologize as he nearly bumps into her in the hotel afterwards, on both occasions looking rather pointedly at her. **It was evident that the gentleman (completely a gentleman in manner)**

admired her exceedingly. It perhaps stretches credulity that modest Anne can find this behaviour so gentlemanly! But of course, Jane Austen's artistic purpose is that Captain Wentworth's admiration be re-ignited, by observing that of another man.

All through the eighteenth century, as wealth increased and good manners were diffused among the population, what it was that made a gentleman was much debated. More people had the means to travel and the leisure to mix with one another in resorts such as Bath, or even at the assemblies of modest provincial towns, with the result that rough edges were knocked off the rustic squirearchy by observing and aping their betters. But not everyone who seemed polished subscribed to the same core values: some were upstarts, on the make, without the chivalrous instincts and fine feelings which should underlie good manners. The subject was susceptible to many treatments. In 1719 Richard Steele in *The Tatler* No. 207 asserted that 'The Appellation of a Gentleman is never to be affixed to a man's Circumstances, but to his Behaviour in them.' Lord Chesterfield's famous letters to his (illegitimate) son, begun in 1737, though designed to make him accepted as a gentleman, are occupied more with etiquette and the social arts than with morals.

In all Jane Austen's novels the characters and the narrator are concerned with what makes a gentleman, but in none more so than *Emma*. This novel has the distinction of containing, in the hero, Jane Austen's idea of a true English gentleman, perfect in his instincts and manners yet not so polished that we do not believe in him as a real man. It is a rare feat to pull off. **'You might not see one in a hundred with gentleman so plainly written'**, says Emma, long before she has recognized her love for him. One of Mr Knightley's virtues is that though he thinks very much about other people's feelings, he seldom bothers about the impression he is making himself. In Emma's view he is too apt to get about on his own two feet, but when he arrives at the Coles' party in his carriage, **'This is coming as you should do'**, **said she, 'like a gentleman'**, to which he retorts that is it lucky they arrived at the same moment or it is doubtful **'whether you would have discerned me to be more of a gentleman than usual'**. As Emma watches him walk across a ballroom, it is **enough to prove in how gentlemanlike** a manner, with what natural grace, he must have danced would he only take the trouble. And when, eventually, he addresses her as his own betrothed Emma, It was in plain, unaffected, gentlemanlike English, such as Mr Knightley used even to the woman he was in love with.

Is Harriet's father a gentleman? Without any evidence, Emma thinks so. 'There can be no doubt of your being a gentleman's daughter.' Is Harriet's suitor, Mr Martin? The evidence suggests that he is: when Emma sees his letter proposing marriage to Harriet, she has to admit to herself that as a composition it would not have disgraced a gentleman, and Mr Knightley, who knows him much better than Emma can do, describes him as 'a respectable, intelligent gentleman-farmer'. But again Emma pays scant heed to evidence. 'I think, Harriet, since your acquaintance with us, you have been repeatedly in the company of such very real gentlemen, that you must yourself be struck with the difference in Mr Martin. At Hartfield, you have had very good specimens of well-educated, well-bred men.... What say you to Mr Weston or Mr Elton? Compare Mr Martin with either of them. Compare their manner of carrying themselves, of walking, of speaking, of being silent. You must see the difference.' Jane Austen would not claim that the criteria Emma cites are unimportant – but, being externals, they are not the *most* important.

Mr Martin is not the only resident of Donwell parish who seems to be acquiring *gentility* through his own efforts and character, rising above the previous generation. It is an upwardly mobile little community, no doubt representative of English society at that time. Highbury boasts a whist-club, established among the gentlemen and half-gentlemen of the place. The latter are probably the more prosperous tradesmen and local professional men, like lawyer Mr Cox and medical man Mr Perry – men with some education, but who need to work for their living. Mr Weston, cited by Emma as a good example of a gentleman, comes from a family which for the last two or three generations had been rising into gentility and property; and the Coles, whose dinner party Emma is prevailed upon to attend, are described as very good sort of people, friendly, liberal and unpretending; but, on the other hand, they were of low origin, in trade, and only moderately genteel. This description is coloured by Emma's own snobbery, or reflects the tittle-tattle of the neighbourhood, but still, with the assistance of money and the lifestyle money buys, the Coles are gradually being accepted, and their children will no doubt be accepted even more. Frank Churchill, brought up in luxury by a rich uncle possessed of **a quiet, indolent, gentlemanlike sort of pride,** is not too proud himself to find the male contingent at the Coles' dinner party **in general a set of gentlemanlike, sensible men.** Just as in *Persuasion,* Jane Austen portrays a society where the rigidities of rank are breaking down, but where, as a consequence, good manners and good feelings are all the more important.

Gentlemanlike is a term much used by Jane Austen, frequently on the first introduction of a character. *Ungentlemanlike* is much more uncommon. It is questionable whether Fanny Price's father belongs to the gentry. We first hear of him as being 'without education, fortune or connections', a lieutenant in the marines by profession – though he is in a position to meet and persuade into marriage a woman with a fortune of seven thousand pounds, who must herself have gentry status (or Sir Thomas would never have married her sister). When Henry Crawford calls on the family in Portsmouth, Fanny is deeply ashamed of her father. **Ungentlemanlike as he looked, Fanny was obliged to introduce him.** His appearance, always coarse and slovenly, is not improved by its being Saturday: that is, he has probably been drinking.

But most of the players in her dramas, whatever qualities or defects remain to be discovered in them later, are stamped indubitably as *gentlemanlike* on first introduction. It is what is immediately registered about them by the other characters. Two or three examples from each of the novels will suffice to show the ubiquity, almost the nothing-meaningness of this term. At the Lower Rooms in Bath, where Catherine Morland knows nobody, the Master of Ceremonies **introduced her to a very gentlemanlike young man** who turns out to be the hero, Henry Tilney. The two men who end up marrying the heroines in *Sense and Sensibility* are neither of them particularly prepossessing, yet one appears in the story as **the brother of Mrs John Dashwood, a gentlemanlike and pleasing young man** and the other is Colonel Brandon, whose **address was particularly gentlemanlike.**

In *Emma*, characters of very different social status – certainly in Emma's own snobbish world view – attract the term: the narrator tells us that the apothecary **Mr Perry was an intelligent, gentlemanlike man** and that the hero's brother **Mr John Knightley was a tall, gentlemanlike and very clever man**. Characters significant and completely insignificant within a novel are so described. Sir Thomas Bertram is, in Mrs Grant's words to her sister Mary, who is yet to meet the absent head of the household, '**a fine-looking man, with most gentlemanlike, dignified and consistent manners**'. This means something; it is a thoughtful and respectful depiction, which Mary listens to with the seriousness it deserves. But she herself draws Fanny's indignation when she writes from London, of Edmund's arrival, '**My friends here are much struck with his gentlemanlike appearance**', her friends being shallow people of fashion.

And when Tom Bertram, seeking a neighbour to fill a part in his play, asserts that '**Charles Maddox is as gentlemanlike a man as you will see**', his words mean nothing. We never do meet Charles Maddox. The praise is on the same level as that of the vulgar John Thorpe for General Tilney, who is as far above him in manners as in understanding: '**A gentlemanlike, good sort of fellow as ever lived**.'

Gentlemanlike for a man almost seems the equivalent of *elegant* for a woman: an empty term, easily bestowed on any acquaintance of the right social standing. Tom Bertram, 'being entirely without particular regard for either ... could speak very handsomely of both' when his father enquires about the Crawfords: '**Mr Crawford was a most pleasant gentlemanlike man – his sister a sweet, pretty, elegant, lively girl**'.

When the narrator uses the word, it is more trustworthy. Elizabeth Bennet's mercantile uncle Mr Gardiner is presented to us as **a sensible, gentlemanlike man**. We need that narrative word to counter the Bingley sisters' and Darcy's doubts that anybody in trade can be classed as a gentleman. Its association with *sensible* gives it particular authenticity; Mr Gardiner is not just affecting manners above his station. He is truly gentlemanly, though this must be a matter of innate good judgement rather than of upbringing, since his two sisters are so silly, verging on vulgar. In these early novels, Jane Austen is not so particular as she would later become about making her sibling-groups plausible; the difference in sense and manners between the Bennet sisters themselves is proof of this, as is that between the Jennings sisters in *Sense and Sensibility*.

From the opening sentence of *Pride and Prejudice*, there is much speculation about, and many hopes invested in, the new tenant of Nertherfield, who makes his first appearance at the Meryton assembly. **Mr Bingley was good-looking and gentlemanlike; he had a pleasant countenance, and easy, unaffected manners** is the way he is introduced to us. His companion Mr Darcy is more complex and unknowable, but in Mr Bingley's case neither we nor the characters have cause to change our 'first impressions' of him, either at the ball or later. This description would fit him as well at the end of the novel as at the beginning.

But in others, appearances are deceptive. When Wickham catches the attention of the Bennet sisters as he walks with an officer along the street of Meryton, he is **a young man, whom they had never seen before, of most gentlemanlike appearance.** Invited with the other officers to dinner at the Philipses, Wickham stands out: **The officers of the shire were in general a very creditable, gentlemanlike set, and the best of them were of the present party; but Mr Wickham was as far beyond them all in person, countenance, air and walk, as** they **were superior to the broad-faced stuffy uncle Philips, breathing port wine.** Mr Wickham has been given **a gentleman's education,** beyond the means of his own father to provide, by the kindness of the elder Mr Darcy, who supported him at school and at Cambridge and left him a legacy. He has the manners but not the morality of a gentleman, as events prove. The same applies to Mr Elliot in *Persuasion*. Both Sir Walter Elliot and Mrs Smith use the term in his praise: the former **did justice to his very gentlemanlike appearance** and the latter asks Anne, **'Where could you expect a more gentlemanlike, agreeable man?'** Only Anne seeks to understand what may lie beneath.

Willoughby, who begins *Sense and Sensibility* by demonstrating **the perfect good breeding of the gentleman,** by the end of the novel has departed **so far from the appearance of every honourable and delicate feeling – so far from the common decorum of a gentleman.** Henry

Crawford will always behave towards his wife, even if he ceases to love her, **with the liberality and good breeding of a gentleman,** according to his sister. *Good breeding* in Jane Austen implies a person's having been brought up to have exquisite manners, rather than anything to do with family or birth (though the two do often go together, of course).

A man can be a perfect gentleman in breeding and deportment, but lack the core qualities of honour, truth and compassion that should underpin his social being, as they do so notably in the case of Mr Knightley. When General Tilney turns Catherine Morland from his door, he acts **neither honourably nor feelingly – neither as a gentleman nor as a parent.** A university education undoubtedly supports a man's claim to gentry status, but is not sufficient in itself, as we see in John Thorpe, an Oxford man, **who, with a plain face and ungraceful form, seemed fearful of being too handsome unless he wore the dress of a groom, and too much like a gentleman unless he were easy where he ought to be civil, and impudent where he might be allowed to be easy.** He is easy with his new acquaintance Catherine Morland, and impudent, downright abusive with his mother and sisters – he has neither judgement nor feeling, and speaks entirely without regard for the truth.

Another formulation common in Jane Austen is *quite the gentleman* and its variants. Mr Shepherd uses 'quite the gentleman' twice in one speech when he is recommending Admiral Croft as a tenant to Sir Walter Elliot: **'quite the gentleman in all his notions and behaviour'.** The Admiral returns the (unheard) compliment later when he says of Sir Walter, **'Very much the gentleman I am sure';** while Sir Walter's verdict on Colonel Wallis, the Bath friend of Mr Elliot, is **'a highly respectable man, perfectly the gentleman'.** Colonel Fitzwilliam, in *Pride and Prejudice*, on introduction is said to be **not handsome, but in person and address most truly the gentleman.** So he should be, as younger son of an earl. When the Crawfords arrive at Mansfield, there is much mutual sizing up to be done. Mary Crawford, not knowing what to expect from her rural relations, is pleased to find **a sister's husband who looked the gentleman;** while Henry Crawford is judged by the Bertram sisters at first to be **not handsome ... but still he was the gentleman, with a pleasing address.** Mr Hurst, in *Pride and Prejudice*, an idle nonentity

without anything interesting to say for himself, **merely looked the
gentleman.**

Emma, taken in by Mr Elton's smooth manners, finds him **quite
the gentleman himself, without low connections,** but at the same time
not of any family who could object to the illegitimate birth of Harriet
Smith, whom Emma designs as his wife. However, Mr Elton, 'so well
understanding the gradations of rank below him' yet 'blind to what rose
above', disdains Harriet, aspires to Emma herself and then, in pique,
chooses his own wife. The upstart, pert and pretentious new Mrs Elton
uses the same terminology as Emma, to Emma's disgust. '**Knightley is
quite the gentleman**', she tells Emma on their first meeting, '**Decidedly,
I think, a very gentlemanlike man.**' On the arrival of Frank Churchill at
Highbury, she assures Mr Weston that she finds his son '**so truly the
gentleman, without the least conceit or puppyism**'. It seems really offensive
to tell a man that his son is a gentleman. She uses the same construction
of *Mrs* Weston when speaking to Emma: '**I was rather astonished to find
her so very ladylike. But she is really quite the gentlewoman.**'

Emma is incensed that Mrs Elton thinks herself qualified to pass
judgement in this way. '**Actually to discover that Mr Knightley is a
gentleman! I doubt whether he will return the compliment, and discover
her to be a lady.... Astonished that the person who had brought me up
should be a gentlewoman!**' What is most interesting in this passage is the
terminology, bringing in the female equivalents of *ladylike, lady* and
gentlewoman. The two nouns seem interchangeable. Frank Churchill
uses the same construction when he makes a personal remark about
his fiancée, Jane Fairfax: '**A most distinguishing complexion! So
peculiarly the lady in it.**'

Notwithstanding both this remark, and Emma's about Mr
Knightley discovering Mrs Elton to be a lady, Jane Austen's usual
practice is to use *gentlewoman* when making a particular point about
rank, and *lady* as a general term for a woman of rank but where
rank is not the question. Mr Dashwood's second wife, for example, is
termed *his present lady*, and such constructions as *Mr Bingley was to
bring twelve ladies and seven gentlemen with him to the assembly* are
very common. *Gentlewoman* would not be a good substitute in either
of these instances, nor in such speeches as Mr Woodhouse's plaintive

'I would always wish to pay every proper attention to a lady', and 'young ladies are delicate plants'.

But Sir Thomas Bertram, in taking the child Fanny Price from her home and accustoming her to the luxuries of Mansfield Park, understands that to make the arrangement 'really serviceable to Mrs Price, and creditable to ourselves, we must secure to the child ... the provision of a gentlewoman' should she fail to marry. She must not be thrown back on her parents, or expected to earn her living as a governess, like Jane Fairfax (another child brought up outside her natural family, in a degree of material comfort beyond their reach), otherwise the transplantation would in the long run be cruel, not kind. Sir Thomas must put money aside for his niece's lifetime's keep – which helps explain his keenness for Fanny to accept Henry Crawford's proposal of marriage.

Sir Thomas, while admitting that he has never seen Fanny dance since she was a little girl, answers William Price's enquiry on the subject with, 'I trust we shall both think she acquits herself like a gentlewoman when we do see her.' In *Northanger Abbey*, the vapid Mrs Allen has few recommendations, one of which is the air of a gentlewoman. Lady Catherine de Bourgh, officiously instructing Mr Collins to find himself a wife, tells him to 'choose a gentlewoman for my sake'. In all these cases *lady* would be too nebulous a term. Identification with rank is spelled out when the widowed Mrs Norris absurdly claims that she has been left with 'barely enough to support me in the rank of gentlewoman'. Henry Crawford, trying to placate Julia Bertram as they cast for the play Lovers' Vows, alights on an ingenious comparison with professional women: 'I consider Amelia as the most difficult character in the whole piece. It requires great powers, great nicety, to give her playfulness and simplicity without extravagance. I have seen good actresses fail in the part. Simplicity, indeed, is beyond the reach of almost every actress by profession. It requires a delicacy of feeling which they have not. It requires a gentlewoman – a Julia Bertram. You will undertake it, I hope?' turning to her with a look of anxious entreaty.

Where *gentlewoman* is used a serious point is usually being made. Though as we have seen, *lady* is usually much more neutral, combined into *great lady* or *fine lady* it has potential for comedy which *gentlewoman* entirely lacks. Becoming acquainted with Lady Catherine de Bourgh, Elizabeth soon perceived that though this great lady was not in the commission of the peace for the county, she was a most active magistrate in her own parish, the minutest concerns of which were carried to her by Mr Collins; and whenever any of the cottagers were disposed to be quarrelsome, discontented or too poor, she sallied forth into the village to settle their differences, silence their complaints, and scold them into harmony and plenty.

There is an amusing exchange between Mrs Elton and Mr Weston. The latter has joked that Mrs Churchill 'does everything that any other fine lady ever did. Mrs Churchill will not be second to any lady in the land for –'

Mrs Elton eagerly interposed with: 'Oh, Mr Weston, do not mistake me. Selina is no fine lady, I assure you. Do not run away with such an idea.'

'Is not she? Then she is no rule for Mrs Churchill, who is as thorough a fine lady as anybody ever beheld.'

Mrs Elton began to think she had been wrong in disclaiming so warmly. It was by no means her object to have it believed that her sister was not a fine lady....

Jane Austen was one of the last writers to be unembarrassed by the adjective *genteel*. The Oxford English Dictionary tells us that a few years before the middle of the nineteenth century the word began to be much ridiculed as being characteristic of those possessed of a dread of being taken for 'common people' or who attach exaggerated importance to supposed marks of social superiority. Of course, Jane Austen has plenty of those! Nevertheless, she uses the word straightforwardly as often as she uses it to mock. For example, Georgiana Darcy's chaperone-companion Mrs Annesley, though a paid employee, is praised as a genteel, agreeable-looking woman, whose endeavour to introduce some kind of discourse, proved her to be more truly well-bred than those fine ladies Mrs Hurst and Miss Bingley. On quitting Mansfield Parsonage after her husband's death, Mrs Norris chooses the smallest habitation which could rank as genteel in a village composed mainly of labourers' cottages. Susan Price, brought up in squalor and negligence in Portsmouth, **had an innate taste for the genteel and well-appointed** that her creator certainly does not disparage. In fact, she rewards it by transplantation to Mansfield.

It is true that these are all matter-of-fact remarks by the narrator, while in the mouths of the characters, *genteel* is likely to be a nothing-meaning term of praise reflecting badly on the discrimination of the speaker. So Mrs Rushworth describes Henry Crawford as '**a very genteel, steady young man**' (steady being exactly what he is not) and Lady Catherine de Bourgh calls Elizabeth Bennet '**a very genteel, pretty kind of girl**' (until she gets to know her better!). It is a favourite term of praise in Mrs Bennet, who calls Sir William Lucas '**so genteel and so easy,**' and similarly describes Mr Bingley, in comparison to Mr Darcy, as '**so much the man of fashion! so genteel and so easy!**' It will be noticed that these speakers are all older women. In this and other respects, Jane Austen has a nice line of discrimination between the generations and their habits of speech.

A different case would seem to be that of Mr Shepherd who in recommending the Crofts as possible tenants of Kellynch Hall, describes Mrs Croft as '**a very well-spoken, genteel, shrewd lady**'. Mr Shepherd is neither old nor indiscriminating, indeed he is as shrewd as the lady he describes, and the narrator endorses his assessment of Mrs Croft; but his terminology is perhaps coloured by the fact that his own claim to gentry status is weak. In talking about the dearth of '**genteel young men in Devonshire**', Nancy Steele certainly betrays her own lack of gentility. And although when Nancy and Lucy Steele arrive at Barton, its mistress, who has never seen them before, is relieved to find **their appearance was by no means ungenteel or unfashionable**, Lady Middleton's judgement is superficial in the extreme. Harriet Smith's '**he is not so genteel as real gentlemen**', is an indictment of the muddle which is her mind.

With her high degree of sensitivity to the most subtle association of words, Jane Austen sometimes seems to anticipate the subversion which the term would, later in the century, come to attract. Edward Ferrars, speaking of his mother's ambitions for him, says '**the law was allowed to be genteel enough**'. In choosing the word *genteel* rather than, say, *fashionable*, Edward gives greater force to his perception of his mother's snobbery. When the Thorpes and the Allens discover in the Pump Room of Bath **that there was not a genteel face to be seen, which everybody discovers every Sunday throughout the season,** the sweeping nature of the criticism is pointed up by the word *genteel*. Mr Elliot, describing his younger self, says that he adopted 'the principle **of its being very ungenteel to be curious'.** His subsequent speech takes on a tone of self-mockery as he dilates on the subject of a young man's notions of 'what is necessary in manners to make him quite the thing', a tone which may have led him to choose the word *ungenteel*. These examples derive from the earliest as well as the latest of Jane Austen's novels.

'I am so little at my ease among strangers of gentility!' claims Edward Ferrars, rather feebly, since he certainly belongs to their number, despite his questionable education at Mr Pratt's. He has, after all, gone on from there to university, or he would not be eligible to be ordained. Susan Price, on her way from Portsmouth to Mansfield, has rather more cause to feel abashed by **visions of good and ill breeding, of old vulgarities and new gentilities.** She will be a quick learner, however. It is Emma Woodhouse who is most preoccupied by the concept of gentility. It is a matter of great satisfaction to her, when she visits Donwell Abbey after an absence of two years, to see again **the residence of a family of such true gentility, untainted in blood and understanding.** Her sister, who has married the younger son of the Abbey – just as Emma will herself marry the elder – has given them 'neither men, nor names, nor places, that could raise a blush'. Jane Austen allows that, to Emma, these are pleasant feelings, but whether she shares them is not quite clear.

Certainly Emma is wrong in condemning Robert Martin for **his entire want of gentility,** when she has only seen him at a distance, and for influencing Harriet against him with such pronouncements as, 'I **had imagined him, I confess, a degree or two nearer gentility.'** But Jane Austen does not seem critical of Emma's reactions – the reformed Emma, at the end of the book – when she finds out that Harriet's father is a tradesman. **Such was the blood of gentility which Emma had formerly been so ready to vouch for! It was as likely to be as untainted, perhaps, as the blood of many a gentleman; but ... the stain of illegitimacy,**

unbleached by nobility or wealth, would have been a stain indeed. Jane Austen, an undisputed member of the gentry herself (more so than many a female novelist of her day), has a lurking respect for its social status – but a much more tenacious and outspoken one for its indispensable moral values.

7

Delicacy

ELICACY IS A favourite word and favourite concept of Jane
Austen's and of those among her characters whom she puts
forward for admiration and emulation. At its best, *delicacy*
implies a scrupulous attention to the feelings of others, coupled with
a high notion of personal honour. At its worst, it conveys mere idle
refinement.

Catherine Morland's introduction to Eleanor Tilney occurs when
Eleanor's chaperone, Mrs Hughes, asks Catherine to make space for
Eleanor and her partner in the line of dancers at the Upper Rooms
in Bath. Eleanor of course thanks Catherine, who makes light of the
obligation **with the real delicacy of a generous mind**. The qualities of
the early Catherine should not be undervalued; here she is at the very
start of her education in Bath, and although it is only a small matter
of politeness, thrown on her own resources she is already proving that
the **real delicacy** of her mind must be innate. Though inexperienced
and ignorant of the ways of the world, she is no vapid Harriet Smith;
when called on to act she always does the right thing, sometimes (as
here) without even stopping to think about it, for when it comes to
matters of morality, her instincts are invariably correct.

Another young person with innate delicacy is Fanny Price. So
powerful is this quality in her that it often acts as a brake on her
speech or actions. In Portsmouth, **delicacy to her parents** makes her
careful not to betray any preference for her uncle's house (caution
completely thrown away on them – they are perfectly free from any
jealousy of Mansfield, and their eldest daughter is as welcome to
wish herself there as to be there). When she restores peace to the

Portsmouth household by purchasing a silver knife for Susan, she does so only after **many hesitations of delicacy,** fearful as she is of appearing to elevate herself into a great lady at home.

Edmund Bertram shows how much his judgement has been blinded by love when he tells Fanny that in her and Mary Crawford's characters **'there is so much general resemblance in true generosity and natural delicacy'.** The more reliable narrator has in fact stated that Mary has **none of Fanny's delicacy of taste, of mind, of feeling.** Henry, falling in love with Fanny, recognizes and expatiates on **the disinterestedness and delicacy of her character (qualities which he believed most rare indeed).** Few women of his acquaintance would be so little influenced by the prospect of the home, income and status which marriage with him holds out.

Delicacy in respect to questions of marrying for advantage appears elsewhere in Jane Austen's work. Elizabeth Bennet's disappointment in her friend Charlotte Lucas, who has just proved herself capable of accepting an obnoxious man's proposal purely to obtain a home and husband of her own, makes her turn with fonder regard to her sister Jane, **of whose rectitude and delicacy she was sure her opinion could never be shaken.** We also see Jane Bennet's *delicacy* in action later in the book, regarding Darcy's involvement in Lydia's marriage, which he had hoped to keep secret: **Jane's delicate sense of honour would not allow her to speak to Elizabeth privately of what Lydia had let fall.**

Another young woman to show delicacy in marriage matters is Jane Fairfax. When, after a quarrel, she writes to Frank breaking off their engagement, he honours the **anxious delicacy** which prevents her informing him of her plans to earn her own living as a governess, and thereby seem to threaten him. Among Emma's many regrets, when she looks back on her conduct towards them both, is that by imparting her mischievous imaginings to Frank, she has been the cause of **material distress to the delicacy of Jane's feelings.**

Mr Knightley has always had a high opinion of Jane's probity, so that when he observes a slight smile and blush in reaction to the word 'blunder' placed before her during the alphabet game at Hartfield, exactly what is going on is beyond his comprehension but he is astonished **how the delicacy, the discretion of his favourite could have** been so lain asleep! He feared there must be some decided involvement. Disingenuousness and double dealing seemed to meet him at every turn. These letters were but the vehicle for gallantry and trick. It was a child's play, chosen to conceal a deeper game on Frank Churchill's part.

It is amusing to observe how rapidly Mr Knightley shifts the blame for what he does not understand from Jane to Frank. Before Frank has even appeared in Highbury, Mr Knightley takes against him, declaring in response to Emma's hopes of finding in him an agreeable new acquaintance that 'He may be very "aimable", have very good manners, and be very agreeable; but he can have no English delicacy towards the feelings of other people – nothing really amiable about him.' After the reconciliation of Frank with Jane, Mr Knightley expresses the hope that when the couple are constantly together, 'his character will improve and acquire from hers the steadiness and delicacy of principle that it wants'.

Jane Fairfax's delicacy of principle sounds rather inward-looking, a fierce control of her own conduct, in contrast to the delicacy towards the feelings of other people which Mr Knightley describes. This more sympathetic quality is precisely what Catherine Morland, Jane Bennet, Fanny Price and Anne Elliot have in common. Anne has delicacy which must be pained by any lightness of conduct in a well-meaning young woman, and a heart to sympathise in any of the sufferings it occasioned. Her friend Lady Russell is of strict integrity herself, with a delicate sense of honour, more like Jane Fairfax. Which is not to say that all these admirable women do not, when occasion requires, demonstrate *both* kinds of delicacy – only that we see them differently in action.

There is also romantic delicacy, a somewhat exaggerated delicacy in affairs of the heart, possessed for example by Mrs Dashwood, in whom it overrides common sense, common care and common prudence in her dealings with the lovesick Marianne. Mrs Dashwood, in refraining from asking Marianne whether she has entered into an engagement with Willoughby, abdicates her responsibility as a parent to a young and inexperienced daughter. At the time Marianne might be glad of her mother's reticence, but in the long run, it is not to her advantage. A young person who suffers from the lack, rather than the surfeit, of **romantic delicacy** in her guardian-figure is Fanny Price. Under siege from Henry Crawford's proposal which has her uncle's full support, she knows that, **romantic delicacy was not to be expected from** Sir Thomas, a man who has proved his unromantic view of the world by permitting his daughter to marry a fool like Mr Rushworth, and who does not make allowances for Fanny's not being in love with Henry Crawford.

However unromantic he may be, Sir Thomas is far from lacking the moral delicacy of fine feelings and good intentions; what Jane Austen describes as 'a general wish of doing right and a desire of seeing all that were connected with him in situations of respectability'; so that when he resolves, after being egged on by Mrs Norris, to bring the child Fanny into his guardianship, he debates about the degree of difference that will always exist between his daughters and his niece, telling her, '**It is a point of great delicacy, and you must assist us in our endeavours to choose exactly the right line of conduct.**'

Mrs Norris – happy indeed to assist in any interference which costs her nothing – sycophantically praises Sir Thomas for '**the generosity and delicacy of your feelings**'. In her mouth, the praise is meaningless. Having no delicacy herself, she has no understanding of the concept: when she asserts that Maria has '**such a strict sense of propriety, so much of that true delicacy which one seldom meets with nowadays**', it only proves how little she comprehends either the true character of her niece or the precise quality she is so mindlessly ascribing to her.

Poor Maria – one has a certain sneaking sympathy with her – is required by the fact of her engagement to be more delicate than most. One of Edmund's arguments against the theatrical venture is that '**it would be imprudent, I think, with regard to Maria, whose situation is a very delicate one, considering everything, extremely delicate**'. Julia, seizing one of her very few advantages over her sister, **did seem inclined to admit that Maria's situation might require particular caution and delicacy – but that could not extend to her – she was at liberty.** When the play is chosen and confirms Edmund's worst fears, he takes Maria to one side and tells her: '**If others have blundered, it is your place to put them right, and show them what true delicacy is.... Say that, on examining the part, you feel yourself unequal to it, that you find it requiring more** exertion and confidence than you can be supposed to have.... The play will be given up, and your delicacy honoured as it ought.'

Henry Crawford possesses an active, sanguine spirit, of more warmth than delicacy, and in his pursuit of her, against her known wishes, Fanny feels that here was again a want of delicacy and regard for others that she had so reprobated at the time of his flirtation with Maria. Courting Fanny, however, teaches him to adapt his attentions more and more to the gentleness and delicacy of her character; and later, although his attentions remain unwelcome, she could not say ... that there was indelicacy or ostentation in his manner. Her uncle, whose standards, though less exacting than Fanny's, are certainly those of a gentleman, approvingly tells her that 'Upon my representation of what you were suffering he immediately, and with the greatest delicacy, ceased to urge to see you for the present'. Both the Crawfords are influenced for the good, to some extent, by Mansfield values, and Henry grows capable of criticizing the thought processes of his uncle Admiral Crawford. He tells Mary that Fanny, in her 'faith and integrity', her 'high notion of honour', is 'the very impossibility he would describe – if indeed he has now delicacy of language enough to embody his own ideas'. But for all his temporary improvement while under Fanny's spell, Henry ultimately shares with his sister what Edmund, after his eyes have been opened by Mary's reaction to Maria's adultery, calls 'faults of principle ... of blunted delicacy and a corrupted, vitiated mind'.

When Elinor Dashwood first becomes acquainted with Edward Ferrars, she defends him against her sister's criticism of his inability to draw by asserting that at least he knows how to look: 'his observation [is] just and correct, and his taste delicate and pure'. After the revelations of Lucy Steele have dashed her own hopes of marriage with Edward, Elinor comes to feel more pity for him than for herself: while she will eventually find peace of mind again, his whole life will be ruined. Arraigning Lucy Steele for the thorough want of delicacy, of rectitude, of integrity of mind, which her attentions, her assiduities and her flattery at the Park betrayed, Elinor asks herself whether Edward could ever be tolerably happy with Lucy Steele; could he, were his affection for herself out of the question, with his integrity, his delicacy, and well-informed mind, be satisfied with a wife like her – illiterate, artful and selfish?

Some minds are incapable of attaining the high notions of honour whence true delicacy should spring. For these less worthy characters, *delicacy* is a mere empty word, useful in some social situations, just as we have seen with Mrs Norris. Mr Collins is another offender. The word is often in his mouth. At his first dinner at Longbourn, he boasts of his ability 'to offer those little delicate compliments which are always acceptable to ladies'. Having selected Elizabeth as his future life's partner, he refuses to dance with anybody else at the Netherfield ball, assuring her that his chief object was by delicate attentions to recommend himself to her, and that he should therefore make a point of remaining close to her the whole evening. The following morning, when Elizabeth is forced by her mother to listen to Mr Collins's proposal, he begins by telling her, 'You can hardly doubt the purport of my discourse, however your natural delicacy may lead you to dissemble'. Her refusal only produces the response, 'Perhaps you have even now said as much to encourage my suit as would be consistent with the true delicacy of the female character.' And when he reports what he believes is his successful suit to her mother, he trusted he had every reason to be satisfied, since the refusal which his cousin had steadfastly given him would naturally flow from her bashful modesty and the genuine delicacy of her character.

When Mrs Bennet boasts of dining with four and twenty families, good manners enable Mr Bingley to keep his countenance, but his sister was less delicate and directed her eye towards Mr Darcy with a very expressive smile. To Mr Darcy himself, in her jealousy, Miss Bingley talks of his supposed marriage with Elizabeth, hoping he will drop hints to his mother-in-law as to the advantage of holding her tongue, cure the younger Bennets of running after the officers, 'and, if I may mention so delicate a subject, endeavour to check that little something, bordering on conceit and impertinence, which your lady possesses'. Such conversation proves that Miss Bingley, like Mr Collins and Mrs Bennet herself (as no such delicacy restrained her mother) has no true conception of delicacy. Nor does Lady Catherine de Bourgh, that arch-interferer in other people's lives, who uses the concept to try to control Elizabeth, asking her, 'Are you lost to every feeling of propriety and delicacy?' when Elizabeth has the temerity to stand up to her. Indeed, in this novel, true delicacy as a matter of honourable behaviour and care for other people's feelings is understood only by Jane Bennet; by the reformed Mr Darcy at Pemberley who **without any indelicate display of regard, or any peculiarity of manner** towards Elizabeth that might embarrass her in front of her uncle and aunt, seeks to make himself pleasant to the whole party; and by Elizabeth herself, when she tells Lady Catherine that to keep younger sisters back until the elder are married 'would not be very likely to promote sisterly affection or delicacy of mind'.

As well as in mind, a person may be delicate in constitution or appearance. For Mr Woodhouse, gallant towards the fair sex and fearful of everybody's health, '**young ladies are delicate plants**'. His daughter Isabella, so much like him, is **delicate in her own health** and nervous about that of her children – unlike her husband, who wishes them to grow up active and hardy.

Before Fanny is sent to Mansfield, her mother warns that the family there will find her **somewhat delicate and puny**. The fresh air, exercise and good food to which she has access over the next eight years go some way to building up Fanny's health, but it does not take much to break it down again, and at Portsmouth **the living in incessant noise was to a frame and temper delicate and nervous like Fanny's an evil which no superadded elegance or harmony could have entirely atoned for.** Fanny has no robustness to shake off the threat to body and mind and is in danger of succumbing to real malady.

When some ladies in a shop in Bath pass remarks on Anne Elliot, they agree that '**she is pretty ... very pretty ... it is not the fashion to say so, but I confess I admire her more than her sister ... but the men are all wild after Miss Elliot. Anne is too delicate for them.**' This female chorus evidently believe that men prefer showier looks. We know that Anne is delicate in appearance because her father has always failed to admire her, **so totally different were her delicate features and mild dark eyes from his own.** (If she takes after her mother, how did he come to marry *her*?) Elinor Dashwood is also compared with her more striking-looking sister: **Miss Dashwood had a delicate complexion** whereas Marianne has 'very brown' skin and a complexion 'uncommonly brilliant'. The delicate features and complexions of Elinor and Anne are the outward manifestations of their delicate minds.

Similarly with Jane Fairfax, though the processes of her mind are less transparent to the reader than those of Elinor and Anne. But Jane shares their modesty of behaviour and rectitude of character. On seeing Jane again after some years, Emma acknowledges that the skin, which she had used to cavil at, as wanting colour, had a clearness and delicacy which wanted no fuller bloom. Later, when Frank Churchill has arrived in Highbury, Emma enters into a spirited defence of Jane's complexion (in a discussion that would seem impolite even to us, with our lower standards of conversational propriety): 'It was certainly never brilliant, but she would not allow it to have a sickly hue in general, and there was a softness and delicacy in her skin which gave peculiar elegance to the character of her face.' He listened with all due deference; acknowledged that he had heard many people say the same; but yet he must confess that to him nothing could make amends for the want of the fine glow of health. (Emma herself is, of course, 'the picture of grown-up health'.) When the truth is out, Frank indulges himself by praising Jane to Emma (this time Jane is in the room): 'Did you ever see such a skin? such smoothness! such delicacy! and yet without being actually fair.... It is a most uncommon complexion, with her dark eyelashes and hair – a most distinguishing complexion! So peculiarly the lady in it! Just colour enough for beauty.' To which Emma replies, archly, 'Do I not remember the time when you found fault with her for being so pale?' and he responds, 'What an impudent dog I was!'

Both these conversations, *and* the one in which Emma talks to Miss Bates about Miss Campbell being very plain, seem themselves to border on the indelicate, not in their vocabulary but in their choice of subject – openly discussing the appearance of other people. But delicacy is not prominent among the virtues of a woman who loves to interfere in other people's lives, and believes she is in the secret of all their hearts. Mr Knightley chides Emma at the very beginning of the book, when she is boasting of having brought Miss Taylor and Mr Weston together, 'Your time has been properly and delicately spent, if you have been endeavouring for the last four years to bring about this marriage. A worthy employment for a young lady's mind!' and at the end of the book Emma accuses herself: How improperly she had been acting by Harriet! How inconsiderate, how indelicate, how irrational, how unfeeling had been her conduct!

All the heroines in their different ways understand and strive for the quality of delicacy, some attaining it more readily than others. But to have any value it must be true delicacy – Mr Knightley's definition of *delicacy towards the feelings of other people* – not some showy, over-refined false modesty imposed on women by fools such as Mr Collins or Lady Catherine de Bourgh.

8

Reason and Feeling

REASON, AND ITS associated adjective *rational* (they have the same Latin root), and *feeling* – noun and adjective – are the two sides of the human personality which Jane Austen, as a true child of the Enlightenment, advocates should be kept in balance. Head and heart, prudence and romance, sense and sensibility – in whatever pairings reason and feeling manifest themselves, all require the check of their opposite quality. '**Every impulse of feeling should be guided by reason**', as Mary Bennet says in one of Jane Austen's little jokes at poor Mary's expense. Mary Bennet's observations are actually usually quite sound – pride and vanity *are* different things, a woman's reputation *is* fragile – it is just so irritating to her companions that she spouts them inappropriately, as if she has read them in a conduct book (as she probably has).

Mary's remark could serve as a motto to *Pride and Prejudice*. Though there is real feeling in parts of the novel, its famous 'light and bright and sparkling' nature implies the hardness and brilliance of a jewel, and this to some extent derives from its bias towards what is *rational*, and mockery of what is *irrational* in the speech and behaviour of so many characters.

The adjective *rational* and adverb *rationally* appear at least ten times. '**It would surely be much more rational if conversation instead of dancing made the order of the day**', Miss Bingley, trying to curry favour with Darcy, tells her brother when he is good-naturedly planning a ball for the neighbourhood, to which he replies with some wit, '**Much more rational, my dear Caroline, I dare say, but it would not be near so much like a ball**'. After Lydia's elopement, Mr Bennet threatens Kitty:

'You are never to stir out of doors, till you can prove that you have spent ten minutes of every day in a rational manner'.

Elizabeth regards herself as a rational being. To Mr Collins she insists that she is no elegant female saying 'no' while meaning 'yes', but 'a rational creature, speaking the truth from her heart'. When Lady Catherine tries to bully her into renouncing all thought of Darcy, Elizabeth declares that 'I am not to be intimidated by anything so wholly unreasonable.' Of all the heroines, she is the one who prides herself on being objective and well-judging, which is why the discovery of her mistake over Wickham and Darcy so mortifies her. 'I have courted prepossession and ignorance, and driven reason away, where either were concerned', she accuses herself when put in possession of the facts.

Charlotte Lucas, who marries Mr Collins without an atom of regard for him, makes the best of her situation and does not lose her calm common sense; in her letters to Elizabeth describing her new life it was Mr Collins's picture of Hunsford and Rosings rationally softened – exactly as it should be. Although optimistic Jane Bennet trusts that the Wickhams will settle so quietly, and live in so rational a manner as to make people forget the imprudence of their elopement, Elizabeth knows that neither rational happiness nor worldly prosperity could be justly expected for her sister. *Rational happiness* is happiness based on good and compatible qualities in the other person, or, as Elizabeth really believes in the case of Bingley, all his expectations of felicity are rationally founded, because they had for basis the excellent understanding, and super-excellent disposition of Jane, and a general similarity of feeling and taste between her and himself. It is notable that the Bingleys' prospect of married happiness depends on the conjunction of both *reason* and *feeling*.

Pride and Prejudice is the work of a clever young woman keen to repudiate absurdity wherever she finds it. *Persuasion*, the last completed novel of Jane Austen's maturity, has a different tone, offering a slight adjustment to the balance between *reason* and *feeling*, head and heart, prudence and romance. It is as if the author, like the heroine, comes to value tenderness of heart more and more as her experiences impress her with the general heartlesssness of the world. What is ridiculous can be laughed at by such as Elizabeth Bennet, but what is cruel and hard can only be combated by seeking out, practising and promoting unselfish goodness. As a girl of **gentleness, modesty, taste and feeling**, Anne Elliot has been forced into prudence in her youth, made to relinquish the man she loves; through the long continuance of her love and regrets, with her ever-present tender **recollections and feelings**, she learns romance as she grows older. At twenty-seven, she has not outlived the age of emotion.

Anne is never irrational, never loses the ability to analyse her motives and perceive her own failings; but *feeling* predominates in her. When she first sees Captain Wentworth after eight years of painful separation, **a thousand feelings rushed on Anne.** She tries not to be silly or feeble: **she began to reason with herself, and try to be feeling less.** Her reasoning – her talking to herself, telling herself why it is absurd to be so agitated – is set out for us at length, but **Alas! with all her reasoning, she found that to retentive feelings, eight years may be little more than nothing.**

In a later episode, when Captain Wentworth silently removes the troublesome toddler Walter from her back, the kindness of the action leaves her with **most disordered feelings.** There is another person in the room to feel uncomfortable, **but neither Charles Hayter's feelings, nor anybody's feelings, could interest her, till she had better arranged her own. She was ashamed of herself, quite ashamed of being so nervous, so overcome by such a trifle, but so it was, and it required a long application of solitude and reflection to recover her.** Unlike Marianne Dashwood in *Sense and Sensibility*, Anne does not wallow in her emotions or expect sympathy from others. It is to her credit that she possesses the feelings of a sensitive person, but equally to her credit that she attempts to calm and conceal them.

It is also to her credit that her mind is furnished with poetry, and on a country walk can amuse itself with repeating **lines of feeling** about the autumn landscape.

In a crowd of people Anne reflects that once, before their estrangement, there would have been **no feelings so in unison** as Captain Wentworth's and her own, not even among the married couples. He is, in fact, like her, a person of deep feelings – though not so practised at concealing them. Indeed, it is because he is a man of feeling that he nurtures anger and resentment when a cooler man would have grown indifferent. Even in their estrangement Anne detects **just that degree of feeling and curiosity about her** which recalls the past; when again he acts with kindness and humanity towards her, she realizes that **he could not forgive her, but he could not be unfeeling.** In the aftermath of Louisa's accident he seems to be overpowered by **the various feelings of his soul.** Anne cannot guess at this point – neither can the reader – that these include the first glimmerings of acknowledging Anne's superiority and deploring his own pride and resentment which have prevented his seeking her again. Yet, looking back over the whole of their experiences at Lyme, Anne senses in him **some instances of relenting feeling, some breathings of friendship and reconciliation** which, even if they lead to nothing more, make her heart rejoice.

But there is better to come. When he hastens to Bath after Louisa's engagement to another man, only to find a rival for Anne's affections in Mr Elliot, the scenes build to a crescendo of feeling. At their first, chance encounter in a shop, **he was more obviously struck and confused by the sight of her than she had ever observed before ... for the first time, since their renewed acquaintance, she felt she was betraying the least sensibility of the two. She had the advantage of him in the preparation of the last few moments. All the overpowering, blinding, bewildering, first effects of strong surprise were over with her. Still, however, she had enough to feel! It was agitation, pain, pleasure, a something between delight and misery.** Their next encounter, at the concert, when he mentions Louisa without regret, is **most important in opening his feelings** to Anne. At the White Hart he speaks to her about the changes that may be wrought in eight years and a half **as if it were the result of immediate feeling.**

The following day, many of the same party are assembled at the White Hart again. Engaged in conversation with Captain Harville on the subject of the relative constancy in matters of love between men and women, Anne speaks **in a low, feeling voice.** Harville asserts that just as men's bodies are the strongest, so are their feelings. **'Your feelings may be the strongest', replied Anne, 'but the same spirit of analogy will authorise me to assert that ours are the most tender.'** Harville describes his own emotions in having to sail away from, and then be reunited with, his wife and children. **'God forbid that I should undervalue the** warm and faithful feelings of any of my fellow-creatures!' cries Anne. Captain Wentworth, at a table a little way off, has overheard her, and writes 'You pierce my soul. I am half agony, half hope. Tell me not that I am too late, that such precious feelings are gone for ever. I offer myself to you again with a heart even more your own than when you almost broke it, eight years and a half ago.' As he is able to tell her in person very shortly afterwards, the jealousy of Mr Elliot which had held him back on arrival in Bath had been vanquished at last by those sentiments and those tones which had reached him while she talked to Captain Harville; and under the irresistible governance of which he had seized a sheet of paper, and poured out his feelings. And, as they talk it over and over, he speaks of travelling to Bath with some degree of hope: 'It was possible that you might retain the feelings of the past, as I did.'

Anne and Wentworth, then, are matched in depth of *feeling*. No other woman character in the novel comes anywhere near to Anne in this quality, but Captains Harville and Benwick almost equal their friend Captain Wentworth. Before the Uppercross party even meet Benwick, he is described by Wentworth as uniting very strong feelings with quiet, serious and retiring manners. When, at Lyme, Anne draws him out of himself by talking about poetry, she finds that though shy, he did not seem reserved; it had rather the appearance of feelings glad to burst their usual restraints. In the course of their evening's conversation he repeats with such tremulous feeling, the various lines which imaged a broken heart, or a mind destroyed by wretchedness that Anne ventures to say that it was the misfortune of poetry to be seldom safely enjoyed by those who enjoyed it completely; and that the strong feelings which could alone estimate it truly were the very feelings which ought to taste it but sparingly. When his engagement to Louisa is announced, Anne has a moment's surprise that the dejected, thinking, feeling, reading Captain Benwick has attached himself to a young woman who seems his opposite.

Captain Benwick almost becomes a suitor for Anne, but chance turns him in another direction. Mr Elliot also makes his interest clear. Before she knows any actual bad of him, Anne considers: Mr Elliot was rational, discreet, polished, but he was not open. There was never any burst of feeling, any warmth of indignation or delight, at the evil or good of others. This, to Anne, was a decided imperfection. Later, Mrs Smith, who has known him so much longer, brings this damning indictment:

'Mr Elliot is a man without heart or conscience; a designing, wary, cold-blooded being, who thinks only of himself; who for his own interest or ease, would be guilty of any cruelty, and treachery, that could be perpetrated without risk of his general character. He has no feeling for others. Those whom he has been the chief cause of leading into ruin, he can neglect and desert without the smallest compunction. He is totally beyond the reach of any sentiment of justice or compassion. Oh! he is black at heart, hollow and black!'

When the astonished Anne hears the full story, she listens to a recital which, if it did not perfectly justify the unqualified bitterness of Mrs Smith, proved him to have been very unfeeling in his conduct towards her; very deficient in both justice and compassion.

But when Anne describes Mr Elliot as being rational, discreet, polished, these are terms of praise, albeit qualified praise. There is nothing wrong with being *rational* in Jane Austen's view, even in this novel; only with being *unfeeling*, as Mr Elliot turns out to be, or possessing 'the heartless elegance' of Sir Walter and Elizabeth Elliot. *Unfeeling* in a different sense from the cold and calculating Mr Elliot is the thick-headed, unfeeling, unprofitable Dick Musgrove, whose deficiencies are not so much of the heart as of the head; he is too stupid to feel properly. Poor Dick is the catalyst for one of the most problematic paragraphs in Jane Austen's writing, when she herself seems to lack heart to sympathize with Mrs Musgrove's 'large fat sighings' over the loss of her son. There are unbecoming conjunctions, writes Jane Austen, which reason will patronise in vain – which taste cannot tolerate – which ridicule will seize. Mrs Musgrove's 'crime' is partly being too fat, partly seeming to care more about her son now than when he was alive. Many readers have felt that Jane Austen carries her love of reason and hatred of sentimentality too far in this instance.

However, the attractive side of *rationality* is well illustrated in this novel by two very different female characters. Lady Russell, whom we are meant to approve if not quite love, had a cultivated mind and was, generally speaking, rational and consistent. Mrs Croft, a sensible, straightforward woman, berates her brother: 'I hate to hear you talking … as if women were all fine ladies, instead of rational creatures.'

Charles Musgrove is a pleasant enough fellow, but does nothing with any zeal but sport, and Anne agrees with Lady Russell that a wife with a higher tone of mind than poor Mary would have given **more usefulness, rationality and elegance to his pursuits.** *Rational pursuits* tend to self-improvement or usefulness to others: they can be justified in reason. Every Jane Austen novel is concerned with how *rationally* people spend their time, or 'employ themselves', as she often calls it. In *Northanger Abbey*, speaking amid the superficial pleasures of Bath, Henry Tilney suggests to Catherine Morland that '**You spend your time more rationally in the country**', though she herself, to his and our amusement, can see no difference, as she walks about in both places. City life is not inimical to *rationality*, however, if intelligent people are concerned. In *Emma*, living with the Campbells in London, Jane Fairfax has shared in **all the rational pleasures of an elegant society, and a judicious mixture of home and amusement;** but when she becomes a governess she will have to **retire from all the pleasures of life, of rational intercourse, equal society, peace and hope.** Nobody suggests that such a retirement will be good for her soul.

With Harriet's infatuation with Mr Elton cured at last by his unfeeling conduct towards her at the Crown ball, Emma reflects complacently, **Harriet rational, Frank Churchill not too much in love, and Mr Knightley not wanting to quarrel with her, how very happy a summer must be before her.** Harriet herself uses the same word when bringing her precious mementos of Mr Elton to burn in Emma's presence '**that you may see how rational I am grown**'.

Emma herself is often guilty of misspending her time, though it is only towards the end of the novel that she realizes this. In the evening after the Box Hill picnic, she reflects on how **it was a morning more completely misspent, more totally bare of rational satisfaction at the time, and more to be abhorred in recollection, than any she had ever passed.** That is just one morning; she has misspent many hours in wrong-headed manipulation of Harriet. She now sees **how inconsiderate, how indelicate, how irrational, how unfeeling had been her conduct!**

If Mr Knightley is lost to her father and herself through marriage to Harriet, she wonders, **what would remain of cheerful or of rational society within their reach?** From the very earliest pages of the novel, we have understood that her father **could not meet her in conversation, rational or playful.** Now, from the depths of her misery, **the only source whence anything like consolation or composure could be drawn, was in the resolution of her own better conduct, and the hope that, however inferior in spirit and gaiety might be the following and every future winter of her life to the past, it would yet find her more rational, more acquainted with herself, and leave her less to regret when it were gone.** When her prospects are suddenly and unexpectedly transformed by Mr Knightley's marriage proposal, Emma finds herself **in dancing, singing, exclaiming spirits; and till she had moved about, and talked to herself, and laughed and reflected, she could be fit for nothing rational.**

Though Emma accuses herself of being *unfeeling*, though she penitently writes to Jane Fairfax **in the most feeling language she could command,** and though in Jane's rejections of her overtures **it mortified her that she was given so little credit for proper feeling;** though Mr Knightley's reproach, **'How could you be so unfeeling to Miss Bates?'** makes her cry, and though she hopes that **no-one could have said to her, 'How could you be so unfeeling to your father?'** to be rational likewise means a great deal to Emma. Among the heroines, if Fanny Price strives to do her duty, and Anne Elliot strives to sublimate her own wishes, Emma Woodhouse, so happy and so happily circumstanced, strives to balance head and heart.

Both Mr Knightley and Emma are in the habit of passing judgement on other people's *rationality* and *feeling*, or lack of them. One female personage who has the balance right is Mrs Weston, who is described at different junctures by Mr Knightley both as **a rational, unaffected woman** and **a woman of her good sense and quick feelings.** Mr Knightley is more critical of Harriet, bluntly saying of Robert Martin's wish of marrying her, **'As to a rational companion or a useful helpmate, he could not do worse.'** Emma has to allow that Robert Martin himself is not only a sensible farmer – she has never doubted that – but that **the young man's conduct, and his sister's, seemed the result of real feeling.** Mr Knightly says of him **'He has too much real feeling to address any woman on the haphazard of selfish passion.'** (It is interesting that he makes a distinction between passion and *real feeling*.) Mr Knightley has his reservations about Jane Fairfax – she is too reserved – but he allows that 'Jane Fairfax has feeling ... I do not accuse her of want of feeling.' Emma is pleased to observe in Frank Churchill the language of real feeling towards Mrs Weston but she is not so pleased with his act of impetuosity in (seemingly) going off to London to have his hair cut: it did not accord with the rationality of plan, the moderation in expense which she had been ascribing to him.

The Knightley brothers both detect in Mr Elton, beneath the smirks and smooth talking, an underlying rationality, verging on cold-heartedness, which totally escapes Emma. 'Elton may talk sentimentally, but he will act rationally,' George Knightley informs her, while John says, 'With men he can be rational and unaffected, but when he has ladies to please, every feature works.' Neither is quite saying that *rationality* itself is wrong, only that Emma has misread his character. Even when thus alerted by Mr Knightley, more than a reasonable, becoming degree of prudence, she was very sure did not belong to Mr Elton. His actions, in pursuing first her and then Augusta Hawkins for their fortunes, are to prove how wrong she is. Mr Elton's prudence *is* present in more than *reasonable* amounts, as it governs his behaviour in areas where the heart and feelings should be paramount.

At the end of *Mansfield Park*, Henry Crawford has to live with the misery of having, by his own misdeeds, lost the woman whom he had rationally, as well as passionately, loved. His love for Fanny Price is *rational* because based on her many good qualities, and passionate because his heart has been truly engaged, as proved by his long pursuit of her despite discouragement. To lose her is to lose not just the object of his love, but a woman who would have led him into a better, more useful, more satisfying way of life.

Fanny herself is the usual compound of *feeling* and *reason* that any Jane Austen heroine must be, though perhaps in her case it is *feeling* which comes most naturally and *reason* which sometimes has to be struggled for. Fanny has delicacy of taste, of mind, of feeling, qualities lacking in Mary Crawford, who nevertheless can see that Fanny 'is as good a little creature as ever lived, and has a great deal of feeling'. When

Fanny is reunited with her brother William after so many years apart, **the first minutes of exquisite feeling had no interruption.** Observing the siblings together, Henry Crawford **was no longer in doubt of the capabilities of her heart. She had feeling, genuine feeling.** And her cousin Edmund, who understands Fanny better than anyone – despite a certain obtuseness – sees that Crawford's courtship of Fanny will not get anywhere **without the assistance of sentiment and feeling.**

But Fanny has a **rational self.** 'This is not like yourself, your rational self', says a puzzled Edmund, faced with Fanny's resolute rejection of Crawford's suit. Aching with her silent love for Edmund himself, Fanny tries to banish all that borders on selfishness in her affection, and to **endeavour to be rational, and to deserve the right of judging Miss Crawford's character and the privilege of true solicitude for him by a sound intellect and an honest heart.**

Edmund has just referred to herself and Miss Crawford as the two dearest objects he has on earth; and moreover, has just made Fanny a present of a gold chain, and had been in the act of writing a note to her when she came in. The author tells us that Fanny **had all the heroism of principle, and was determined to do her duty; but having also many of the feelings of youth and nature, let her not be much wondered at if, after making these good resolutions on the side of self-government, she seized the scrap of paper on which Edmund had begun writing to her, as a treasure beyond all her hopes.**

She feasts her eyes on the four words of his writing, 'My very dear Fanny'; after which, **having regulated her thoughts and comforted her feelings by this happy mixture of reason and weakness, she was able, in due time, to go down and resume her usual employments.** Jane Austen's brilliance is in showing us in specific circumstances and action Fanny's competing intellect and heart, thoughts and feelings, reason and weakness – all of which dualities occur within a few sentences. The gift of the chain and Edmund's note are small things in themselves but, in Fanny's reactions all the contradictions, strengths and shortcomings of her character are displayed. In most readers, her **mixture of reason and weakness** will elicit a sympathetic response. Eighteen-year-old Fanny has her share of normal human imperfections, but she does endeavour to do the right thing.

She is in full contrast to Julia Bertram, labouring under somewhat similar circumstances of jealousy. Julia indulges her *feelings* without the check of *rationality*. Passed over by Henry Crawford at the time of the play, Julia neither attempts to maintain social niceties, as is her duty, nor makes **any endeavour at rational tranquillity for herself.** Her feelings are allowed to go unchecked, as she sulks and throws a gloom over the company and, even worse, secretly hopes to see her sister punished by some distressing end to Henry's attentions, some public disturbance at last. Julia is suffering **under the disappointment of a dear, though irrational hope with a strong sense of ill-usage. Her heart was sore and angry, and she was capable of only angry consolations.** Not only does she not attempt to control her feelings, but the nature of those feelings is much less excusable than Fanny's.

In agreeing to dispense with Fanny's services so that she can go to Portsmouth, Lady Bertram is influenced by Sir Thomas's appeal **to her reason, conscience and dignity.** We might not think that Lady Bertram possesses much of any of these qualities, but Sir Thomas makes sure his will does prevail. *Feeling* and *reason* are invoked as the twin motivators of decent behaviour when Fanny becomes acquainted with her family in Portsmouth. Sam, despite his faults of being loud and overbearing, is the best of her younger brothers, **Tom and Charles being at least as many years as they were his juniors distant from that age of feeling and reason which might suggest the expediency of making friends and of endeavouring to be less disagreeable.** Her sister Susan, whose remonstrances **though very reasonable in themselves** are ill-timed and tactless, begins to impress Fanny. **That a girl of fourteen, acting only on her own unassisted reason, should err in the method of reform was not wonderful; and Fanny soon became more disposed to admire the natural light of the mind which could so early distinguish justly, than to censure severely the faults to which it led.** When Fanny is allowed to take Susan back with her to Mansfield Park, the day is hardly long enough for their preparations and packing, which they do without help from their mother or servants: left to their own judgement, **everything was rationally and duly accomplished, and the girls were ready for the morrow.**

The whole course of Edmund's infatuation with Mary Crawford is *irrational*, in the sense that his judgement cannot approve her way of thinking; its character is given in the Sotherton passages, when, discussing distances, **he still reasoned with her, but in vain. She would not calculate, she would not compare. She would only smile and assert. The greatest degree of rational consistency could not have been more engaging.** But at the end of the book, when Fanny (somewhat meanly, but unchastised by her author) gives him to understand the part that his brother's illness (and possible death) played in Mary's wish of a reconciliation, **his vanity was not of a strength to fight long against reason.** He submits to feeling that she never loved him for himself. In this he is mistaken, for Mary is long in finding anyone whose character and manners are such as to put Edmund Bertram out of her head. Her only recourse is to live with Mrs Grant, and allow herself to be soothed by **the true kindness of her sister's heart, and the rational tranquillity of her ways.** Like other worthy characters in Jane Austen's novels, Mrs Grant successfully combines the virtues of head and heart, reason and feeling, conducive to the happiness of herself and those around her.

9

Person and Countenance

TOGETHER WITH AIR and *address* (the subjects of the next chapter) *person* and *countenance* relate to a character's physical presence and presentation of themselves to the world. These four terms are often grouped together in Jane Austen, most frequently when a new character appears. The early chapters of *Sense and Sensibility*, which introduce three men into the heroines' lives, are rich in such examples. Other novelists might give particulars of appearance, but Jane Austen deals in general terms. Elinor admits of Edward Ferrars, 'At first sight, his address is certainly not striking, and his person can hardly be called handsome', but this is negated by what she perceives as 'the general sweetness of his countenance'. Of Colonel Brandon the narrator tells us: though his face was not handsome, his countenance was sensible, and his address was particularly gentlemanlike. When Willoughby first appears in Marianne's life, his person and air were equal to what her fancy had ever drawn for the hero of a favourite story.

Often Jane Austen uses *person* as we would use it today, simply meaning an individual, a human being. Mrs Norris considers that the child Fanny may be consigned to the care of any creditable person who may chance to be going up to London by public coach, and on her arrival at Mansfield Park Fanny finds something to fear in every person and place. In a double use of the word, 'I pay very little regard,' says Mrs Grant, 'to what any young person says on the subject of marriage. If they profess a disinclination for it, I only set it down that they have not yet seen the right person.'

Person in this common sense seems to be the singular of 'people'.

But it can also be used itself in the plural, as in this description of Henry and Eleanor Tilney: **they were viewing the country with the eyes of persons accustomed to drawing.** We are less likely to use this construction today, more likely to choose the synonym 'people'.

Much more interestingly in Jane Austen's novels, *person* signifies the body, specifically the *appearance* of the body. She never uses the term *person* when the *health* of the body is in question, rather than its looks. Then she plumps for *body* itself. '**That would be exercise only to my body, and I must take care of my mind**', Henry Crawford tells his sister. Sir Thomas, had he known the unhealthiness of life for Fanny at Portsmouth, **might have thought his niece in the most promising way of being starved, both mind and body.**

At the beginning of *Northanger Abbey*, when the narrator is impressing on the reader how unfit to be a heroine her heroine is, we learn that Catherine **had a thin awkward figure, a sallow skin without much colour, dark lank hair, and strong features – so much for her person.** Today we are more likely to say 'so much for her appearance'. Such usage as Jane Austen's is now virtually obsolete, remnants only to be found in the phrase 'personal remarks', i.e. remarks about somebody's physical appearance, and the adjective 'personable', meaning pleasant-looking. Indeed, Mrs Clay develops this usage in *Persuasion* when, in her flattery of the vain Sir Walter, she ventures to say that (unlike him), men who have to work for a living in any profession '**lose something of their personableness when they cease to be quite young**'.

The description of Catherine Morland is unusually detailed for Jane Austen. It is not hard to see why, in this case, she deviates from her usual practice: it is part of her burlesque of commonplace novels. There is no equivalent description of the hero of *Northanger Abbey*. From the beginning, Catherine admires Henry Tilney's **person and manners,** but we are left to imagine what he might look like for ourselves.

When Mary Crawford first hears her sister's plans for her to marry the elder son of Mansfield Park, she knows, having seen Mr Bertram in town, **that objection could no more be made to his person than to his situation in life.** On her own return to London, and Edmund's arrival there, she writes to Fanny, '**Mrs Fraser (no bad judge) declares she knows but three men in town who have so good a person, height and air;**

and I must confess, when he dined here the other day, there were none to compare with him.' Fanny is disgusted. 'The woman who could speak of him, and speak only of his appearance! What an unworthy attachment!' she reflects.

When Fanny first comes to Mansfield, malnourished perhaps from Portsmouth, we are told that there was **as striking a difference between the cousins in person, as education had given to their address; and no-one would have supposed the girls so nearly of an age as they really were.** On Sir Thomas's return from several years abroad he sees an improvement in this aspect of Fanny, which Edmund blunderingly conveys to her: '**You will hear compliments enough** [from your uncle]: **and though they be chiefly on your person, you must put up with it, and trust to his seeing as much beauty of mind in time.**' Fanny herself sees alterations in the appearance of her beloved brother William after he has been at sea during his growing-up years, and when they meet again she has first to get over **the disappointment inseparable from the alteration of person** – the alteration involved in maturing into a young man from the boy she remembers. Sir Thomas, too, sees in William **a very different person from the one he had equipped seven years ago,** but the meaning here is ambiguous; Sir Thomas might be thinking of William's appearance but more likely, perhaps, of his whole being and bearing in the world.

There is no such doubt in the early summary of Sir Walter Elliot's character at the beginning of *Persuasion*: **Vanity was the beginning and the end of Sir Walter Elliot's character: vanity of person and of situation. He had been remarkably handsome in his youth; and at fifty-four, was still a very fine man. Few women could think more of their personal appearance than he did.** Here we have both the noun and the semi-repetition of its adjective, meaning not 'their individual appearance' but 'their physical appearance'. Similarly, in the same novel, *personal size* means 'bodily size' rather than 'individual size', a fine distinction: **personal size and mental sorrow have certainly no necessary proportions. A large bulky figure has as good a right to be in deep affliction as the most graceful set of limbs in the world.**

When Jane Austen says of Mary Musgrove that **in person she was inferior to both sisters** her meaning is not that *as* a person, Mary is inferior; the remainder of the sentence shows that *in person* means *in appearance*: 'and had, even in her bloom, only reached the dignity of being "a fine girl"'. (Poor Mary is still only twenty-three, rather young to have lost her 'bloom' – though she has experienced pregnancy and childbirth twice.) Similarly, the widowed Mrs Clay's **personal misfortunes** are nothing to do with her marital or financial situation; they refer solely to her appearance. This is made clear in an interesting exchange which takes place fairly early in *Persuasion*, when Anne attempts to put her sister on her guard about Mrs Clay's possible designs on their father. Elizabeth immediately takes offence, saying: **'If Mrs Clay were a very beautiful woman, I grant you, it might be wrong to have her so much with me; not that anything in the world, I am sure, would induce my father to make a degrading match, but he might be rendered unhappy. But poor Mrs Clay who, with all her merits, can never have been reckoned tolerably pretty, I really think poor Mrs Clay may be staying here in perfect safety. One would imagine you had never heard my father speak of her personal misfortunes, though I know you must fifty times. That tooth of hers and those freckles.... You must have heard him notice Mrs Clay's freckles.'**

To which the wiser Anne replies, **'There is hardly any personal defect ... which an agreeable manner might not gradually reconcile one to.'**

When Emma meets Harriet Smith she is **as much pleased with her manners as her person.** A full description of Harriet has just been given, seen through Emma's eyes. Harriet is 'short, plump, and fair, with a fine bloom, blue eyes, light hair, regular features and a look of great sweetness'. Despite all these attributes of beauty, after this description it is impossible that the reader should nurture as many hopes of Harriet as Emma does. Is it the shortness, the plumpness or the sweetness that prevents our taking Harriet seriously, even before we hear her conversation or see how she behaves? Similarly but conversely, when Emma sees Mr Martin for the first time, the cautious reader reserves judgement. **His appearance was very neat, and he looked like a sensible young man** [what more do we need in order to approve him?] **but his person had no other advantage.** Emma's candidate for supplanting Mr Martin in Harriet's affections is Mr Elton, of whom we have no concrete description, just that **he was reckoned very** handsome; his person much admired in general, though not by her, there being a want of elegance of feature which she could not dispense with.

Person and *mind* are often contrasted and linked in this novel. 'Mr Elton is the standard of perfection in Highbury, both in person and mind', Emma tells the newly arrived Jane Fairfax – without, of course, subscribing to this view herself. Emma does admit that Jane herself possesses elegance which, whether of person or of mind, she saw so little in Highbury. Emma has been surveying and assessing Jane's body in all its detail: height, figure, eyes, eyelashes, skin.

Emma loves to look at Jane (and at Harriet) just as Mr Knightley loves to look at Emma. 'You would rather talk of her person than her mind, would you?' he says to Mrs Weston, who starts praising Emma's looks to divert Mr Knightley from criticizing her behaviour. 'I have not a fault to find with her person,' he admits, though he certainly has a fault to find with her *as* a person. He continues, 'I do not think her personally vain'. In modern discourse, this would equate to something rather vague like, 'I do not think she is herself vain', but Mr Knightley's next sentence makes his more specific application clear: 'Considering how very handsome she is, she appears to be little occupied with it; her vanity lies another way.'

An important aspect of the *person* is the *countenance*, which may relate to the facial features or, more often, to the facial expression – habitual or transitory, mobile or settled. In this portrait of old Mrs Ferrars, *countenance* is what a lifetime of indulging in her own worst traits has made it: her features were small, without beauty, and naturally without expression; but a lucky contraction of the brow had rescued her countenance from the disgrace of insipidity, by giving it the strong characters of pride and ill nature. The brow has set hard, and as severely limits the range of emotions its owner can now express as hardness of heart limits feeling. As Cardinal Manning was to write, 'God made your features, but you made your countenance'.

So closely linked is facial expression with the personality, or at least with other people's interpretation of the personality, that where an individual is liked or disliked, so is their countenance likely to be – but it is hard to say which comes first. When Catherine Morland is introduced to Henry Tilney she finds he **had a pleasing countenance, a very intelligent and lively eye, and if not quite handsome, was very near it.** Some weeks later Frederick Tilney appears in Bath, and Catherine, taking a dislike to him from the start, allows that while **some people might think him handsomer than his brother... in her eyes his air was more assuming, and his countenance less prepossessing.** Catherine is developing better powers of discrimination than those she first brought to Bath. Anne Elliot immediately likes and respects Captain Harville for having **a sensible, benevolent countenance.** Another significant first impression is Emma's of Frank Churchill: **his countenance had a great deal of the spirit and liveliness of his father's – he looked quick and sensible.** Reading the *countenance* is the first step to reading the character, and very often in Jane Austen it is a reliable one.

But not always. When Bingley and Darcy make their first appearance in Meryton society, Bingley **was good looking and gentlemanlike; he had a pleasant countenance and easy, unaffected manners** – a true reading of what Bingley turns out to be. But his friend, though equally or even more handsome, is soon **discovered to be proud, to be above his company, and above being pleased; and not all his large estate in Derbyshire could then save him from having a most forbidding, disagreeable countenance.** In contrast, Wickham, on first introduction, **had all the best part of beauty, a fine countenance, a good figure, and a very pleasing address.** Not only Elizabeth but the whole of Meryton make their disastrously erroneous judgements on little more than a superficial impression of *countenance*.

Only in *Persuasion* is *countenance* occasionally used to signify the arrangement of facial features themselves, and their transmission through the generations, for surely this is what Mary Musgrove must mean when she burbles about **the Elliot countenance** being recognizable in their estranged cousin, Mr Elliot. Anne thinks she speaks nonsense, and so do we. When Lady Russell says movingly to Anne that '**you are your mother's self in countenance and disposition**', she too may be speaking of facial resemblance – we know that Anne looks nothing like her father, and so must have taken her 'mild dark eyes and delicate features' from her mother – but the collocation with disposition suggests that Lady Russell might equally be referring to the expression – gentle, modest and quietly intelligent – which Anne habitually shows to the world.

On other occasions in the novels, *countenance* quite clearly expresses a temporary mood. **Catherine had not read three lines before her sudden change of countenance** alerts her companions to the fact that she is receiving news to distress her. The normally cheerful **Eleanor's countenance was dejected, yet sedate** when she leads Catherine towards her late mother's room at Northanger. **Isabella's countenance was once more all smiles and good humour** when she gets her own way. On the carriage ride to Sotherton, seated on the barouche box beside Henry Crawford, **when Julia looked back, it was with a countenance of delight;** a rare enough expression for the slighted Julia Bertram, almost always playing second fiddle to her sister.

As well as reading the character from a person's habitual countenance, it is often necessary to read or receive the truth from a passing expression. So Emma, unable to withstand the happy looks of Mr Weston in announcing his son's imminent arrival, is yet glad to have the news confirmed **by the words and countenance of his wife, fewer and quieter, but not less to the purpose.** After Mr Knightley's rebuke on Box Hill and the penitent Emma's visit to Miss Bates the next morning, she finds Mr Knightley on her return home to Hartfield, just waiting to bid adieu before setting off for London: **she could not be deceived as to the meaning of his countenance ... she had fully recovered his good opinion.** And later, when Mr Knightley brings her news which he is not sure whether she will class as good or bad (in fact, the engagement of Harriet and Robert Martin), she is certain that what he has to tell her must be good news: **'I see it in your countenance. You are trying not to smile.'**

Communication has flowed in the other direction when Emma is impatient to thank him for dancing with Harriet at the Crown ball: **though too distant for speech, her countenance said much, as soon as she could catch his eye again.**

Sometimes the communication is involuntary. Anne Elliot has no idea of what her face might be betraying until Mrs Smith asserts, **'Your countenance perfectly informs me that you were in company last night with the person you think the most agreeable in the world.'** (She is not imagining it; Anne, with hope in her heart again, has been indulging in 'musings of high-wrought love and constancy' as she walks to Mrs Smith's lodgings; her face is probably what we would call radiant.)

When Colonel Brandon alludes to a lady in his past, he cannot quite conceal his emotion, and **his countenance gave rise to conjectures, which might not otherwise have entered Elinor's head.** And when Lucy Steele relates her story of being engaged to Edward Ferrars, the horrified, half-disbelieving Elinor **looked earnestly at Lucy, hoping to discover something in her countenance; perhaps the falsehood of the greatest part of what she had been saying; but Lucy's countenance suffered no change.**

For, as this last phrase suggests, while some characters are trying to read the truth in others' countenances, those others may be trying to conceal it, or else to assume a particular expression for purposes (good or bad) of their own. Elinor herself, responding to Lucy, **was careful in guarding her countenance from every expression that could give her words a suspicious tendency.** Elinor is rather mistress of hiding her feelings. For the sake of politeness and comfortable feelings all round, when Edward Ferrars calls at Barton Cottage following – as the inhabitants believe – his marriage to Lucy, Elinor tries to keep any suggestion of resentment or distress from her face or manner: **with a countenance meaning to be open, she sat down again and talked of the weather.**

When Mrs Weston is fearful that Emma's heart will be broken by the news of Frank's engagement to Jane Fairfax, Emma assures her that is not the case. Mrs Weston has been assiduously bent over her sewing, to allow Emma a moment of privacy in which to absorb the distressing news she has to tell; on hearing Emma's assurances **Mrs Weston looked up, afraid to believe; but Emma's countenance was as steady as her words.** In this case it is not to preserve another person from seeing or sharing distress that Emma keeps a steady countenance, but to convince her companion of the truth of her reaction. Increasing her efforts, she goes on to greet *Mr* Weston **with a smiling countenance** so that he too may be convinced. Smiling is more convincing than steadiness, more difficult to assume if the heart is distressed, more easily seen through by people familiar with the usual smiles and expressions of that individual. The face more than the words here can be relied on to speak the simple truth.

However, the simple truth is exactly what Frank Churchill is determined to conceal when he and Jane Fairfax are interrupted in her grandmother's sitting-room by the arrival of Emma and other ladies; ostensibly mending old Mrs Bates's spectacles (and really indulging in a little love-talk with Jane): **busy as he was, however, the young man was yet able to show a most happy countenance on seeing Emma again** when he must have longed for five more minutes without her!

At other times it is not so much subterfuge as social necessity which dictates concealment of real feelings. Mr Elton, Mr John Knightley and Emma have shared a carriage to Randalls, the two men in very different moods according to their taste for dining out. **Some change of countenance was necessary for each gentleman as they walked into Mrs Weston's drawing-room; Mr Elton must compose his joyous looks, and Mr John Knightley disperse his ill-humour. Mr Elton must smile less, and Mr John Knightley more, to fit them for the place.** Eleanor Tilney speaks **with a command of countenance** which smooths over an embarrassing moment with the General. It behoves polite characters to keep their countenance, that is, to avoid betraying laughter or scorn, when in company with fools. **Nothing but concern for Elizabeth could enable Bingley to keep his countenance** when her mother is speaking at her silliest; and Mr Bennet, while listening with the keenest inward enjoyment, maintains **a resolute composure of countenance** during Mr Collins's absurd utterances.

However, to be put *out of countenance*, meaning to be disconcerted, annoyed or abashed, is sometimes the unavoidable reaction to the breaking of social proprieties by others. **Catherine heard all this, and quite out of countenance, could listen no longer** to the flirtatious whisperings of Isabella and Captain Tilney. Tom Bertram, the master of the social anecdote, tells of a young lady who **stared me out of countenance, and talked and laughed,** while Isabella Thorpe (again) is the transgressor when she appeals to Catherine, '**You and John must keep us in countenance**', as she plans some minor infringement of the social rules with Catherine's brother James, in which she hopes to enlist the other couple's participation. In all these examples, *countenance* has become metaphorical.

That **countenance** is not exactly or usually a synonym for *face* is clear from its sometimes being deliberately distinguished from it. Catherine Morland's first impression of Eleanor Tilney is of **a good figure, a pretty face, and a very agreeable countenance.** A pretty face could be marred by a disagreeable countenance, but the expression on Eleanor's face evinces her friendly, pleasant and unselfconscious approach to the world. A little way into their relationship, Edmund Bertram analyses Mary Crawford's charms to his reluctant confidante Fanny, having drawn from her the admission that Mary is 'so extremely pretty'. '**It is her countenance that is so attractive**', he explains (to himself as much as to Fanny). '**She has a wonderful play of feature**'. The features are pretty, but it is their expression of the mind behind them that captivates Edmund, for whom prettiness would be insufficient to seduce him from the path of perfect righteousness.

In the same novel, Henry Crawford also separates the concepts of features and countenance in this exchange with Mrs Grant, who begins by telling him:

'**You like Julia best.**'

'**Oh! yes, I like Julia best.**'

'**But do you really? For Miss Bertram is in general thought the handsomest.**'

'**So I should suppose. She has the advantage in every feature, and I prefer her countenance – but I like Julia best. Miss Bertram is certainly the handsomest, and I have found her the most agreeable, but I shall always like Julia best, because you order me.**'

(Incidentally, it will be noticed that Jane Austen has no inhibition about using the superlative, rather than the comparative, even though she is comparing two rather than three young women. Just so is Emma Woodhouse introduced as 'the youngest of the two daughters of a most affectionate, indulgent father'.)

Released from the necessity of keeping a secret which has intensified her natural tendency to reserve, Jane Fairfax presents a different face to Emma at the end of the novel. **There was consciousness, animation and warmth; there was everything which her countenance or manner could ever have wanted.** Sometimes *countenance*, used alone without any further description, seems to mean this ability to express feeling – or indeed the inability to suppress it – rather than the expression of any one particular personality trait or mood. It is therefore possible to possess this attractive attribute to a greater or lesser extent. When the Bertram sisters meet Henry Crawford they regard him as 'absolutely plain' but a second meeting modifies their view: **he was plain, to be sure, but then he had so much countenance, and his teeth were so good.** To understand the concept of *countenance* as it stands alone here we should think of the noun attached to the reformed Jane Fairfax, 'animation'. It is a good synonym to bear in mind. The phrase **so much countenance** is also used by Sir Thomas of Fanny, after his return from Antigua, when as Edmund tells her, '**your uncle never did admire you till now – and now he does. Your complexion is so improved! and you have gained so much countenance!**' Henry Crawford also links complexion and countenance when he begins to revise his opinion of Fanny, telling his sister, '**I used to think she had neither complexion nor countenance; but in that soft skin of hers, so frequently tinged with a blush as it was yesterday, there is decided beauty; and from what I observed of her eyes and mouth, I do not despair of their being capable of expression enough when she has anything to express.**'

The fact that the complexion itself can show emotion, by a blush or a glow, inspires the linkage in Henry's ideas, which are reinforced and reiterated when Fanny's beloved brother William arrives. Observing them together, Henry finds that **Fanny's attractions increased – increased twofold – for the sensibility which beautified her complexion and illuminated her countenance, was an attraction in itself. He was no longer in doubt of the capabilities of her heart.** What Fanny is so unselfconsciously displaying are the same qualities that Jane Fairfax shows Emma, 'consciousness, animation and warmth'. That Jane Austen herself possessed these attributes, including a readiness to blush, is known to us from her brother Henry's *Biographical Notice* in which, describing his late sister's appearance, he paraphrases John Donne: 'Her complexion was of the finest texture. It might with truth be said, that her eloquent blood spoke through her modest cheek.'

10

Air and Address

WHEN USED OF a person's physical presence, the word *air* denotes such qualities as carriage, demeanour, attitude, style, mood; the general appearance and bearing of an individual, either fleeting or habitual; the expressiveness of any part of their body, including what we might today term body language.

Sometimes the *air* of a person is consciously cultivated to make the right impression. Lucy Steele is a case in point, having **a smartness of air, which though it did not give actual elegance or grace, gave distinction to her person.** Another such is Isabella Thorpe. Catherine is instantly impressed by **the fashionable air of her figure and dress,** while the younger Miss Thorpes, inferior in beauty and self-assurance, by **imitating her air, and dressing in the same style** do well enough in Bath. Mr Bingley's sisters, with their London education, have cultivated **an air of decided fashion** which enable them to look down on the more uncouth ways of country-town society.

One of the very few attributes in Mrs Allen's favour, one of the very few reasons why a man might choose to marry her – though hardly a sufficient one – is **the air of a gentlewoman.** At the most, this means that she has good bearing; but she certainly would not have fulfilled the Bingley sisters' criteria for the truly accomplished woman, which demand she have '**a certain something in her air and manner of walking, the tone of her voice, her address and expressions**'.

Gentlemen, too, may cut a good figure in the world with an air of fashion. Sir Walter Elliot praises Mr Elliot's **very gentlemanlike appearance, his air of elegance and fashion,** while what gratifies Anne is his **air of good sense.** Mr Palmer has **an air of more fashion and sense** than his wife, the silly if good-humoured younger daughter of vulgar Mrs Jennings. These are both sophisticated men who know how to behave as men of the world, and by combining sense with fashion, they escape some of the censure we are directed to feel for the female tribes of Bingley, Thorpe, Jennings, Hawkins and Steele. Jane Austen has plenty of ridiculous male characters, but no true fop – that fashionable but vacuous stereotype in the novels and drama of the period.

Air is not always assumed. Often enough it is the person's natural way of being. When the child Fanny Price arrives at Mansfield, **her air, though awkward, was not vulgar.** She is self-conscious, and untutored, but not brash or offensive in the way she moves and speaks. One of the best grown-up airs is that of Eleanor Tilney, which **though it had not all the decided pretension, the resolute stylishness of Miss Thorpe's, had more real elegance.** Emma Woodhouse has a high regard for elegance, but there is something even more lovely, and more natural, in the picture Mrs Weston paints: **'there is health not merely in her bloom, but in her air, her head, her glance'.** Emma is not preoccupied with her looks; she does not cultivate these attractions, they are an intrinsic part of herself. While Mrs Elton draws Emma's disgust: **neither feature nor air, nor voice, nor manner were elegant,** Emma approves Frank because **his manner had no air of study or exaggeration.**

In conversation with Harriet, Emma does her best to define *air*. Mr Martin, she asserts, is **'so very clownish, so totally without air'.** She is sure that Harriet must have been struck by his awkward look and abrupt manner, and the uncouthness of what she calls his unmodulated voice. **'Certainly'**, says Harriet, **'he is not like Mr Knightley. He has not such a fine air and way of walking as Mr Knightley.'** Emma replies, **'Mr Knightley's air is so remarkably good that it is not fair to compare Mr Martin with** him.' But, she adds, **'What say you to Mr Weston and Mr Elton? Compare their manner of carrying themselves, of walking, of speaking, of being silent.'** All these add up to *air*.

Though a person's air, like any other personal attribute, may be good or bad, sometimes merely the possession – or lack – of it is what matters, as with Emma's assertion that Mr Martin is **totally without air.** A good synonym for *air* when used this way would be *presence*.

Lady Dalrymple allows that Captain Wentworth has '**more air than one generally sees in Bath**', and that other arch-snob, Elizabeth Elliot, in issuing him with an invitation to her party, '**had been long enough in Bath to understand the importance of a man of such an air and appearance as his.... Captain Wentworth would move about well in her drawing-room.** Henry Crawford, too, **though not handsome, had air and countenance.** Or, as we might gloss this, a commanding presence and animation of eyes and mouth which are attractive in themselves.

When we read, on Wickham's appearance in Meryton, that **all were struck by the stranger's air,** we are called on to imagine a general look of smartness, agreeableness and self-assurance that, because unusual in a country town, even among the stationed militia, impresses itself on his beholders. This is made more explicit when, at their next meeting, at the Philipses' dinner party, Elizabeth acknowledges Wickham's superiority to all the other gentlemen **in person, countenance, air and walk.** Later, when Darcy has laid charges to his door the truth of which the shocked Elizabeth must at least consider, she can recollect no actual good of Wickham in word or deed, though she can **see him instantly before her, in every charm of air and address.**

But *air* meaning little more than bearing, neither good nor bad, must be what is meant when Elinor and Marianne on a country walk see a male figure in the distance which Marianne immediately assumes must be Willoughby. While Elinor protests, '**the person is not tall enough for him and has not his air**', Marianne insists, '**I am sure he has. His air, his coat, his horse**'. Of course, this is total self-delusion, made all the more odd because Edward Ferrars – whom the traveller turns out to be – possesses none of the graces of person or air in Marianne's eyes with which she endows Willoughby.

Air with a specific qualifying noun or adjective may be either a permanent characteristic of someone or evidence of a passing mood. *Pride and Prejudice* furnishes good examples of both. When Lady Catherine is first encountered, **her air was not conciliating,** which remains true of her throughout, culminating in her arriving at Longbourn **with an air more than usually ungracious.** Mr Collins's **air was grave and stately** from the moment of his first introduction, and after he has been rebuffed by Elizabeth he has **an air more stately**

than usual. In both cases, offence has been taken and has intensified the habitual nature of the *air*. Amusingly, the very same adjective is used of Mr Darcy: '**There is something a little stately in him,**' says Mrs Gardiner after their first meeting, '**but it is confined to his air, and is not unbecoming**'. The owner of Pemberley, cleverer as well as richer than most of the people around him, has more right to be stately than a stupid, fawning country clergyman. By '**confined to his air**', Mrs Gardiner draws the distinction between Darcy's bearing, which he can hardly help, and his conversation, which is under his own control and is as 'polite and unassuming' as Mr Gardiner could desire.

These are settled characteristics of the person's presentation of themselves to the world, as is Jane Bennet's admirable **serenity of ... countenance and air.** That this outward calmness might mask inner suffering is lost on the world at large: as Darcy explains to Elizabeth, trying to exculpate his own behaviour in separating Bingley from Jane, '**There was a constant complacency in her air and manner, not often united with great sensibility**'.

But when Mr Collins approaches Darcy, against Elizabeth's advice, with **the determined air of following his own inclination,** and Darcy replies **with an air of distant civility,** or when Darcy listens to Elizabeth's accusations with **an air which proved him wholly unmoved by any feelings of remorse,** their body language, though wholly in character, is applicable to that moment only. The **air of indifference** with which Wickham questions Elizabeth about her better knowledge of Darcy is obviously assumed. And when Darcy, on first hearing of Lydia's elopement with Wickham, walks about the room in the Lambton inn with **his brow contracted, his air gloomy,** this is (though Elizabeth does not read him correctly) less a revelation of character than evidence of his immediate thought processes, simultaneously self-accusatory and deeply anxious to involve himself in putting matters right.

A character's temporary *air* can confirm facts, or it can mystify. On Captain Wentworth's arrival in Bath, he is staggered to discover Mr Elliot's intimacy in the family, and his dangerous proximity to Anne. Wentworth recognizes Mr Elliot from the encounter in Lyme, when he was a stranger to them all, the very same man who admired Anne then **except in the air and look and manner of the privileged relation and** friend. Captain Wentworth is able to read this instantly, as could any observant looker-on. But not long afterwards, when a friendly conversation in the Octagon Room begins to give Anne hope that Captain Wentworth's tenderness for her is returning, and they are then divided for the concert, he reappears with a grave and irresolute demeanour, puzzling to Anne. **The difference between his present air and what it had been in the Octagon Room was strikingly great. Why was it?** Anne is left to her own deductions, uncertainties and fears.

The more self-aware characters manipulate others, or attempt to do so, by introducing a certain quality into their *air*. Emma having, as she thinks, made Frank Churchill a little in love with her, but not wishing it to go further, begins to wonder when it might be **necessary for her to throw coldness into her air.** Henry Crawford, dashing Maria's hopes of a proposal of marriage in a very public way by talking to her brother Tom of his plans to leave Mansfield, turns to her and repeats his story **with only a softened air and stronger expressions of regret. But what availed his expressions or his air? He was going....**

Mr Elton, at the height of his hopes of Emma, also turns to her **with a soft air.** Mr Elton's body language is one of the more obnoxious things about him, whether he is in fawning, resentful or exulting mode. After Emma has refused him, and on the rebound he has gained the hand of Augusta Hawkins, Emma finds him not **improved by the mixture of pique and pretension now spread over his air.** Poor Harriet's regrets are kept alive and feelings irritated by constantly catching sight of him, **his air as he walked by the house, the very sitting of his hat, being all proof of how much he was in love.** And when he returns with his bride, **he had the air of congratulating himself on having brought such a woman to Highbury, as not even Miss Woodhouse could equal.**

However, Augusta Hawkins, from mercantile Bristol, can only call on **all her airs of pert pretension and underbred finery** to impress the country neighbourhood. *Airs* in the plural generally evokes pretension, a usage that has not entirely died out. Louisa Musgrove declares that she would not be held back from doing what was right by **the airs and interference of such a person,** that is, her snobbish sister-in-law Mary, while the Miss Bertrams, knowing how to preserve the good opinion of the neighbourhood, **gave themselves no airs.** They have no shortage of vanity, being pleased with their own looks and their situation in life, but they are careful to keep their vanity from becoming apparent.

Air does not always refer to the person. Sometimes it describes a domestic interior or grounds. The Musgrove sisters are busy giving their old-fashioned home **the proper air of confusion by a grand pianoforte and a harp, flower-stands and little tables placed in every direction.** At Pemberley, admiring the unadorned landscape, Elizabeth is pleased by **a simple bridge, in character with the general air of the scene,** while at Hunsford Parsonage, neatly fitted up and arranged by its new mistress, **when Mr Collins could be forgotten, there was really a great air of comfort throughout.** The meaning seems to be variously *appearance*, *character* or *feeling*, terms that we are more likely to use in such contexts today.

When Henry Tilney is introduced to Catherine Morland as a dancing partner by the Master of Ceremonies at the Lower Rooms, we are told that **his address was good, and Catherine felt herself in high luck.** The Tilneys have their lodgings in Milsom Street, which is certainly a good address in our understanding of the term, but what it means to Catherine is not that at all. Henry speaks to her pleasantly and politely – he addresses her well. For a young woman whose previous admirer has been the boorish John Thorpe, this is a promising start.

If *air* relates to something intangible (*aura* might be a good synonym), *address* concerns speech and the approach that one person makes towards another. Jane Austen uses it to indicate a manner of speaking when she does not wish or need to give the conversation itself. When Emma beholds the long-awaited Frank Churchill, among his other attractions **height, air, address, all were unexceptionable ... she felt immediately that she should like him.** On being introduced to the wealthy Mr Rushworth, **there was nothing disagreeable in his figure or address,** thinks Maria Bertram, which is enough for her to become engaged to him; later, of course, she realizes how very unprepossessing his address actually is.

Henry Crawford, despite not being handsome, has **a pleasing address.** Another man whose appeal does not lie in his looks is Colonel Brandon: **though his face was not handsome his countenance was sensible,** and his address was **particularly gentlemanlike.** A few pages later, Elinor defends him from the criticism of Marianne and Willoughby, pronouncing him **a sensible man, well-bred, well-informed, of gentle address.** By contrast, Edward Ferrars, on first introduction to the ladies at Norland, was **not recommended to their good opinion by any peculiar graces of person or address.** It is not long, however, before Mrs Dashwood, learning to see Edward through Elinor's eyes, finds that **even that quietness of manner which militated against all her established ideas of what a young man's address ought to be,** is no longer uninteresting when she understands that underneath his shyness is warmth of heart.

Mrs Dashwood herself speaks with the **sweetness of address which always attended her,** and which soon overcomes Edward's reserve. This habitual, and wholly natural, **sweetness of address** plays a large part in the 'captivating manners' which, Jane Austen tells us, make any man who is in love with either of her daughters extend the passion to herself. Charles Bingley is another character who is **blessed with greater sweetness of address** than other men, at least according to Jane Bennet.

Possessing a pleasing *address* is usually the sign of a lovable personality, but occasionally it masks absolutely the reverse. George Wickham numbers **a fine countenance, a good figure and a very pleasing address** among his attributes, and has **every charm of person and address that can captivate a woman.** Naturally, he is aware of his powers. Confident in his superiority over Darcy in this point at least, he asks Elizabeth, who has returned from Kent with an altered perception of Darcy (whom they have previously denigrated together), '**Is it in address that he improves? Has he deigned to add aught of civility to his ordinary style?**' Elizabeth replies to the effect that in essentials Darcy is what he has always been, but that with increasing acquaintance comes greater understanding of his character.

Nothing abashes Wickham for long. When he and Lydia, after running away together and having to be bribed into marriage, are received at Longbourn, Elizabeth and Jane blush for them, but Lydia and Wickham themselves show no shame. But while Lydia's bravado extends to boasts and exultations, Wickham is more self-aware and knows better than to offend in this way. **His manners were always so** pleasing, that had his character and his marriage been exactly what they ought, his smiles and his easy address, while he claimed their relationship, would have delighted them all.

That these are almost all male examples (with the exception of Mrs Dashwood) can be accounted for by the fact that, like other personal qualities, *address* is most frequently described by Jane Austen when a new male character is introduced, the heroines having to reach an assessment of him. But it is by no means solely a male attribute. Miss Bingley, in describing the truly accomplished woman (trying to make Elizabeth feel inferior) says **'She must possess something in her air and manner of walking, the tone of her voice, her address and expressions.'** The three girl cousins Maria, Julia and Fanny, when first they come to live together, display among other differences that which **education had given to their address.**

If *address* sometimes means speech in general, on other occasions, as the context makes clear, it implies a particular speech. We use the word in this sense today of a public lecture, for example. In Jane Austen it refers to a much shorter passage of speech than a lecture, but is differentiated from the to-and-fro of normal conversation by the fact that only one person is speaking. **Henry's address, short as it had been,** by representing the probabilities of the situation, and describing the kind of society they inhabit, opens Catherine's eyes to the folly she has been indulging in by imagining General Tilney has murdered his wife.

Sir Thomas Bertram is accustomed to laying down the law in his household; the child Fanny is in awe of him; and as he makes his farewells on leaving for Antigua, although the purport of his message to her is kind, **would he only have smiled upon her and called her 'my dear Fanny' while he said it, every former frown and cold address might have been forgotten.**

Mr Elton makes a misjudged speech begging Mrs Weston's influence to prevent Emma visiting Harriet's sick-room: **Emma saw Mrs Weston's surprise, and felt that it must be great, at an address which, in words and manner, was assuming to himself the right of first interest in her.** Henry Crawford is better-judging, adapting his speech not only to the person he is talking to, but to those who might overhear. As he details to Fanny his scheme for renting a house in Northamptonshire, **Sir Thomas heard and was not offended. There was no want of respect in the young man's address.**

Elizabeth Bennet is astonished by the change in Darcy's mode of speech when she encounters him at Pemberley: **what a contrast did it offer to his last address in Rosings Park, when he put his letter into her hand!** Contrast of a more unwelcome nature occurs when the Dashwood sisters find themselves in company with Willoughby at a London gathering and, all his old intimacy gone, he enquires in a hurried and formal manner after their mother and how long they have been in town: even Elinor did not expect this. **Elinor was robbed of all presence of mind by such an address.**

John Thorpe, meeting his mother in Bath, greets her with 'Where **did you get that quiz of a hat? It makes you look like an old witch. Here is Morland and I come to stay a few days with you, so you must look out for a couple of good beds somewhere near.' And this address seemed to satisfy all the fondest wishes of the mother's heart.** Later, with Catherine oblivious to his heavy hints of being in love with her, **she hurried away, leaving him to the undivided consciousness of his own happy address and her explicit encouragement.**

Mr Collins, in demanding Elizabeth hear his proposal, says **'Allow me to assure you that I have your respected mother's permission for this address.'** The case of Mr Collins, whose next speech is some five hundred words in length, beginning 'My reasons for marrying' and ending 'when we are married', brings us to the more specific expression *paying one's addresses*, i.e. making a proposal of marriage.

'Here is a young man wishing to pay his addresses to you with everything to recommend him', says Sir Thomas uncomprehendingly when he understands that Fanny means to refuse Henry Crawford. In continuation of the same sentence, he uses the word in its more general meaning when he lists the points in Henry's favour: **'not merely situation in life, fortune and character, but with more than common agreeableness, with address and conversation pleasing to everybody'**.

Having rejected Darcy at Rosings, and finding him so much improved at Pemberley, Elizabeth has to ask herself whether **she should employ the power, which her fancy told her she still possessed,**

of bringing on the renewal of his addresses. (This is before the debacle with Lydia changes everything.) It is clear that the word *addresses*, in the plural as here, means proposals.

Similarly, as a verb, *to address*, though it might simply mean to speak to, may carry the more particular meaning of proposing marriage. At the end of *Persuasion*, Captain Wentworth, now high in his profession and with a fortune of twenty-five thousand pounds, is **esteemed worthy to address the daughter of a foolish, spendthrift baronet.** As every reader understands from the context, this does not mean worthy to speak to her, but worthy to make her an offer of marriage. Incidentally, it is unclear quite whose viewpoint this is. Neither Sir Walter nor Elizabeth, nor even Lady Russell, is likely to admit he is a foolish, spendthrift baronet, even this late in the story; while Anne and her narrator have never thought Wentworth unworthy. It can only be the public at large.

Address sometimes carries the more specific meaning of *adroitness* in working on others to gain one's ends. A benign case occurs when Elinor Dashwood offers to sit out a round of cards so that she can help Lucy Steele make a filigree basket for the spoilt daughter of the Middletons, not because she cares about the child or the basket but because she wants some private conversation with Lucy. **Elinor joyfully profited by the first of these proposals** [to sit out the first round], **and thus by a little of that address, which Marianne could never condescend to practise, gained her own end, and pleased Lady Middleton at the same time.** Marianne, of course, will never say anything she does not mean, and so could not utter Elinor's 'I should like the work exceedingly', or pretend to enjoy Lucy's company because she wants to extract information from her.

Seeing Charlotte Collins for the first time in her new married home, Elizabeth retires at night to meditate upon her friend's **address in guiding, and composure in bearing with her husband, and to acknowledge that it was all done very well.** Elizabeth admires Charlotte's skill in managing her husband without overtly criticizing him, showing any dissatisfaction in public, or causing friction in the home.

Both Elinor and Charlotte are given credit for their quiet good sense and cleverness, but this kind of *address* is not always so unexceptionably applied. Twice we encounter the word in connection with Frank Churchill. Emma perceives that **it was not without difficulty, without considerable address at times** that Frank can get away from Enscombe or introduce an acquaintance for a night. Although there is nothing unreasonable or malevolent about Frank's wishes, he has become used to manipulating people for his own ends – manipulating them with charm, no doubt. On the other, more light-hearted occasion, Frank uses the word of his own methods: **'I will attack them with more address'**, he remarks of his dull companions on Box Hill, whom his silly chatter is failing to rouse into liveliness. It is appropriate that Frank, with his French name and connotations, should use the word in this sense. (Mr Knightley has said of Frank that he can only be *aimable* in French, not amiable in English; and Frank himself admits at one point to being sick of England.) The connection with French wiles is made more explicit when Mary Crawford tells her sister Mrs Grant that **'If you can persuade Henry to marry, you must have the address of a Frenchwoman. All that English abilities can do, has been tried already'**, going on to tell how three of her friends, their mothers, her aunt and herself have long been trying to reason, coax or trick him into marrying. The implication must be that a Frenchwoman could do this more subtly, without the object of her artifice being aware. With her love of English straightforwardness, Jane Austen is evidently suspicious of the kind of manoeuvring implied by this sense of the word *address*.

11

Mind

WHILE *PERSON, COUNTENANCE, air* and *address* are the terms by which Jane Austen assesses the outward appearance and presentation of the individual, *mind*, together with *spirit* and *temper*, the subjects of the next two chapters, are used by her to dissect the personality within. *Mind*, for her, is a large concept, comprising both intellect and capacity for feeling. When she speaks of **the greatest powers of the mind** in her praise of the novelist's art in *Northanger Abbey*, she is implying not only the learning that comes from being well-read, but a native psychological acuity, a sense of proportion and even a sense of fun, the qualities of course that she herself possessed in abundance.

To fall in love with a person properly, not superficially, must be to fall in love with the *mind*. The more intelligent of the lovers and suitors in the novels not only observe the externals of behaviour, but also penetrate the deeper qualities of the *mind* which underpins it. Henry Crawford loves Fanny for '**the sweetness of her temper, the purity of her mind**', for her **modest and elegant mind** and for **a youth of mind as lovely as of person**. Anne Elliot is, in her cousin's view, **a most extraordinary young woman: in her temper, manners, mind, a model of female excellence.**

Mr Elliot is morally flawed; but his good opinion of Anne's mind is reciprocated: within ten minutes of listening to his conversation, she has decided that **his tone, his expressions, his choice of subject, his knowing where to stop; it was all the operation of a sensible, discerning mind.** These are important qualities in a husband – they are lacking in, for example, young husbands like Mr Collins, Mr Rushworth and

Mr Elton – but though they go a long way, they are not sufficient security for a young woman's happiness. Anne is not quite satisfied, though it requires further observation before she can identify why her cousin, for all his sense and discernment, makes her feel uneasy.

While both Mr Elliot and Mr Crawford turn out to be unworthy of the heroines they pursue, the fact that they are attracted by more than looks and manners is in their favour. Not that they praise the women they love more highly than those women deserve: Fanny, the narrator tells us, has delicacy of taste, of mind, of feelings, unlike the lively but more shallow Mary Crawford. Again in contrast to Mary, as Edmund eventually acknowledges, Fanny's **mind, disposition, opinions and habits wanted no half-concealment**, and he also speaks of her **beauty of mind.**

As for Anne, the heroine that Jane Austen called 'almost too good for me', she is early praised for **the nice tone of her mind** and **elegance of mind and sweetness of character.** At the age of nineteen she is considered by Lady Russell, the only person who appreciates her qualities except for Captain Wentworth, to be, **with all her claims of birth, beauty and mind,** too good to marry him – or to throw herself away, as Lady Russell expresses it. Sad and misunderstood though Anne often is, she reflects that she would not exchange **her own more elegant and cultivated mind** for all the advantages enjoyed by the Musgrove sisters – envying only their closeness as sisters. When Captain Wentworth's love is gradually rekindled by observing, among her many other quiet virtues, Anne's **presence of mind** and **resolution of a collected mind** in an emergency, as well as her emotional intelligence, sympathy and unselfishness, he comes to acknowledge **the perfect excellence of the mind with which Louisa's could ill bear comparison.**

Mind may be glossed as intellect, intelligence, or way of thinking, feeling and reacting to the world around. The mind may be well stocked with learning and reflection, or it may be empty and uncultivated. The former must bring greater depth and resources to a life partnership. Elizabeth Bennet, reflecting on her sister Jane's right to be beloved by Mr Bingley, considers **her understanding excellent, her mind improved, and her manners captivating.** Jane's mind is improved, presumably, by reading, since the Bennet girls have received no other kind of education. When Darcy and Miss Bingley are discussing what makes a truly accomplished woman, Darcy adds to the more showy qualities enumerated by Miss Bingley, 'something more substantial, in the improvement of her mind by extensive reading'. And Edmund Bertram's attentions to his young cousin Fanny are of the highest importance in assisting the improvement of her mind, and extending its pleasures. He knew her to be clever, to have a quick apprehension as well as good sense, and a fondness for reading, which, properly directed, must be an education in itself.

However, when Edmund tells Fanny, who is afraid that she must go and live with an unlovable aunt, that 'Your being with Mrs Norris will be as good for your mind as riding has been for your health', he certainly has no intellectual improvement in view for Fanny. Even Edmund, with the best will in the world, cannot think that Mrs Norris's conversation will enlarge Fanny's mind intellectually. Rather, he considers that Fanny will learn to exert herself more in a small household, and enjoy being important as a companion to someone: with increasing self-confidence, she will grow out of what is elsewhere called the common timidity of her mind. Edmund, as so often, is deluding himself. Fanny does, indeed, grow out of her timidity, but not until Portsmouth forces her to act as a responsible adult, an older sister exercising her better judgement for the good of the family. Beginning to understand the worth of Susan and the difficulties of her position, Fanny entertains the hope of being useful to a mind so much in need of help, and so much deserving it. Fanny takes on the educative role, introducing Susan to books, ideas and knowledge of the wider world. Under Fanny's gentle influence, Susan's mind is improved both intellectually and morally. We see how excellent Fanny will be as a parent.

There are some qualities of the mind which are specifically masculine. Captain Harville possesses a mind of usefulness and ingenuity, enabling him to add comfort to his home; while the younger sailor, William Price, inspires respect for having gone through such bodily hardship, and given such proofs of mind: that is, proofs of exertion, endurance and heroism. On the journey to Portsmouth with Fanny, everything supplied an amusement to the high glee of William's mind, and he was full of frolic and joke, in the intervals of their higher-toned subjects: a good companion for serious Fanny. As a young man, one of Captain Wentworth's attractions for Anne is **fearlessness of mind**; Lady Russell equates this with dangerous self-confidence and imprudence. She is wrong. It advances him in his career, and it is by acting 'with the activity and exertion of a fearless man' that Captain Wentworth restores Anne's friend Mrs Smith to some of her fortune at the end of the story.

Of the Musgrove family, we read that **their children had more modern minds and manners**. There might be an element of education in the *minds* referred to here, since the younger generation have received more than their parents; but the word could be glossed as ways of thinking rather than mental endowments, young people commonly being more up-to-date in their ideas than their elders, as Jane Austen had observed.

When in reaction to the engagement of Captain Benwick to Louisa Musgrove, Captain Wentworth fears there is **too great a disparity, and in a point no less essential than mind**, he means that, not only in intelligence and knowledge, but in thoughtfulness and seriousness of feeling, Louisa differs from her lover. In terms of the plot, the Benwick-Louisa match is convenient, but unconvincing. But Captain Wentworth's remark to Anne is given to indicate his realization, at last, of the limitations of Louisa's mind; she would never have satisfied him as a wife. He now regards Louisa, while 'not deficient in understanding' as lacking Benwick's 'something more. He is a clever man, a reading man'. Only a man equally clever and well-read could estimate Benwick this way (Charles Musgrove, though liking him well enough, is incapable of appreciating him properly) for as, in another novel, Emma Woodhouse says of Mr Elton's presumption to her hand, **perhaps it was not fair to expect him to feel how very much he was her inferior in talent, and all the elegancies of the mind. The very want of such equality must prevent his perception of it.** This is a telling observation. Anyone, however plain themselves, can see different levels of physical attractiveness in others; financial and social status are easily appreciated by those more lowly situated; but not everybody has the power to estimate another person's mental endowments if they are at a level some way above their own.

And yet – to return to *Persuasion* – only months earlier, Frederick Wentworth has told Louisa, with some degree of warmth, to '**cherish all her present powers of mind**', and has said of her more malleable sister, '**Happy for her, to have such a mind as yours at hand!**' Mind here must bear quite a different meaning from the way Wentworth subsequently uses it – nothing to do with being clever or well-read. It recalls Maria Bertram's assertion that '**I cannot but think that good horsemanship has a great deal to do with the mind**', having in the same context just praised Mary Crawford's 'spirits ... and energy of character' – similar qualities to those which Wentworth fancies he sees in Louisa. Even in this, he is mistaken – Louisa just likes having her own way – but he has his own reasons, as we know, for overestimating the quality of unpersuadableness. As Anne reflects, after Louisa's self-willed behaviour on the Cobb at Lyme Regis, leading to her accident, **like all other qualities of the mind, it should have its proportions and limits.**

The habitual state of the *mind* may be *composed* – Lady Russell; *eager* – Mrs Dashwood; *illiberal* – Mrs Bennet; or *trifling* – Mrs Allen. These are all mature women, though it is only the twenty-seven year old Anne Elliot who is credited with actual **maturity of mind.** Frank Churchill speaks of Jane Fairfax's having '**the most upright female mind in the creation**'. Edmund Bertram too has **uprightness of mind** and Fanny Price has **propriety of mind** – examples of the word's conveying moral rather than intellectual qualities. This is made even more specific when, at the end of *Mansfield Park*, Sir Thomas realizes too late that the education of his daughters had been too superficial and could have had **no moral effect on the mind.**

Edmund is infatuated by Mary Crawford, seeing in her **the mind of genius** and what he calls '**the finest mind**', appreciating her wit and cleverness; but he is also afraid of those very same qualities: criticizing her levity to Fanny, he lays the blame with her London acquaintance and says '**it does appear more than manner; it appears as if the mind itself was tainted**'. Here the most fundamental question of a person's goodness seems to reside in the mind. '**Hers are faults of principle, Fanny, of blunted delicacy and a corrupted, vitiated mind**', Edmund eventually acknowledges, when his courtship is finally over. He even tells the lady herself that **as far as related to mind, it had been** a creature of my own imagination, not Miss Crawford, that I had been too apt to dwell on for many months past. This is not only rather cruel but it is not strictly true, since he has always had reservations about the moral aspects of Miss Crawford's mind. And Fanny has her own criticisms to make of Miss Crawford's mind, calling it, in her own thoughts, **a mind led astray and bewildered, and without any suspicion of being so; darkened, yet fancying itself light.** This is Fanny at her most priggish and least attractive.

Henry Crawford likewise has **a mind unused to make any sacrifice to right.** Fanny uses the same word of his mind as Edmund has used of Mary's. '**Never happier than when behaving so dishonourably and unfeelingly! Oh, what a corrupted mind!**' is her silent reflection on his retrospective enjoyment of the theatricals – which amused Henry's **sated mind.** And in *Sense and Sensibility*, observing Lucy Steele's assiduous, flattering ways with her social superiors, Elinor reflects on **her thorough want of delicacy, of rectitude, and integrity of mind.** After Willoughby's long explanation of his conduct, she reflects with greater feelings of sadness **on the irreparable injury which too early an independence and its consequent habits of idleness, dissipation, and luxury, had made in the mind, the character, the happiness of a man who, to every advantage of person and talents, united a disposition naturally open and honest, and a feeling, affectionate temper.**

Elinor is almost being *too* lenient to Willoughby here. Another heroine who equates mind with morality is Anne Elliot, who, in thinking of her cousin, **saw that there had been bad habits ... that there had been a period of his life (and probably not a short one) when he had been, at least, careless in all serious matters; and, though he might now think very differently, who could answer for the true sentiments of a clever, cautious man, grown old enough to appreciate a fair character? How could it ever be ascertained that his mind was truly cleansed?**

But the mind also seems to be the seat of emotion, especially painful emotion. When Maria Bertram realizes that Henry Crawford is not going to ask for her hand in marriage, as his attentions have led her to hope, **the agony of her mind was severe.** Being left alone at her two aunts' beck and call on a very hot day, while all the other young people are out enjoying themselves, Fanny develops a headache, and as she retreats to the sofa after dinner feeling neglected and even jealous, before Edmund returns to speak up for her, **the pain of her mind had been much beyond that in her head.** On Box Hill, listening to Frank flirting more outrageously than ever before with Emma, Jane Fairfax suffers **the agony of a mind that could bear no more.** Emma herself, in a sudden burst of self-knowledge, finds that **her mind was in all the perturbation** that such a realization as her love for Mr Knightley and doubt of its return must bring.

'**Poverty has not contracted her mind**', Emma says generously (and truly) of Miss Bates, even though as a general rule '**a very narrow income has a tendency to contract the mind, and sour the temper**'. On another occasion, in sarcastic mode, Emma speaks of Miss Bates's '**powerful, argumentative mind**'. Though occasionally castigating herself for not having the simple and affectionate nature of her father, Isabella, Harriet or even Miss Bates, Emma is generally pleased enough with her own mind. '**Mine is an active, busy mind, with a great many independent resources**', she tells Harriet – sounding somewhat like Mrs Elton. She foresees a happy future as an unmarried woman: '**Woman's usual occupations of eye, and hand, and mind, will be as open to me then as they are now.**' Like Fanny Price, whose 'own thoughts were habitually her best companions', (yet whose **mind had seldom known a pause in its alarms or embarrassments**), Emma's is **a mind delighted with its own ideas** and, even at the moment when life in Highbury seems particularly uneventful – enough to bore anyone – Emma has the advantage of **a mind lively and at ease,** which creates her own enjoyment out of nothing. This is in stark contrast to **the many vacancies of Harriet's mind.** Of course, Emma's mind often leads her astray, but it is usually capable of correcting itself.

In this novel, the mind is not confined to the private sphere. Those with the most active or powerful minds use them, consciously or unconsciously, to control and judge other people. They are almost a social tool. Emma employs **all the force of her own mind** to direct something as simple as Harriet's purchases, not to mention her choice of husband. Reluctant though she is to give any credit to Robert Martin, having read his letter she concedes '**I understand the sort of mind. Vigorous, decided, with sentiments to a certain point not coarse**'.

(But still not good enough to marry Harriet.) To Mr Knightley, Robert Martin's '**mind has more true gentility than Harriet Smith could understand**'.

Jane Fairfax's **higher powers of mind** are felt by the Campbells, though without resentment, in comparison to their own daughter; and Mr Knightley explains to Emma that '**Miss Fairfax awes Mrs Elton by her superiority both of mind and manner**'. He is very scathing about the **little minds** of the wealthy, domineering Churchills and sure that Frank could bend them to his will if he would only do his duty by his father. Mr Knightley himself always acts **with the alertness of a mind which could neither be undecided nor dilatory**. In matters of the heart, a state of indecision **must be more intolerable than any alternative to such a mind as his**.

His brother resembles him, having **all the clearness and quickness of mind** which his wife lacks. **The strength, resolution and presence of mind of the Mr Knightleys** are a source of comfort to the nervous Mr Woodhouse. Quickness of comprehension is also a quality of Emma's mind: **A mind like hers, once opening to suspicion, made rapid progress.** This is when she is admitting to herself her love – which she fears must be unrequited – for Mr Knightley. Wretchedly blaming herself for all her misdealings with other people, she reflects that, apart from her acknowledgement of Mr Knightley's superiority, **every other part of her mind was disgusting**. (Disgusting then had the milder meaning of distasteful.) But even at a moment of crisis in her own emotions, Emma is supported, and enabled to act so as not to cause pain to Mr Knightley, by the qualities of her mind: **There was time only for the quickest arrangement of mind. She must be collected and calm.**

Once past childhood, can the qualities of a mind be altered by the influence of others? John Dashwood and Charles Musgrove are two rather lightweight young men who, their author assures us, would have been improved in character had they married more amiable and well-judging women. Early in his marriage Mr Bennet despairs of **enlarging the mind of his wife**, a woman characterized by her **weak understanding and illiberal mind**, incapable of looking beyond its own petty concerns. But his daughter Elizabeth, with more promising material to work on in Mr Darcy, considers (when she thinks she has lost him) that **by her ease and liveliness, his mind might have been softened, his manners improved.** A softened mind in this instance is clearly not an enfeebled one, but one less severe, more open to amusement: more able, like Elizabeth, to delight in absurdity. We see this process in action after their marriage, to the astonishment of his sister Georgiana, whose own **mind received knowledge which had never before fallen in her way ... that a woman may take liberties with her husband.** Darcy tells Elizabeth that he learnt to admire her 'for the **liveliness of your mind'** – another suitor who makes qualities of the *mind* the most important criteria in a partner (notwithstanding the fact that 'clever' Emma Woodhouse does not believe that men **'fall in love with well-informed minds instead of handsome faces').**

Or, as Jane Austen says in *Northanger Abbey*, tongue firmly in cheek: **to come with a well-informed mind is to come with an inability of administering to the vanity of others, which a sensible person would always wish to avoid. A woman especially, if she have the misfortune of knowing anything, should conceal it as well as she can.**

12

Temper

WHEN IT IS the turn of Susan Price to be transplanted to Mansfield, she brings to her post of resident niece **a readiness of mind** which gives her **quickness in understanding the tempers of those she had to deal with**. This is not to imply that the inhabitants of Mansfield Park are what we would call bad-tempered (Mrs Norris has, after all, been banished by this time). *Temper*, in most contexts in Jane Austen, signifies *temperament*, a morally neutral measure. Or in eighteenth century parlance, the 'particular Temper which the Mind has by Nature, or which has been established by Education, Example, Custom or some other means'.

The term comes from the Latin *temperare*, meaning to keep, manage or combine in due proportion, to bring to a proper or suitable condition (as in the Lord tempers the wind to the shorn lamb). From this, the noun, when used of a person, came to mean the disposition as composed of a combination of elements – in good order or not, as the case may be. When someone is *out of temper* or *ill-tempered* it is because mental balance and composure fail under provocation. While our modern understanding of the word has limited it to this negative sense, Jane Austen employs a richer panoply of meaning.

There are certainly occasions when she uses the word as we would today. **He was not an ill-tempered man, not so often unreasonably cross as to deserve such a reproach; but his temper was not his great perfection.** This is our introduction to John Knightley, given in the narrator's voice but reflecting his sister-in-law's judgement. Amusingly, Mrs John Knightley is oblivious to her husband's chief defect. Praising Mr Weston, she says to her husband, '**I believe he is one of the very best-**

tempered men that ever existed. Excepting yourself and your brother, I do not know his equal for temper'. Mr Weston says that Mrs Churchill has 'a devil of a temper', prompting Isabella to say, in all innocence, 'To be constantly living with an ill-tempered person must be dreadful. It is what we happily have never known anything of.'

As the guests at the Westons' dinner party take their carriages to depart, Emma hopes to see John Knightley recover his temper and happiness when this visit of hardship were over. 'Capable of sometimes being out of humour', is another way of putting this kind of *temper*, which on the part of John Knightley occasionally manifests itself in 'a rational remonstrance or sharp retort equally ill-bestowed'. The same *temper/ humour* parallel is drawn in *Persuasion*, when Charles, though in very good humour with her, was out of temper with his wife. In *Emma*, attention is drawn to the phrase itself, when the heroine perceives that Frank Churchill's state of irritability 'might best be defined by the expressive phrase of being out of humour'. Mary Crawford, criticizing her brother-in-law Dr Grant, says that if the cook makes a blunder, he 'is out of humour with his excellent wife'. Edmund agrees that this is 'a great defect of temper', and he links the two terms again shortly afterwards in speaking to Fanny as Mary leaves them: 'There goes good humour I am sure', he said presently. 'There goes a temper which would never give pain!' Even when his eyes have been opened to her moral shortcomings, he can still distinguish and say 'Hers are not faults of temper'.

Mansfield Park places considerable stress on questions of *temper* in the sense of self-control, politeness and the preservation of domestic harmony. When vexed, Julia Bertram's temper was hasty. As Sir Thomas realizes too late, his daughters had never been properly taught to govern their inclinations and tempers. So when Maria, having run away with Henry Crawford, realizes that he has no intention of marrying her, the disappointment and wretchedness arising from the conviction rendered her temper so bad, and her feelings for him so like hatred, as to make them for a while each other's punishment, and then induce a voluntary separation. After which, obliged to make a home with her aunt Norris, shut up together with little society, their tempers became their mutual punishment.

Mansfield inhabitants are glad to get rid of Mrs Norris. **Since Mrs Rushworth's elopement, her temper had been in a state of such irritation as to make her everywhere tormenting.** Mrs Norris and Mrs Rushworth are left to torment each other, while their author hastens to 'restore everybody, not greatly in fault themselves, to tolerable comfort'. It is worth remarking that while Mrs Rushworth and Mrs Norris are mutually bad-tempered when things do not go their way, only Mrs Rushworth suffers from this defect while living with Mr Crawford – as far as we know, his good manners are preserved. Earlier, Fanny, endeavouring to do him justice, **thought he was really good-tempered** despite his more serious faults. When Sir Thomas, astonished by Fanny's refusal of Mr Crawford's hand, asks **'Have you any reason, child, to think ill of Mr Crawford's temper?'** she has to reply 'No, Sir'; and as negotiations proceed, Sir Thomas is left with **'a most favourable opinion of his understanding, heart and temper'.**

In *Emma*, after Mrs Churchill's death proves she has been truly ill, it is generally admitted in Highbury society that **continual pain would try the temper** and she is thought of more kindly than before. Emma also acknowledges, of those less fortunate than herself, that **a very narrow income has a tendency to contract the mind, and sour the temper.** More severely, because he has nothing to complain about, she instructs Frank Churchill to **believe your temper under your own command.** She herself has **difficulty in behaving with temper** when Mr Elton oversteps the boundaries of correct behaviour towards her; but with some effort, she succeeds in preserving her own good manners. All these are examples of the word implying crossness and failure of common courtesy for one reason or another.

But there can be as many adjectives attached to *temper* as there can be kinds of temperament, and many are peaceable and pleasant. Mrs Allen, that nonentity, has **a great deal of quiet, inactive good temper.** Mrs Weston, while Emma's governess, hardly exercised any restraint because of **the mildness of her temper.** Her husband has a **sanguine temper** and **social temper**; once Emma even has occasion to deplore **the unmanageable good will of Mr Weston's temper.** Miss Bates is popular because of her **universal good will and contented temper** and Mrs Grant is characterized by **a temper to love and be loved.**

Amongst parents, Mr Woodhouse has **an amiable temper** and **a general benevolence of temper.** Lady Bertram possesses **a temper remarkably easy.** Another character whose **temper was cheerful and sanguine** is Mr Dashwood, father of Elinor and Marianne, and **no temper could be more cheerful than** Mrs Dashwood's in 'seasons of cheerfulness' as she possesses 'that sanguine expectation of happiness which is happiness itself' – though she can equally be carried away by sorrow. More stable are Mr and Mrs Morland, the only intact set of parents belonging to a heroine: **their tempers were mild, but their principles were steady.**

Their daughter Catherine has **'a temper cheerful and open'.** Willoughby and Marianne are alike in having **tempers so frank.** Captain Wentworth has a **decided, confident temper,** not unlike Mr Knightley, whose **temper was much the most communicative** of the Knightley brothers. Frank Churchill on first coming to Highbury appears **to have a very open temper – certainly a very cheerful and lively one.** At the end of the novel, when Jane Fairfax has become reconciled after their quarrel, she blames herself for taking his flirtation with Emma too seriously, and not making allowance for the nature of his **temper and spirits** which had originally bewitched her.

Henry Crawford has **a temper of vanity and hope,** Edmund an **unsuspicious temper,** both very specific natures. William Price has a **bolder temper** than Fanny and their sister Susan's **temper was open.** This is a good thing, as the well-judging Mr Knightley makes clear in his critique of Jane Fairfax: **'Her sensibilities, I suspect, are strong, and her temper excellent in its power of forbearance, patience and self-control; but it wants openness.... I love an open temper.'**

On the other hand, Susan has **an imperfect temper,** which Fanny is careful not to irritate, bringing us back to the other meaning of *temper.* As does this early description of Mrs Bennet: **a woman of mean understanding, little information and uncertain temper.** This, of course, does not mean that her personality is an unknowable one but that, like Susan, though with less excuse, she lacks equanimity. The **want of temper** included in the list of disqualifications for being agreeable possessed by those present at the Dashwoods' dinner party in London, suggests that some of them have indulged their bad-temperedness so habitually as to be incapable of socializing in any other mode. Elinor and Marianne move in the most unpleasant social circle of any of the heroines – and not, of course, by choice.

Fanny later realizes that, as a child, she probably alienated the love of her mother **by the helplessness and fretfulness of a fearful temper.** Even in maturity she is **a gentle-tempered girl** with **a frame and temper delicate and nervous.** Fanny has **an obliging, yielding temper** and **a supine and yielding temper** – as a rule, almost too supine; only when her deepest feelings are in revolt does she (at much cost to herself) discover an iron will, astonishing all who know her. Then Sir Thomas is brought almost to accusing her of **wilfulness of temper, self-conceit:** a most unfair charge.

Two pairs of Bennet sisters are compared in terms of *temper.* Kitty is **not of so ungovernable a temper as** Lydia. Elizabeth has **less pliancy of temper than her sister** Jane. One of the most attractive qualities of Elizabeth is that she has **a temper to be happy.** She adjusts to changed circumstances, like the curtailment of travelling plans, without complaint. When travelling with her uncle and aunt, they all have **health and temper to bear inconveniences** which ensures the pleasantness of their holiday.

More contrasts are made between the Elliot sisters in *Persuasion,* one being drawn near the beginning and one near the end of the book. We are early told that **Mary had not Anne's understanding nor temper** (while her husband Charles is **in sense and temper ... undoubtedly superior to his wife**) and later Anne doubts how her sister Elizabeth's **temper and understanding might bear the investigation of** Mr Elliot, if he is disposed to marry her.

With all these disparate qualities coming under the term *temper,* it is clear that, whilst the word often has nothing whatsoever to do with irritability or its reverse, it does sometimes carry a residue of that meaning. Many characters, for example, are said to have **sweet tempers.** Fanny reflects on her aunt Bertram's **having the sweetest of all sweet tempers** (not that she has much to try her!) while Fanny herself is also praised for **the sweetness of her temper** by those who love her, including the narrator, on several occasions. Isabella Knightley has **extreme sweetness of ... temper** while Jane Bennet's **steady sense** and sweetness of temper exactly adapted her for attending to her little nephews and nieces. She will make a good mother – a better one perhaps than Isabella Knightley, since Jane has both sweetness *and* sense.

Though the male temper is not so often characterized as sweet, Mr Weston has a **warm heart and sweet temper** and Mr Bingley is a **sweet-tempered, amiable, charming man.** As such he is contrasted with Fitzwilliam Darcy, as the latter proudly admits himself when asked to name his faults. **'My temper I dare not vouch for.'** This does not mean that he is liable to fly into a rage but, as he goes on to explain, **'I cannot forget the follies and vices of others so soon as I ought, nor their offences against myself.... My temper would perhaps be called resentful. My good opinion once lost is lost for ever.'** Later Elizabeth recalls, **'I do remember his boasting one day, at Netherfield, of the implacability of his resentments, of his having an unforgiving temper. His disposition must be dreadful.'** And yet Elizabeth is not satisfied with the other extreme represented by Bingley: **She could not think without anger, hardly without contempt, of that easiness of temper, that want of proper resolution** that allows him to be influenced by his friends. **The easiness, openness and ductility of his temper** are among Bingley's recommendations as a friend to Darcy, but in Elizabeth's opinion (and that of her father, though half-joking) they can be carried too far – and Jane will not exert any contra-influence, being so similar herself.

That he was not a good-tempered man, had been her firmest opinion of Darcy for many months, and is Elizabeth's chief reason for rejecting his proposals, for no intelligent woman would knowingly entrust her happiness to a man with such a disposition: Mrs Grant is a portrait of a good wife, even a loved wife, who suffers from a bad-tempered husband. But, at Pemberley, Elizabeth has to rethink her opinion when hearing from the housekeeper that Darcy **'was always the sweetest-tempered, most generous-hearted boy in the world'**, a statement given with corroborating evidence. Gradually she comes to realize that **his understanding and temper, though unlike her own, would have answered all her wishes.** She is using the word *temper* in its more general sense of disposition. When Darcy eventually admits to Elizabeth that **'As a child I was taught what was right, but I was not taught to correct my**

temper', it does not mean that he threw tantrums, any more than did his earlier boast; but that he grew up 'to think meanly of all of the rest of the world'. This does not tally with the housekeeper's impression, but it hardly matters and readers hardly notice the discrepancy, for it is clear he has confronted his faults in a way few people are capable of, and is a reformed man.

The question of whether similarity of *temper* is essential or desirable in marriage partners, settled so easily by Elizabeth in the negative (and likewise, but less convincingly, by Jane Fairfax), is also raised by Fanny Price, hoping to win Edmund to her opinion that she is not suited to Henry Crawford. Edmund replies to her objections, **'There is a decided difference in your tempers, I allow. He is lively, you are serious; but so much the better; his spirits will support yours'**, adding **'I am perfectly persuaded that the tempers had better be unlike; I mean unlike in the flow of spirits, in the manners, in the inclination for much or little company, in the propensity to talk or to be silent, to be grave or to be gay.'** His thoughts have slipped to himself and Mary Crawford. And though he later retracts this opinion, as he switches his affection to Fanny, having in her case **no fears from opposition of taste, no need of drawing new hopes of happiness from dissimilarity of temper**, it is clear that the *temper* Edmund speaks and thinks of on both occasions is a far more wide-ranging summation of character than the simple matter of being good- or bad-tempered, important though that is.

13

Spirit

IN SUGGESTING THAT Henry Crawford and Fanny would
complement each other as marriage partners, Edmund Bertram
describes 'the flow of spirits, the propensity to talk or to be silent, to
be grave or to be gay', as marking one of the discernible differences
between personalities, without privileging one way of being over
the other. *Spirits* are usually a blessing to possess, attractive to other
people and conducive to one's own happiness; yet to be noticeably
lacking in them, like Fanny or like Anne Elliot, whose spirits were not
high, is no moral failing – no more than it would be to have a poor
state of health. (Fanny and Anne are the two physically weakest of
the heroines, suggesting a symbiosis between *spirits* and health.) It is
important to make a distinction. Neither Fanny nor Anne could be
called weak-spirited like Kitty Bennet, who is weak-spirited, irritable
and completely under Lydia's guidance. Fanny and Anne are far from
lacking in moral fibre or strength of character. This is the meaning
of *spirit* in the singular; whereas in the plural it conveys liveliness, a
sense of fun, and an eager response to life.

As such it is perfectly possible to overdo them: Lydia Bennet has high
animal spirits and exuberant spirits which make her uncontrollable, and
lead to her own downfall and the anguish of her family. Mrs Bennet's
spirits fluctuate too much, between spirits oppressively high when
things go well for her, to a spiritless condition when they do not. In this
family, it is Elizabeth who has the happy spirits which had seldom been
depressed. Looking forward to the Netherfield ball, Elizabeth's spirits
were so high on the occasion that she could not help asking her cousin
whether he intends to dance, which brings on a request that she be his

partner: 'her liveliness had been never worse timed. There was no help for it however.' Looking forward to seeing Wickham at the ball, she **dressed with more than her usual care, and prepared in the highest spirits for the conquest of all that remained unsubdued of his heart.** Wickham stays away, but **though every prospect of her own was destroyed for the evening, it could not dwell long on her spirits.** When she travels into Kent, **every object in the next day's journey was new and interesting to Elizabeth; and her spirits were in a state for enjoyment.** Finally, after the serious thankfulness with which she accepts and contemplates Darcy's second proposal, her **spirits soon rising to cheerfulness again** she can resume being her usual delightful, teasing self.

Spirits in the plural are a perceptible indicator of character, denoting the robustness or otherwise with which a person copes with life. Mrs Weston, knowing that she must be missed at Hartfield, comforts herself in the knowledge that **dear Emma was of no feeble character, she was more equal to her situation than most girls would have been, and had sense and energy and spirits that might be hoped would bear her well and happily through its little difficulties and privations.** Indeed, Emma has need of spirits enough for two, her father being a constant drain on hers. **His spirits required support. He was a nervous man, easily depressed.**

The possession of good *spirits* may be a settled characteristic in an individual, or may vary with the occasion. Something may happen to put someone in **a flutter of spirits,** or for a while a set of characters may be **rendered spiritless by the ill success of all their endeavours.** As Anne Elliot is driven away from Kellynch Hall for the last time by Lady Russell, they feel an equal sense of desolation: though Lady Russell is usually the more robust of the two, on this occasion Anne's **friend was not in better spirits than herself.** However, on a subsequent drive into Bath, the two women diverge markedly in feeling. The sights and sounds of the city are unpleasant to Anne, giving her a sense of doom and imprisonment, and she retreats into herself; but to Lady Russell such sights and sounds **belonged to the winter pleasures; her spirits rose under their influence.**

When Anne visits Uppercross, the various members of the Musgrove family are introduced to us in terms of their *spirits*. Mary's are the most volatile, with the least excuse. **While well, and happy, and properly attended to, she had great good humour and excellent spirits; but any indisposition sunk her completely.** Luckily, and admirably, her husband Charles **had very good spirits, which never seemed much affected by his wife's occasional lowness.** His sisters, Henrietta and Louisa, are at first undistinguished one from the other: **their faces were rather pretty, their spirits extremely good, their manner unembarrassed and pleasant.** Later, when Anne is trying to fathom which of the sisters interests Captain Wentworth more, she reflects that **Louisa had the higher spirits; and she knew not** *now,* **whether the more gentle or the more lively character were most likely to attract him.** Anne, who once understood the workings of Wentworth's mind so well, has an intense personal interest in this question, being decidedly gentle rather than lively herself. Later she seizes the chance to oppose **the too common idea of spirit and gentleness being incompatible with each other** when Admiral Croft expresses surprise that with his 'soft sort of manner' Captain Benwick should yet be 'a very active, zealous officer'. Anne, drawing the distinction between high *spirits*, which may be unthinking, and *spirit* in the sense of courage, grit and resolution, replies '**I should never augur want of spirit from Captain Benwick's manners**'.

Being *out of spirits* may happen to anybody. Mr and Mrs Musgrove, while they are normally jolly enough, are temporarily laid low by one circumstance early in the novel: '**papa and mamma are out of spirits this evening, especially mamma; she is thinking so much of poor Richard! And we agreed it would be best to have the harp, for it seems to amuse her more than the pianoforte**', reports Louisa, the change of musical instrument strangely proposed as balm for this recent reminder of a dead son. Mary Crawford's fundamental kindness is demonstrated when, after Mrs Norris has brought tears to Fanny's eyes by urging her to join in with the theatricals, Mary speaks kindly to Fanny and **with pointed attention continued to talk to her and endeavour to raise her spirits, in spite of being out of spirits herself.**

Although Mr Elton's unwelcome proposal during the carriage drive from Randalls leaves Emma for the rest of that evening in an **indescribable irritation of spirits**, she soon recovers: **to youth and natural cheerfulness like Emma's, though under temporary gloom at** night, the return of day will hardly fail to bring return of spirits. More momentously, at Emma's lowest point, when she is contemplating the loss of Mr Knightley to Harriet, she imagines herself left, for the remainder of his life, **to cheer her father with the spirits only of ruined happiness;** but Mr Knightley's proposal soon restores her – not just to her normal level of cheerfulness, for now she has an exquisite source of happiness – but to extraordinary **dancing, singing, exclaiming spirits.** These, however, she has the tact to indulge only when alone; she is scrupulous neither to unsettle her father, nor to gloat over Harriet. Indeed, it is because Harriet's own fate is happily settled at last, as the betrothed of Robert Martin, that Emma's satisfaction in her own engagement is at last unalloyed.

In religious terms, of course, *spirit* in the singular implies that core of the self which survives after the decay of the body; and although Jane Austen does not use it thus in her novels, which – for all her commitment to Christian values – avoid the more supernatural aspects of religion, she does occasionally use the word to express a sense of one's own or someone else's selfhood. **'His sturdy spirit to bend as it did!'** remembers Mary of her influence over Edmund regarding the theatricals. For a while, she has seemingly come close to actually changing his nature, though it reasserts itself later as his eyes are opened. Mr Knightley and Emma debate her character in terms of her **vain spirit** and her **serious spirit**: two sides of her personality. **'My spirit is humbled, my heart amended'** Marianne assures Elinor when, as she sincerely believes, her sufferings have transformed her very being.

As one attribute among others, *spirit* could be construed as backbone, courage, determination, pride, stubbornness; to possess some measure of it is usually a good thing for the person concerned – though not all those who do possess it in Jane Austen are good people. For example, the Miss Churchill who marries the young Mr Weston in defiance of her family's wishes **though she had one sort of spirit, she had not the best. She had resolution enough to pursue her own will in spite of her brother, but not enough to refrain from unreasonable regrets at that brother's unreasonable anger, nor from missing the luxuries of her former home.** Maria Bertram, who lacks 'neither pride nor resolution', suffers the dashing of her hopes as Henry Crawford speaks publicly of leaving Mansfield: **her spirit supported her, but the agony of her mind was severe.** Her *spirit* enables her to conceal what she is suffering, not only from her family, but from the object of her passion, and we have to respect her for that. Her passion may be an unlawful one, and she has pursued it careless of others; but at least she does not bewail her lot. Elizabeth Bennet has something of the same kind of *spirit* – though her moral framework is in infinitely better order than Maria's. When Darcy makes his rude remark about her at the Meryton ball, she is left with no very cordial feelings towards him, but **she told the story however with great spirit among her friends; for she had a lively, playful disposition, which delighted in anything ridiculous.**

Liveliness is one of the happier attributes of *spirit* and is often present in the young male character, who may or may not turn out to be the hero. When Catherine Morland is introduced to Henry Tilney, **he talked with fluency and spirit – there was an archness and pleasantry in his manner which interested, though it was hardly understood by her.** Anne Elliot is first drawn to Captain Wentworth because he has **a great deal of intelligence, spirit and brilliancy.** Marianne Dashwood, hearing that new acquaintance Willoughby once danced until four in the morning without sitting down, asks eagerly, **'Did he indeed? And with elegance, with spirit?'** By her use of the term *spirit* she is demanding to know whether Willoughby danced with energy and evident enjoyment, rather than listlessly or grudgingly just to satisfy convention. As so often in Jane Austen, *spirit* here denotes an attractive degree of vivacity, of experiencing life to the full.

In the dark eyes of Marianne herself **there was a life, a spirit, an eagerness, which could hardly be seen without delight.** Her criticism of Edward includes the fact that **his eyes want all that spirit, that fire, which at once announce virtue and intelligence** – though she is wrong, for Edward's conduct proves that he is both virtuous and intelligent: much more so in fact than Willoughby, even though this 'hero of a favourite story' **read with all the sensibility and spirit which Edward had unfortunately wanted.** As for poor Colonel Brandon, Marianne is very quick to declare **'that he has neither genius, taste nor spirit. That his understanding has no brilliancy, his feelings no ardour, his voice no expression.'** Brilliancy, eagerness, sensibility and fire: *spirit* is associated with extremely attractive, though not wholly reliable, qualities. Even Captain Wentworth, though Anne never ceases to love him, is not the most reliable or consistent of men; and Willoughby, Henry Crawford and Frank Churchill are downright charmers.

Henry Crawford possesses **an active, sanguine spirit, of more warmth than delicacy** and learns to court Fanny **in the language, tone and spirit of a man of talent.** The word may apply to a period of time or an event as well as to people. Looking back on the theatricals, before he has realized Fanny's distaste, Henry remembers fondly, 'There **was such an interest, such an animation, such a spirit diffused! Everybody felt it. We were all alive.**' Emma Woodhouse likewise, when Frank Churchill's first visit to Highbury ends, reflects **certainly his being at Randalls had given great spirit to the last two weeks – indescribable spirit; the idea, the expectation of seeing him which every morning had brought, the assurance of his attentions, his liveliness, his manners!**

Of all Jane Austen's male characters, Frank Churchill is perhaps the best endowed with *spirits*; his are generally harmless and appealing, though occasionally they get out of control. At their first meeting, Emma notices that **his countenance had a great deal of the spirit and liveliness of his father's – he looked quick and sensible.** At the impromptu dance at the Coles', he and she lead off the dance **with genuine spirit and enjoyment.** His subsequent wish of reviving the custom of balls at the Crown Inn, irrespective of the kind of company it might attract, she passes off as **an effusion of lively spirits.**

When Emma sees him again on his return to Highbury after a gap of several months, **he was in high spirits; as ready to talk and laugh as ever,** although at the same time **his spirits were evidently fluttered; there was a restlessness about him. Lively as he was, it seemed a liveliness that did not satisfy himself,** to which Emma ascribes totally the wrong reasons. The climax comes on Box Hill, when his **spirits now rose to a pitch almost unpleasant. Even Emma grew tired at last of flattery and merriment.**

It is the last straw for poor Jane Fairfax, who the day before has confessed, '**Miss Woodhouse, we all know what it is to be wearied in spirits. Mine, I confess, are exhausted.**' At Box Hill she is tried beyond endurance, and that evening writes to Frank to break off their engagement. When, after some delays and mishaps, he has won her anew, she blames herself for intolerance and gives an insight into why she first fell in love with him, permitting herself the secret engagement which she always knew to be wrong. Mrs Weston repeats Jane's words to Emma: **'I did not make the allowances'**, said she, **'which I ought to have done, for his temper and spirits – his delightful spirits, and that gaiety, that playfulness of disposition, which, under any other circumstances would, I am sure, have been as constantly bewitching to me as they were at first.'** By now, the reader may be feeling that Frank's famous spirits, fine on first introduction, would be less than bewitching to have to endure for the rest of one's life; but love is unaccountable, and Jane Austen makes a reasonable hand of matching Frank with Jane. It is the same sort of complementary match that one between Fanny and Henry would have been; but though both young women are extremely level-headed, only Fanny escapes. Jane is left to her fate: but a) it is not such a bad one, and b) she is not the heroine after all – we do not care so *very* much about her.

Some of Jane Austen's shallowest and most conceited females pride themselves on their *spirit* or *spirits*. Isabella Thorpe says, **'my spirit, you know, is pretty independent'**, and **'You know I have a pretty good spirit of my own.'** Her mode of behaviour consists of defying men in order to attract them; this is what she calls *spirit*. She tells the innocent Catherine that men in general **'are often amazingly impertinent if you do not treat them with spirit, and make them keep their distance'.** Mrs Elton, who often boasts about her vivacity, cries, **'I am in a fine flow of spirits, ain't I?'** Mary Crawford, altogether a more engaging character, declares **'I shall stake my last like a woman of spirit.'** She is speaking in the context of a game of cards, but half-wishes to be understood metaphorically, in terms of courtship.

Spirit can go hand-in-hand with spite. Old Mrs Ferrars, who expects to have her own way, eyes Elinor **with the spirited determination of disliking her** and later, **'with a very natural kind of spirit'** in her son-in-law's view, punishes her son Edward for marrying the wrong woman by giving his inheritance to his younger brother. When the news of Lydia's marriage filters through to the neighbourhood, replacing the earlier news of her disgrace, **all the spiteful old ladies of Meryton lost** but little of their spirit in this change of circumstances because with such a husband, her misery was considered certain.

There are several instances in Jane Austen's novels of the older generation repressing the spirits of the younger. The chief error in Sir Thomas Bertram's system of raising his children is that though a truly anxious father, he was not outwardly affectionate, and the reserve of his manner repressed all the flow of their spirits before him. As a consequence he does not know their true characters, cannot effectively guide them, and misses out on the pleasures of family life: 'their father was no object of love to them, he had never seemed the friend of their pleasures, and his absence was unhappily most welcome'. General Tilney is a worse example, a check upon his children's spirits out of sheer tyranny. Catherine puzzles over this after she has spent a day in Milsom Street, for he seems charming enough: he could not be accountable for his children's want of spirits, or for her want of enjoyment in his company. But gradually she realizes that he is indeed accountable. Invited to accompany the family to Northanger Abbey itself, after the unpleasant bustle of leaving the Milsom Street lodgings, the party dividing into two vehicles, Catherine's spirits revived as they drove from the door; for with Miss Tilney she felt no restraint; and once at the Abbey, when the General turns back from showing her the grounds Catherine was shocked to find how much her spirits were relieved by the separation. Elizabeth Bennet, however, even in the repressive presence of Lady Catherine, is able to converse with Colonel Fitzwilliam with great spirit and flow.

Like Emma, Elizabeth is borne happily through life by her *spirits*. Another woman whose *spirits* keep her in a state of cheerfulness despite every drawback in her circumstances is Mrs Smith, in *Persuasion*. At the end of the novel, we learn that her spring of felicity was in the glow of her spirits, as her friend Anne's was in the warmth of her heart. Anne sees in her not just fortitude and resignation, but 'that elasticity of mind, that disposition to be comforted, that power of turning readily from evil to good, and of finding employment which carried her out of herself, which was from nature alone. It was the choicest gift of Heaven.' This is as good a definition of *spirits* as any, and all the more convincing by being formulated in the mind of one whose own *spirits* are not so robust.

Even Anne, however, has her moments. When first she gets the chance to be alone with Captain Wentworth following the letter of love he has secretly slipped to her, the two of them indulge in **smiles reined in and spirits dancing in private rapture.** It is on a par with Emma's **dancing, singing, exclaiming spirits** and Elizabeth's irrepressible **spirits soon rising to cheerfulness again.** For all of them, the right marriage partner has been found. Even the two subdued heroes of *Sense and Sensibility,* for so long so lacking in *spirits,* find them incomparably improved by their respective marriages. **If Edward might be judged from the ready discharge of his duties in every particular, from an increasing attachment to his wife and his home, and from the regular cheerfulness of his spirits, he might be supposed no less contented with his lot** than his brother Robert; while his brother-in-law Colonel Brandon finds **his mind restored to animation, and his spirits to cheerfulness** by the regard and society – and eventually the love – of Marianne herself.

14

Sensibility, Sense and Sentiment

IT WAS PART of Jane Austen's genius to take the commonplace
novelistic concerns of her day and breathe life, wit and common
sense into them. In the 1790s many popular novels featured
heroines who feel everything more acutely than those around them:
their appreciation of nature, their loves, joys and sorrows, are all more
highly developed than in other people. This is the quality of *sensibility*
– natural or assumed. Admired by their authors and emulated by
their readers, these frail vessels of exaggerated feeling fell victim to
the youthful Jane Austen's critical intelligence. Much of her juvenilia
is a burlesque on this mode of fiction. She clearly saw that to strive to
heighten feeling out of a belief that it made one a more interesting or
more admirable character, was both dangerous and absurd.

The story of Marianne Dashwood exemplifies this view. **Her
sensibility was potent enough!** as she weeps and starves herself into
illness on the defection of Willoughby. Even before Willoughby
appears, while Marianne is still heart-whole, **Elinor saw, with concern,
the excess of her sister's sensibility** and her determination openly
to grieve, or rejoice, or indulge in raptures without moderation or
consideration of those around her.

It is, in fact, the excess, rather than the quality itself, which Elinor
and her author deplore, and after she has made her extended case
in *Sense and Sensibility*, bringing Marianne almost to death's door,
Jane Austen relinquishes much of her opposition to *sensibility*. Her
two most delicate heroines, created in her mature years, are imbued
with the quality, yet have the strong approval of their author. Anne
Elliot, at the time of her mother's death, is **a girl of fourteen, of strong**

sensibility and not high spirits, and by the end of her story, knowing herself beloved by Captain Wentworth, we see her **glowing and lovely in sensibility and happiness.** Fanny Price, as a small bewildered child transplanted to Mansfield, is perceived by her cousin Edmund to be **entitled to attention by great sensibility of her situation.** When, some years later, he does her a particular kindness, as is his habit, she feels it **with all, and more than all, the sensibility which he, unsuspicious of her fond attachment, could be aware of.** Later still, Henry Crawford, who has moral taste enough to value the picture, falls under her spell as he watches her affectionate reunion with her brother William: **Fanny's attractions increased – increased twofold – for the sensibility which beautified her complexion and illumined her countenance was an attraction in itself. He was no longer in doubt about the capabilities of her heart. She had feeling, genuine feeling. It would be something to be loved by such a girl, to excite the first ardours of her young, unsophisticated mind!**

The more robust heroines, Elizabeth Bennet and Emma Woodhouse, don't have much truck with sensibility. Yet even that most downright and unromantic of heroes, Mr Knightley, betrays the quality at a moment of heightened emotion. As he walks in the shrubbery with Emma, **she found her arm drawn within his, and pressed against his heart, and heard him thus saying, in a tone of great sensibility, speaking low, 'Time, my dearest Emma, time will heal the wound.'** Henry Tilney, too, finds himself speaking **with the embarrassment of real sensibility** to Catherine's mother when he comes to apologize for his father's behaviour. Both cases turn out to be the immediate precursor to a proposal of marriage. No wonder that both these men of sense are, for the moment, overcome by an unusual degree of sensibility, a little slippage in their habitual command of the situation.

The *sense* that Jane Austen opposes to *sensibility* in the title of her first-published novel is an indispensable quality in any character worthy of our interest and esteem. Strangely, in the initial character sketches which introduce the contrasting sisters in that novel, the word *sense* is not attached to Elinor; rather the *elements* of sense, 'strength of understanding and coolness of judgement', are said to be hers (and lest these qualities appear too alienating, they are counterbalanced by 'an excellent heart'). In the following paragraph we read that 'Marianne's abilities were, in many respects, quite equal to Elinor's. She was sensible and clever; but eager in everything; her sorrows, her joys, could have no moderation. She was generous, amiable, interesting; she was everything but prudent.'

So it is Marianne who, in these introductory paragraphs, merits the description *sensible*. This is an adjective that can derive from either noun, sense *or* sensibility. An *insensible* person is not silly but one who has no feeling, no awareness (or even no consciousness, if they have fainted or been concussed, like the Musgrove sisters). But a *sensible* person may be either the opposite of this, fully alive to the nuances of what is going on; or alternatively they may be, as we would assume from the word today, well endowed with common sense. Which kind of sensible is Marianne? Because the phrase is **sensible and clever** and it is followed by the ominous 'but...' describing Marianne's lack of moderation, we must read it as meaning that Marianne possesses a fundamental good sense.

Of the third sister, Margaret, we learn that **as she had already imbibed a good deal of Marianne's romance, without having much of her sense, she did not, at thirteen, bid fair to equal her sisters at a more advanced period of life.** Closing down the possibility of improvement for Margaret represents a rare artistic failure on the part of the author; but it is interesting that what is emphasized, once again, is Marianne's sense.

Mrs Dashwood is not always a good role model for her girls: at a time of crisis, **common sense, common care, common prudence, were all sunk in Mrs Dashwood's romantic delicacy.** Yet despite the various deficiencies of three of the four Dashwood women, the first quality Willoughby notes in them collectively is *sense*. It takes only a little observation to assure him of **the sense, elegance, mutual affection and domestic comfort of the family to whom accident had now introduced him.** Willoughby himself is no fool, nor is he (despite his subsequent behaviour) heartless; it is a mark in his favour that he is drawn not only to the bewitching Marianne, but to the very way of life at Barton Cottage, surely the most harmonious and cultivated household in all Jane Austen's work.

It has to be Elinor who has the highest and most consistent value for sense. Defending the rather dull Colonel Brandon from the strictures of Willoughby and Marianne, she asserts that he 'is a sensible man; and sense will always have attractions for me'. At first relieved to find Lady Middleton less garrulous than her husband or mother, Elinor needed little observation to perceive that her reserve was a mere calmness of manner with which sense had nothing to do. When it is Elinor's turn to suffer romantic heartache, she conceals her distress from her family: she was stronger alone, and her own good sense so well supported her, that she retains her usual appearance of cheerfulness.

The kind of good sense displayed by Elinor, here and elsewhere, has a moral dimension. It comprises not only intelligence and level-headedness, but right-mindedness – the ability to judge right from wrong and to act consistently on that judgement. This is certainly what Sir Thomas means when he reflects with satisfaction on the character of Edmund, his strong good sense and uprightness of mind. Fanny Price, too, possesses this strength of character. Good sense, like hers, will always act when really called upon, the narrator tells us of Fanny at a moment of acute embarrassment – the appearance of Henry Crawford at the home she is ashamed of in Portsmouth. Fanny pulls herself together, as it were, and performs the necessary introductions. But it is not only that trial and suffering have developed this quality in Fanny, though undoubtedly they have strengthened it; right from the beginning, when she is only a child, Edmund, the only one of the family to penetrate her shyness, knew her to be clever, to have a quick apprehension as well as good sense.

Mr Bennet, rarely one to show his feelings, is glad to welcome back his two eldest daughters from Netherfield: the family circle had lost much of its animation, and almost all its sense, by the absence of Jane and Elizabeth. Mrs Gardiner warns Elizabeth, when she seems in danger of falling in love with the penniless Wickham, 'You have sense, and we all expect you to use it'. Mr Knightley, quarrelling with Emma about her interference in Harriet's life, says, 'Better be without sense than misapply it as you do', which at least acknowledges that, for all her follies and mischief, she does possess fundamental good sense (as he observes daily in her treatment of her father).

Mr Knightley himself is introduced to us without preamble as **a sensible man about seven- or eight-and-thirty.** As is the case with Colonel Brandon, we are assured from the beginning of his sense – it just remains for a 'faulty' heroine to realize it. But with some of the other heroes, the qualities of the mind are more ambiguously described on introduction. Darcy is compared with Bingley: 'in understanding Darcy was the superior. Bingley was by no means deficient, but Darcy was clever'. Captain Wentworth, when Anne first meets him, has 'a great deal of intelligence', while Henry Tilney is immediately perceived by Catherine to have 'an intelligent eye'. Understanding, cleverness and intelligence are desirable gifts, essential in a man worth loving; but from these early descriptions, can we yet be sure that the gentlemen concerned have the right attitude to those around them? These introductory remarks might lead only to arrogance and superciliousness; we must wait to see how they behave under pressure, and therefore whether they are worthy to be heroes.

When Henry Tilney says that, if his brother Frederick marries Isabella Thorpe, he '**will not be the first man who has chosen a wife with less sense than his family expected**', he does not mean that the chosen one will have less sense – Isabella, like Lucy Steele, does have sense of a shrewd, self-seeking kind – but that the *choice* will be made with less sense – Frederick being unable to see beneath her superficial charms. (Just such a pitfall as was not avoided by Mr Bennet and Mr Palmer, intelligent men who find themselves married to silly, vacuous wives.) In fact, Frederick Tilney, no fool, *can* see that Isabella is not worth having; his heart is not touched, his mind not tempted for a moment; it is the inexperienced James Morland who is thoroughly taken in by her posturing. His claim that '**she has so much good sense, and is so thoroughly unaffected and amiable**', convinces the reader, who has already been witness to Isabella's shallow self-promotion in talk and conduct, not of any undetected merit on her side, but of a great deal of naivety on his.

For us to rely on it, *good sense* must be attributed by the author, or at the very least by a character whose judgement we can trust. In the same novel, towards its denouement, Mrs Morland advances **a great deal of good sense** for the use of Catherine in reconciling herself to home after her adventures in Bath and at Northanger, culminating in the unkindness of General Tilney in dismissing her from his house, which Catherine's mother advises her to put into perspective by considering the longstanding friendship of such people as the Allens. The Morlands are, in fact, the only parents who have anything really useful or helpful to say to their heroine offspring; the only ones whose speech and conduct demonstrate *good sense*, even if it is ineffectual in this instance. It has not occurred to them that Catherine may be in love. The senior Morlands' apprehension is limited, despite their principles being sound.

When Fanny Price refers to Dr Grant as **a sensible man** who cannot preach every week without being improved by his own sermons, she may be being idealistic, but she is not being foolish. She is giving him credit for being self-aware, and therefore aware of his duty, at least in his better moments, when greed, his prevailing fault, is not getting the better of him. Mary Crawford may laugh at her (kindly enough), but Edmund does not correct her.

Having received a university education and been ordained, however, and even being in the habit of writing sermons, is not sufficient to guarantee the possession of sense in Jane Austen's world. '**Can he be a sensible man, sir?**' Elizabeth Bennet asks her father when the reverend Mr Collins's pompous yet servile letter of introduction is read out to the family; and after the arrival of the man himself, the narrator begins a new chapter bluntly: **Mr Collins was not a sensible man.** In fact he is something of a caricature, as must be all those characters in Jane Austen's early books who have no sense or very little: Charlotte Palmer, Mrs Allen, Sir William Lucas – but supremely, because he has a lot more to do and say, Mr Collins himself. Entertaining to encounter in a novel, almost Dickensian, in fact – but perhaps not ringing entirely true. Be that as it may, and each reader must decide for themselves, every speech and action of Mr Collins betrays a total lack of any kind of sense, both common (held in common by well-judging people) and the higher kind of sense sometimes called by Jane Austen, as we have seen, *good sense* (found in the smaller number of people who have truly sound values).

In his inability to regulate his conversation to what is appropriate for the occasion, Mr Collins is the antithesis of another gentleman, encountered by a heroine in a different novel. **There could be no doubt of his being a sensible man. Ten minutes were enough to certify that. His tone, his expressions, his choice of subject, his knowing where to stop – it was all the operation of a sensible, discerning mind.** The novel is *Persuasion*, and this is Anne reflecting on her first opportunity for conversation with her cousin. Though far more agreeable to be with than Elizabeth Bennet's cousin, Mr Collins, Mr Elliot's being *sensible* turns out to be more of a smokescreen than an indication of real worth. After having been in company with him several times, Anne acknowledges to herself, **that he was a sensible man, an agreeable man – that he talked well, professed good opinions, seemed to judge properly as a man of principle – this was all clear enough. He certainly knew what was right.** Yet she continues to feel uneasy and, as she puts it to herself, is afraid to answer for his conduct or his true sentiments, which she guesses may be cunningly concealed beneath the unfaltering correctness of his social demeanour.

Another potential marriage partner whose conversational sense and general intelligence cannot be faulted, but whose morals can, is of course Henry Crawford. On his arrival in Mansfield, in immediately deciding to make the Miss Bertrams like him, **he did not want them to die of love; but with sense and temper which ought to have made him judge and feel better, he allowed himself great latitude on such points.** He is gifted with **sense and temper**; he is not obtuse, not unaware of what he is at. Later, in falling genuinely in love with Fanny, he comes closest to achieving the best self it is in him to be, aided again by his *sense*: **Henry Crawford had too much sense not to feel the worth of good principles in a wife, though he was too little accustomed to serious reflection to know them by their proper name.**

As with these several examples, in the three late novels Jane Austen often seems to be ramping up the moral dimension of the terms *sense* and *sensible*. A woman who consistently makes the effort to be **sensible and well-judging** is Lady Russell. As a person **of sense and honesty**, her primary concern at the beginning of the novel is that her friend Sir Walter should repay his debts by making economies, even though the public will be witness to those economies: 'The true dignity of Sir Walter Elliot will be very far from lessened, in the eyes of sensible people, by his acting like a man of principle', she reasons. By sensible people she means, of course, right-minded people, who put honesty before show. If the public are not *sensible*, perhaps because they are too snobbish, or too shallow, their good opinion is not worth having.

But the word does not always carry such serious import. On reading John Knightley's letter of calm congratulation to his brother on their engagement, Emma says, 'He writes like a sensible man'. She has the humility to acknowledge that greater praise of her would not be well-judged – it would be insincere, it would be silly. Like her assertion to Harriet that 'a single woman of good fortune is always respectable, and may be as sensible and pleasant as anybody else', the meaning here is straightforward, the simple opposite of 'silly'.

Sensible in its other sense – being alive to or aware of – is used at least as often by Jane Austen. They were both ever sensible of the warmest gratitude towards the persons who ... had been the means of uniting them are the closing words of *Pride and Prejudice*. The family at Mansfield Park speak of the child Fanny, after she has gone to bed, as seeming so desirably sensible of her peculiar good fortune in being transplanted among them (though in fact she is sobbing herself to sleep). As time passes and Sir Thomas does what he can to help the other young Prices, Fanny, though almost totally separated from her family, was sensible of the truest satisfaction in hearing of any kindness towards them, or of anything at all promising in their situation and conduct. Much later, when she has refused the offer of marriage from Henry Crawford, mystifying and displeasing her uncle, the kind expressions and forbearing manner with which, after a little while, he endeavours to calm her tears were sensibly felt by her.

The word may be used as a synonym for *aware* or *conscious* without the emotional freight of the examples above. 'I am not sensible of having done anything wrong', declares Marianne Dashwood on occasion when her conduct is criticized by her sister. It is not surprising that Emma, after continually praising Mr Elton to Harriet, finds her young friend becoming decidedly more sensible than before of Mr Elton's being a remarkably handsome man, with most agreeable manners.

But how to construe the word when used of Lady Bertram's reaction to the return of Sir Thomas after his long absence? **By not one of the circle was he listened to with such unbroken unalloyed enjoyment as by his wife, who was really extremely happy to see him, and whose feelings were so warmed by his sudden arrival as to place her nearer agitation than she had been for the last twenty years. She had been almost fluttered for a few minutes, and still remained so sensibly animated as to put away her work, move Pug from her side, and give all her attention and all the rest of her sofa to her husband.** Does this mean that Lady Bertram herself is aware of her own unusual degree of animation? Or that her animation takes a discernible form that makes the rest of the family aware of it (amid all their other concerns)? Or that it makes her act with unwonted common sense – that is, making room for her husband, which is the sensible thing to do?

Insensible is always the adjective of *insensibility*, there being no negative form of sense (except for nonsense, when the adjective becomes **nonsensical**, a word Mr Knightley uses, fondly enough, to describe Emma, when they have agreed to disagree). The double negative is employed in the construction **Harriet was not insensible of manner** – that is, tutored by Emma, she is aware of manner in the men around her. But when the same young lady **had been partially insensible** after her encounter with the gypsies, enabling Frank to recount the story unheard by her, she is in fact partially unconscious. This is even more the case with Henrietta Musgrove who, sinking under the conviction that her sister is dead, **lost her senses too, and would have fallen on the steps** if not caught by the others, and who a little later **was kept, by the agitation of hope and fear, from a return of her own insensibility.** Even more dramatically, Catherine imagines the drugged Mrs Tilney being taken for concealment in one of the old monastic cells of Northanger Abbey: **down that staircase she had perhaps been conveyed in a state of well-prepared insensibility!**

More frequently, *insensibility* is merely the opposite of *sensibility*: lack of sensitivity or feeling. Marianne, while believing that a man of Colonel Brandon's advanced years must have outlived all acuteness of feeling, favourably but somewhat grudgingly compares his attentive listening to her music with **the horrible insensibility of the others.** The tender-hearted Fanny Price, grieving that she cannot grieve over the departure of her uncle on a dangerous sea voyage and an absence of many months, accuses herself of **a shameful insensibility**. The narrator of *Northanger Abbey*, poking fun at female obsession with dress, warns of **the insensibility of man towards a new gown**. The adjective is used in the same novel to denote that which can hardly be discerned: **The lenient hand of time did much for her by insensible degrees.**

Two other words from the same group are *sensation* and *sentiment*, both in their different ways denoting feeling. *Sensation* is occasionally physical. Marianne and Margaret Dashwood, walking on the downs and glorying in the wind in their faces, **pitied the fears which had prevented their mother and Elinor from sharing such delightful sensations.** Emma Woodhouse, stepping into the garden after having been kept indoors by rain, finds that **never had the exquisite sight, smell, sensation of nature, tranquil, warm and brilliant after a storm, been more attractive to her.** More often, *sensation* denotes emotion. Emma tells Harriet, with all the smug self-satisfaction with which she is so well-endowed at the beginning of the novel, that **'I shall be very well off, with all the children of a sister I love so much to care about. There will be enough of them, in all probability, to supply every sort of sensation that declining life can need. There will be enough for every hope and every fear ...'.** As here, specific sensations are often listed. Emma later thinks she must be in love with the recently departed Frank Churchill, which would account for **'this sensation of listlessness, weariness, stupidity, this disinclination to sit down and employ myself, this feeling of everything's being dull and insipid about the house!'** Harriet, on first learning of Mr Elton's engagement to another, becomes subject to **sensations of curiosity, wonder and regret, pain and pleasure.**

(Just once in Jane Austen's novels, *sensation* is used the way we are so familiar with today. **'Cannot you imagine, Mr Knightley, what a sensation his coming will produce? There will be but one subject throughout the parishes of Donwell and Highbury; but one interest – one object of curiosity; it will be all Mr Frank Churchill; we shall think and speak of nobody else.'** To which Mr Knightly responds bluntly, 'You will excuse my being so much overpowered.')

But it is romantic love which is the emotion most commonly

indicated when the word *sensation* stands alone. Emma, having learnt to know herself, feels **ashamed of every sensation but ... her affection for Mr Knightley.** Looking at Darcy's portrait at Pemberley, **there was certainly at this moment, in Elizabeth's mind, a more gentle sensation towards the original, than she had ever felt at the height of their acquaintance.** Henry Crawford, asked by his sister to recount the progress of his courtship of Fanny, has **in fact nothing to relate but his own sensations.** Fanny herself is incredulous to find Henry expects her **to believe that she had created sensations which his heart had never known before.** Marianne thinks that a man of Colonel Brandon's age, **if he were ever animated enough to be in love, must have long outlived every sensation of the kind.** Anne Elliot, experiencing a momentary wobble when Lady Russell relays Mr Elliot's admiration of her mind and manners, **could not know herself to be so highly rated by a sensible man, without many of those agreeable sensations which her friend meant to create.**

If *sensations* are often felt in the heart, and are created by somebody or something else – the loved one, or a picture, or an influential friend – perhaps *sentiments* belong in the head, and are more fixed, innate, characteristic of the individual's mode of thinking. '**You know the weak side of her character, and may imagine the sentiments and expressions which were torturing me**', Edmund confides to Fanny of his last interview with Mary Crawford. Sir Thomas, meeting Mr Rushworth for the first time and temporarily deceived by his opinion that it is disagreeable to be always rehearsing and much better to be sitting comfortably doing nothing, responds, '**I am happy to find our sentiments on this subject so much the same**'. It does not take many more hours in the company of Mr Rushworth for Sir Thomas to perceive not only his wrong assessment, but his daughter Maria's contempt for the man to whom she is engaged. After her downfall, he blames himself: **he felt that he ought not to have allowed the marriage, that his daughter's sentiments had been sufficiently known to him to render him culpable in authorizing it.**

Mr Bennet, mocking his wife, says '**I had hoped that our sentiments coincided in every particular**'. When Lydia denies that Wickham could ever have cared for Mary King, 'such a nasty little freckled thing', but only for her ten thousand pounds, **Elizabeth was shocked to think that, however incapable of such coarseness of expression herself, the coarseness of the sentiment was little other than her own breast had harboured and fancied liberal!** Marianne Dashwood disdains **to aim at the restraint of sentiments which were not in themselves illaudable.** In all these cases, *opinion* is what is meant.

Sentiments may be specified, in which case the word becomes a synonym for feeling: when Elizabeth stands in front of the portrait of Darcy, **she thought of his regard with a deeper sentiment of gratitude than it had ever raised before.** Mrs Bennet is raised from the depths of self-pity to the heights of exultation when she hears that runaway Lydia is to be married after all: **no sentiment of shame gave a damp to her triumph.** After Edmund Bertram has proved so kind to his child cousin Fanny, **her sentiments towards him were compounded of all that was respectful, grateful, confiding and tender.**

Sometimes the word comes closer to its fellow *sensibility* by implying indulgence in excessive or imaginary feeling, which is usually what the adjective *sentimental* signifies to us now. Mr Knightley intends this meaning when he says, '**Elton may talk sentimentally, but he will act rationally**'. Emma, gratified to observe in Mr Elton that **there was a great deal of sentiment in his manner of naming Harriet,** correctly identifies the sentimental aspect of his talk, without identifying its true object (herself). In *Northanger Abbey*, Catherine finds it awkward to be in company with her friend Isabella and her brother James, as **they were always engaged in some sentimental discussion or lively dispute,** with **their sentiment conveyed in such whispering voices, and their vivacity attended by so much laughter,** that she feels excluded.

Sentiment may be false or exaggerated, as in Mr Elton and Isabella, or it may be a true symptom of tenderness of heart. When Edmund Bertram starts paying regular visits to hear Mary Crawford play the harp at Mansfield Parsonage, everything conspires to make him susceptible to falling in love. **A young woman, pretty, lively, with a harp as elegant as herself, and both placed near a window, cut down to the ground, and opening on a little lawn, surrounded by the rich foliage of summer, was enough to catch any man's heart. The season, the scene, the air, were all favourable to tenderness and sentiment.**

Wishing Henry Crawford to succeed in his courtship of Fanny, Edmund is pleased when his friend shows that he can speak thoughtfully on serious subjects: This would be the way to Fanny's heart. She was not to be won by all that gallantry and wit and good nature together could do; or at least, she would not be won by them nearly so soon, without the assistance of sentiment and feeling, and seriousness on serious subjects. When Henry travels to Portsmouth to see Fanny, and they walk with her family on the ramparts, Fanny comes closer to finding him acceptable than at any other point in the trajectory of their relationship. They often stopped with the same sentiment and taste, leaning against the wall some minutes to look and admire; and considering he was not Edmund, Fanny could not but allow that he was sufficiently open to the charms of nature, and very well able to express his admiration.

Fanny, in her love of nature and her stubborn adherence to her 'first attachment' is another Marianne. She has *sensibility*, and she has *sentiment*, and is blamed for neither, perhaps because she keeps them to herself. Or perhaps because her author is more mature and less judgemental than she had been when, as a reaction to the absurdities of current fiction, she created the heroines of *Sense and Sensibility*.

15

Firmness, Fortitude and Forbearance

BESIDES BEING PLEASINGLY alliterative, these three qualities are linked by a sense of resoluteness, steadfastness, quiet inner strength. But whereas *fortitude* and *forbearance* are always to be admired in Jane Austen's moral universe, *firmness* is more liable to misapplication. It depends, of course, on what the person is being firm about; and nowhere is this more evident than in *Persuasion*, when being firm to the point of obstinacy over a matter of no importance – a silly jump – leads Louisa Musgrove to lose first her senses (and almost her life) in a fall, and then, as a consequence of the pause in his courtship which that fall entails, her chance of capturing Frederick Wentworth as her husband. Yes, she gets the perfectly agreeable James Benwick instead; but there is no doubt in the reader's mind, because we feel as Anne Elliot feels, that Wentworth is the more thrilling man, and Louisa would have got him if she could.

It is Wentworth, of course, who has misguidedly encouraged Louisa to cultivate the habit of *firmness*. In one speech, overheard by Anne, he tells Louisa, '**yours is the character of decision and firmness, I see.... Let those who would be happy be firm.... My first wish for all whom I am interested in, is that they should be firm.**' Louisa cannot fail to get his message.

We – and Anne – know where this is coming from. It is part of his angry reaction to Anne's having been persuaded to give him up eight years before, which he puts down to feebleness of character, weakness and timidity. His requirements now in seeking a wife are 'a strong mind, with sweetness of manner', and in his slight arrogance, without realizing quite what effect he is having on another human being – and a young, impressionable one at that – he is somewhat carelessly seeing whether he can mould Louisa to suit him. But when he advises Louisa not to jump, and she has the choice between two ways of increasing her appeal to him – deferring to his masculine judgement, or stubbornly maintaining her own way, she disastrously chooses the latter course. As Anne Elliot later wonders, did it ever occur to him now **to question the justice of his own previous opinion as to the universal felicity and advantage of firmness of character; and whether it might not strike him that, like all other qualities of the mind, it should have its proportions and its limits.**

Henry Tilney makes the same point, albeit in a less serious context. Isabella Thorpe, having declared that, as an engaged woman whose fiancé is absent, she will not dance at the Assembly Rooms, is next seen dancing with Frederick Tilney, to the astonishment of Catherine, who expects people to keep to their word. Henry responds to Catherine's exclamations:

'The fairness of your friend was an open attraction; her firmness, you know, could only be understood by yourself.'

'You are laughing; but I assure you, Isabella is very firm in general.'

'It is as much as should be said of anyone. To be always firm must be to be often obstinate. When properly to relax is the trial of judgement; and, without reference to my brother, I really think Miss Thorpe has by no means chosen ill in fixing on the present hour.'

Henry *is* laughing, indeed. But also, not unpleasantly, demonstrating that better knowledge of the world which is continually giving Catherine useful lessons.

The most admirable kind of firmness is that quiet and considered kind demonstrated by, for example, Colonel Brandon who, in arranging to fetch Mrs Dashwood to the sickbed of Marianne, **acted with all the firmness of a collected mind.** Marianne herself, returning in chastened state to Barton Cottage, **turned her eyes around it with a look of resolute firmness, as if determined at once to accustom herself to the sight of every object with which the remembrance of Willoughby could be connected.** She goes to the piano, sees music on it bearing his name (why did not Mrs Dashwood put it away?), runs her fingers over the keys, and closes the instrument, **declaring however with firmness as she did so, that she should in future practise much.**

Elinor has always been able to summon up firmness when she has needed it. Listening with mounting horror and conviction to Lucy's confidences, she remains capable of answering her **with a firm voice;** and afterwards, she endeavours to behave as normal and to conceal her suffering from her family. Their sorrow and sympathy would only aggravate her distress: **she was stronger alone; and her own good sense so well supported her, that her firmness was as unshaken, her appearance of cheerfulness as invariable, as with regrets so poignant and so fresh, it was possible for them to be.**

In *Pride and Prejudice*, the usually mild-mannered Jane **was firm where she felt herself to be right.** Readers, in love with the more acerbic Elizabeth, might be inclined to belittle Jane for being too sweet and easy, but it is a mark in her favour that she is not to be persuaded against her better judgement. Elizabeth herself demonstrates **firmness** in all she thinks and does, though only once is it an effort for her to speak **with tolerable firmness;** that is when, struggling for politeness, she congratulates Charlotte Lucas on her engagement.

Fanny Price – as deceptively meek in her outward demeanour as Jane Bennet is mild – represents the other exemplar of *firmness* among Jane Austen's female creations. Edmund, the only person who understands her worth (though he does not always understand her feelings) praises her as '**a woman who, firm as a rock in her own principles, has a gentleness of character so well adapted to recommend them**'. This summation of Fanny's attractions in male eyes foreshadows Captain Wentworth's recipe for the ideal wife, with its combination of *firmness* or strength of character with *sweetness* or gentleness of manner.

It is, in fact, in Anne Elliot, his original love, that Wenworth rediscovers and confirms what he is looking for. This time the term used is *fortitude*: Anne's character possesses, he acknowledges at the end of the book, **the loveliest medium of fortitude and gentleness.**

Fortitude is the mental or moral strength to stick to one's principles or bear difficulties whatever blandishments are on offer. It differs from *firmness*, perhaps, in terms of duration, being more often required or demonstrated over an extended period. Frequently called for in matters of religious faith, fortitude is one of the four cardinal virtues. Anne, somewhat idealistically perhaps, muses on 'what instances ... of heroism, fortitude, patience, resignation' are to be witnessed in a sick chamber; though her companion, the more worldly Mrs Smith, replies that, more often, 'it is selfishness and impatience rather than generosity and fortitude that one hears of'.

Fortitude is not in itself sufficient to make its possessors happy, except insofar as they know they are doing their duty. (This is the kind of happiness, or hard-won contentment rather, than heroines Elinor, Fanny and Anne have to be satisfied with during the greater part of their respective stories.) Mrs Smith herself, despite her ill health and penury, is usually cheerful. Anne, observing her, decides that **this was not a case of fortitude or resignation only.** Fortitude would supply resolution and patience, but Mrs Smith is blest with an elasticity of mind that enables her to turn from evil to good and to be carried out of herself by interest in her fellow-creatures.

When the difficulties are small, or imaginary, Jane Austen often mocks a person's claim to fortitude, but she usually does it kindly. Emma Woodhouse is **delighted with the fortitude of her little friend – for fortitude she knew it was in her to give up being in company and stay at home.** Emma herself, when told that she cannot lead off the dance at the Crown, because the obnoxious Mrs Elton must be shown that distinction as a bride, **heard the sad news with fortitude.** Darcy too, on asking to be introduced to Elizabeth's companions at Pemberley, and finding that they are the very relations *in trade* against whom his pride had earlier revolted, sustains the realization **with fortitude.**

As for Fanny Dashwood, she shows (according to her husband) nothing less than **the fortitude of an angel** on the discovery of her brother's secret engagement to Lucy Steele; this though he has just said that she has been in hysterics all day. Even Elinor's **high-minded fortitude** in lingering about on the landing-place in order to give Edward and Lucy more time alone together in Mrs Jennings' drawing-room, is presented as a semi-farcical moment. For Jane Austen, *fortitude*, despite being such a worthy attribute, often allies itself with comedy. It is not hard to see why. *Fortitude* was something of a cliché in the novels she grew up with.

In the early part of *Northanger Abbey*, an explanation occurs while Catherine in her everyday dilemmas is still being compared with the high-flown heroines of novels: **To be disgraced in the eyes of the world, to wear the appearance of infamy while her heart is all purity, her actions all innocence, and the misconduct of another the true source of her debasement, is one of those circumstances which peculiarly belong to the heroine's life, and her fortitude under it what particularly dignifies her character. Catherine had fortitude too; she suffered, but no murmur passed her lips.** She is at a ball; her partner, John Thorpe, has walked off, and Catherine is left to the apparent disgrace of being without a partner. Not a disaster: but Catherine's behaviour is as good, under her circumstances, as a 'real' heroine's is under hers.

Strangely, perhaps, the word *fortitude* never appears in *Mansfield Park*, though Fanny is surely the heroine (after the more mature Anne) who is best endowed with this virtue – or at least, the one whose many trials require her to practise it, and enable her to perfect it over a long period of years. In Fanny, as in Anne Elliot and Elinor Dashwood, Jane Austen *shows* fortitude in operation.

Not surprisingly, Marianne Dashwood has only a **small degree of fortitude** on the evening of Willoughby's departure from Devon, and this is quite overcome merely by her mother's silently pressing her hand with tender compassion; Marianne bursts into tears and leaves the room. When Mrs Dashwood writes to London after Marianne's hopes of Willoughby are finally dashed, her letters **express her anxious solicitude for Marianne, and entreat she would bear up with fortitude under this misfortune.** Is it Elinor or Jane Austen whose thoughts are reflected in the succeeding wry observation: **Bad indeed must the nature of Marianne's affliction be, when her mother could talk of fortitude!**

Although the besotted Colonel Brandon speaks of **concern for her unhappiness, and respect for her fortitude under it** at a time when Marianne is showing no fortitude at all, she is subsequently transformed by her illness, and brought to a better knowledge of herself: '**I saw that my own feelings had prepared my sufferings, and that my want of** fortitude under them had almost led me to the grave.' Nothing could be more serious than this. But in comparing the two sisters, perhaps their mother's should be the last word. Suddenly awakened to the real and sustained sufferings of her eldest daughter, Mrs Dashwood fears that **she had been unjust, inattentive, nay, almost unkind, to her Elinor – that Marianne's affliction, because more acknowledged, more immediately before her, had too much engrossed her tenderness, and led her away to forget that in Elinor she might have a daughter suffering almost as much, certainly with less self-provocation, and greater fortitude.** Among the things that come right for Elinor at the end of the book, it satisfies the reader's sense of justice that she should receive this overdue acknowledgement from her mother.

Forbearance involves the exercise of self-restraint in the interests of harmony between people who have to rub along in close proximity to one another. It is not surprising then that it is one of the virtues most strongly advocated by Jane Austen. While people cannot help what they feel, she shows us, they can certainly help what they say. Her ideal is the resolve expressed by Marianne Dashwood at the end of her story: always to **'practise the civilities, the lesser duties of life, with gentleness and forbearance'.**

Her sister Elinor, of course, numbers *forbearance* among her virtues: as Marianne asks in remorse, **'Did I imitate your forbearance?'** Anne Elliot thoroughly understands the importance of practising *forbearance*. Made the confidante at Uppercross of both branches of the Musgrove family, who come to her with their grievances, she tries, in her gentle way, to **give them all hints of the forbearance necessary between such near neighbours.** And, in warmly assuring Captain Harville that she believes men like him are equal to **every domestic forbearance** in their married lives, she demonstrates her understanding of the patience, tolerance and courtesy required within marriage as within any close relationship.

Emma Woodhouse's greatest criticism of her brother-in-law John Knightley is **want of respectful forbearance towards her father.** John Knightley is not always so much in control of his tongue as he should be, though Emma herself can see that the provocation from her well-meaning but fussy father is sometimes almost irresistible. She herself is invariably patient with her father, as is John's brother George, for his is the superior character in this and every other respect.

When Emma is tempted to argue with her brother-in-law over his reflection on Mr Weston's over-sociable habits, she struggles, and lets it pass: 'She would keep the peace if possible' – a family imperative for Jane Austen. We believe in Emma for having to struggle, and we admire her for succeeding. To assist her willpower, Emma ruminates on John's own admirable domestic self-sufficiency, whence springs his criticism of the very different Mr Weston, allowing that this quality in John has **a high claim to forbearance.**

Amid her family, Emma's *forbearance* springs from this resolve to keep the peace, and in the wider world (that is, Highbury society) from her wish of always appearing gracious and exquisitely polite. A rare lapse occurs when she does not forbear to mock Miss Bates on Box Hill, much to her subsequent chagrin, especially when Mr Knightley tells her, **'I wish you could have her honouring your forbearance in being able to pay her such attentions, as she was forever receiving from yourself and your father, when her society must be so irksome'.** Emma knows she does not deserves this, and she is all contrition.

When Elizabeth Bennet is still the dupe of Wickham, she is inclined to think that **attention, forbearance, patience with Darcy was injury to Wickham** and can hardly even be polite to the former as they dance together. Later she realizes that Darcy has in fact, throughout their dealings, behaved with **forbearance and liberality** towards Wickham even while deploring his wickedness. It turns out that Darcy, who had seemed so supercilious, is a model of gentlemanly forbearance. After his engagement is announced, not only does he bear 'with admirable calmness' the obsequious civility of Mr Collins, and with 'decent composure' the compliments of Sir William Lucas, but **Mrs Philips's vulgarity was another, and perhaps a greater tax on his forbearance,** making Elizabeth look forward to their removal from Hertfordshire and society so little pleasing to either her fiancé or herself.

Unlike her sister, Mrs Bennet is too much in awe of Darcy to speak much to him, but she exercises no such restraint in her dealings with the more amenable Bingley. His reaction is admirable. He **bore with the** ill-judged officiousness of the mother, and heard all her silly remarks with a forbearance and command of countenance for which Jane is grateful. Both Darcy and Bingley are demonstrating good husband material.

The standard of perfection in a husband, according to Mary Crawford, is Sir Thomas Bertram. This must be because of the forbearance he consistently shows his wife, bearing with her extreme indolence without apparent impatience or reproach. Mary Crawford goes on to name her own sister, Mrs Grant, as her standard of perfection in a wife; and again, it is her forbearance with the irritable Dr Grant that Mary admires. In Sir Thomas and Mrs Grant, Jane Austen repeatedly and in varying circumstances *shows* forbearance in action rather than telling us it is so.

We are occasionally told that Sir Thomas exercises *forbearance*, but towards other erring members of his family. When he finds his private rooms being used as a stage by his children in his absence, it needed all the felicity of being again at home, and all the forbearance it could supply, to save Sir Thomas from anger. When Fanny bewilders and disappoints him by refusing Mr Crawford, he begins by being dreadfully severe, but though indubitably master of his household, he is not a tyrant; soon her uncle's kind expressions ... and forbearing manner give her some ease, and, to her great relief, she is spared Mrs Norris's reproaches on the same subject because he pressed for the strictest forbearance and silence towards their niece. In so doing, Sir Thomas mixes politeness with policy: the forbearance of her family on a point respecting which she could be in no doubt of their wishes might be their surest means of forwarding it, he considers. It is with the same mixture of kindness and ulterior motive that he despatches her to Portsmouth.

Fanny herself demonstrates the qualities of a good wife. So Henry Crawford thinks, noticing how continually exercised her patience and forbearance are by almost all members of the family at Mansfield Park. But Fanny is human, especially in her jealousy of Mary Crawford. Just like another heroine, Emma, she has to resolve to bite her tongue. She could have said a great deal, but it was safer to say nothing... lest it should betray her into any observations seemingly unhandsome. Miss Crawford's kind opinion of herself deserved at least a grateful forbearance.

Before travelling to Portsmouth, Fanny remembers how her mother had never shown her much affection in her infancy, but her mature judgement tells her that this was probably her own fault, for being unreasonable in wanting a larger share of her attention than any one among so many children could deserve. But now, thinks Fanny, **when she knew better how to be useful and how to forbear ... they should soon be what mother and daughter ought to be to each other.** In Portsmouth, Fanny is disappointed all over again in her slatternly mother, but to counterbalance this disappointment, she begins to make friends with a sister who, at fourteen, and of a very different temperament from Fanny, has *not* yet learnt to forbear. Susan sees that much is wrong at home, and wants to put it right. She is assertive and argumentative with her mother in a way that shocks Fanny, for whom outward respect for elders is an absolute obligation. Fanny cannot cease to feel that Susan's manner is often wrong, her looks and language very often indefensible; and yet, **while seeing all the obligation and expediency of submission and forbearance, Fanny saw also with sympathetic acuteness of feeling all that must be hourly grating to a girl like Susan.** Jane Austen shows us that while *forbearance* certainly keeps the peace, it does not right wrongs, and she goes so far as suggesting that Susan's assertiveness is in fact more beneficial to the household than Fanny's *forbearance*. Fanny's example does do good among her younger, still impressionable siblings, but on her mother's ways she has no effect whatsoever.

For when forbearance is unilateral, the other person has no motivation to reform. Lady Bertram remains indolent, Dr Grant repeatedly indulges in bad temper, because their spouses make no protest. Jane Austen, with her deep attachment to the virtue of forbearance, does not exactly point this up – but the interaction of the characters, so psychologically truthful, shows it happening before our eyes.

Mary Crawford, listening in silence to Sir Thomas's plans for Edmund, which run counter to her own, finds herself subject to **that involuntary forbearance which his character and manner commanded ... not daring to relieve herself by a single attempt at throwing ridicule on his cause.** Mary, rich and independent, with hardly any relations she cares for, is not accustomed to practising forbearance; charm is more her style in social situations. Jane Austen's phrase **involuntary forbearance**, while being something of an oxymoron, sums up the strangely tongue-tied state in which this most self-confident of young women finds herself. Mary seems to be as surprised by her own silence on this occasion as she is at finding herself in a country parsonage month after month.

The *forbearance* of another self-confident young woman, Emma Woodhouse, is by contrast voluntary, but still has its price to pay. The occasion is when Mr Weston proposes that Mrs Elton's picnic party should merge with their own, and Emma silently reacts: **Every feeling was offended; and the forbearance of her outward submission left a heavy arrear due of secret severity in her reflections on the unmanageable goodwill of Mr Weston's temper.**

And there is sometimes a more serious price to pay than annoyed afterthoughts. Practised over an extended period, *forbearance* may intensify suffering. Never to be able to give vent to one's feelings may cause pent-up agony, as we see to some extent in Fanny Price, but even more in Jane Fairfax. On her entry into the story she is justly praised by Mr Knightley for having a '**temper excellent in its power of forbearance, patience, self-control**' and Frank Churchill later blithely acknowledges Jane's '**spirit of forbearance which has been so richly extended towards myself**' as if it costs her nothing. But in fact it drives Jane to the point where she can bear no more, and she suffers a complete breakdown of health and spirits.

Forbearance, usually so admirable, is not without its shortcomings and drawbacks.

16

Propriety and Decorum

ALIEN TO OUR modern culture with its overriding emphasis
on the rights of the individual to 'do their own thing,' these
concepts are all too apt to carry connotations of deadening
conformity and hypocrisy. Utilized by one level of society to put
another in its place, they are seen as having been harmfully restrictive
of human self-expression. In recent decades such attitudes have been
discredited, or at the very least driven underground, by mockery and
sit-com humour. It would be hard to use such words seriously today.

Jane Austen's society, having more recently emerged into the sunlit
uplands of civility from what they regarded as a barbarous past, when
people were continually giving offence by their uncouth manners, put a
much higher store on *propriety* and *decorum* as the essential means of
preserving that degree of social harmony within which the individual
is enabled to lead the most useful and happiest life of which he or she
is capable. *Propriety* is the more general concept, covering a wider
swathe not only of behaviours but of moral and mental tendencies;
indeed, it can be applicable to everything that a person does or
thinks, and certainly every decision made; while *decorum* is more
narrowly affixed to the visible aspects of conduct. For some modern
readers, this framework of rules and the concomitant tendency to be
judgemental, provide an insuperable barrier to Jane Austen's world.
For others, they add immeasurably to its appeal.

The intriguing thing is that Jane Austen herself was by no means
blind to the misuse of rules of *propriety* and *decorum* to wield
power and assert status. Anything that elevates the individual ego
at the expense of other people is anathema to her. So too is mean-

spiritedness sheltering behind a mask of social convention. But she does attach an extremely high value to good manners and honourable behaviour when they proceed from attention to the comfort of others. Her novels are full of this differentiation.

Lady Russell is **most correct in her conduct, strict in her notions of decorum, and with manners that were held to be a standard of good-breeding.** Were this all, she might be one of those starchy dowagers who disapprove of all youthful deviation from her own rigid ideas of behaviour, and indeed, there *is* something of this tendency in her, with the Miss Musgroves being considerably in awe of her as a result. But the author takes care to tell us that Lady Russell is also 'a benevolent, charitable, good woman, and capable of strong attachments', so we know her heart is in the right place and she is worthy of Anne's warm regard.

Mrs Rushworth senior, however, 'civil, prosing, pompous', a widow in similarly comfortable circumstances, is without either feeling (except for herself and her son) or understanding. She has none of Lady Russell's intelligence, culture or desire to do the right thing, but on the marriage of her son she takes herself off with **true dowager propriety to Bath, there to parade over the wonders of Sotherton in her evening parties.** She does the right thing in the wrong spirit. Jane Austen's scorn is palpable. She had met many such women at her aunt's card tables in Bath, forever boasting about their former lives and possessions.

In *Emma*, when the wealthy Miss Churchill marries the more humbly born Captain Weston, her relations **threw her off with due decorum**, an ironic use of the term since the action is the very opposite of how people should behave. In *Persuasion*, Lady Russell praises Mr Elliot for being able to judge for himself in everything essential **without defying public opinion in any point of worldly decorum.** The adjective is interesting here. *Decorum*, Lady Russell is rounded enough to know, applies to things of this world, and important though those are, they are not the most important.

That members of the gentry class are schooled in *decorum* in the sense of moving and speaking in certain constrained ways, is clear from something that Edmund Bertram says when amateur theatricals are under discussion at Mansfield. While he loves to see professional acting as much as anybody, Edmund says, he would not cross the room to watch the efforts of ladies and gentlemen who have **all the disadvantages of education and decorum to struggle through.** This kind of decorum is evidently a matter of externals, of conforming to society's expectations. Certain characters are prepared to defy these expectations, relying on their own judgement instead.

Marianne Dashwood is one such. She replies warmly to a semi-serious jest of Elinor's after Willoughby's first visit, '**I have erred against every commonplace notion of decorum; I have been open and sincere where I ought to have been reserved, spiritless, dull and deceitful – had I talked only of the weather and the roads, and had I spoken only once in ten minutes, this reproach would have been spared.**' That Elinor could possibly want her sister to behave like the insipid, formal Lady Middleton is of course impossible, though she does see some dangers in this early instance of Marianne's flouting of social norms. What Marianne so scornfully terms **every commonplace notion of decorum** has, in fact, developed to protect people – especially young women – from drawing too much attention to themselves, or worse, dashing headlong into dangerous intimacies with strangers.

Elizabeth Bennet shares with Marianne a reliance on her own taste and judgement in matters of behaviour. Usually, she strikes a happy medium between the indecorous conduct of her sister Lydia – a character who shows the danger of paying no attention whatsoever to decorum in any action of her life – and the overly ceremonious, snobbish characters like Lady Catherine and the Bingley sisters. The latter criticize Elizabeth for showing **a most country town indifference to decorum.** Elizabeth has just splashed through puddles in her haste to reach an ill sister, arriving hot and dirty at Netherfield. The reader knows that the Bingleys' is not the kind of decorum we are expected to endorse: the sisters condemn themselves out of their own mouths for caring more about appearances than feelings, while Elizabeth, by getting her priorities right, endears herself to us. (As does Mr Bingley in defending her against their censure.)

In reply to Elizabeth's enquiry why she should not marry Darcy, the dictatorial Lady Catherine pronounces in her most overbearing tones,

'**Because honour, decorum, prudence, nay, interest, forbid it.**' Neither Elizabeth nor the reader can see that any of these principles would be violated by a marriage between a gentleman and a gentleman's daughter of equal (if different styles of) intelligence and social deportment. (In fact the whole novel has illustrated how Elizabeth can teach Darcy a thing or two about the latter, his practice not living up to his theoretical knowledge.) Lady Catherine is the widow *par excellence* in Jane Austen's gallery for dictating to others on matters little and great.

Countering her aunt's criticism of Wickham, that he has been indelicate in pursuing Miss King as soon as she inherits a fortune, having cared nothing for her before, Elizabeth says rather flippantly, '**A young man in distressed circumstances has not time for all those elegant decorums which other people may observe.**' It is not the case, however, that Elizabeth cares nothing for decorum. She respects what is due to the feelings of a friend, and although her astonishment on hearing of Charlotte's agreement to marry Mr Collins is so great **as to overcome at first the bounds of decorum** in her exclamations, she soon recollects herself, and makes the effort to utter the phrases more conventionally used to greet an engagement.

Much more importantly, Elizabeth has long been painfully aware of something wrong in her father's behaviour that she cannot laugh off: **the continual breach of conjugal obligation and decorum which, in exposing his wife to the contempt of her own children, was so highly reprehensible.** This is a matter of real weight. In promoting, for his own amusement, the violation of the commandment to respect one's mother and father, he does deep disservice not only to the wife whom he has vowed to love and cherish, but to the developing consciences of his offspring. Two major religious imperatives, not to mention his ordinary social and paternal duties, are set at naught by him – all for the sake of privately enjoying his own mental superiority. Other characters in Jane Austen are more mean-spirited or even cruel – but no other character, with intelligence enough to know what he is about, offends so gravely against the tenets of the Christian religion.

In direct contrast is another father, Sir Thomas Bertram, whose behaviour to a stupid wife is exemplary, but whose heavy-handed method of educating his children in the principles of their religion proves almost as faulty as Mr Bennet's opposite tack. Those children are in full agreement that **his sense of decorum is strict**; Fanny dreads the effect of Maria's adultery on **Sir Thomas's parental solicitude, and high sense of honour and decorum**; and Sir Thomas himself, on making the acquaintance of the shallow Mr Yates, finds **much to offend his ideas of decorum and confirm his ill opinion.**

Edmund, the only one of his children to resemble Sir Thomas in seriousness of reflection, in the early stages of his infatuation with the lively Miss Crawford, acknowledges to Fanny that her remarks about her uncle were '**very wrong – very indecorous**'. It is judgements like these, coming from a young man, that have turned some readers against Edmund, made many think he is a prig (and Fanny, his pupil and sympathizing listener, just as bad). Not much later Edmund attempts unsuccessfully to put a stop to the theatricals by appealing to his eldest sister: '**In all points of decorum**, your **conduct must be law**'. For a moment her vanity is tickled; Maria loves to lead, but she loves the licence to flirt with Mr Crawford even more, and turns Edmund's appeal on its head by claiming that if she were to 'harangue' the others on the subject, '**there would be the greatest indecorum, I think**'.

Interestingly, the negative form is also used in a different novel when a character is squirming to justify a decision they know is unworthy. John Dashwood, having been persuaded by his wife to go back on his promise to his dying father to provide financially for his stepmother and half-sisters, **finally resolved, that it would be absolutely unnecessary, if not highly indecorous, to do more for the widow and children of his father, than such kind of neighbourly acts as his own wife pointed out.**

The word receives its most serious treatment in any Jane Austen novel when Henry Crawford, having to his own astonishment so deeply fallen in love with Fanny that he wants her for his wife, acknowledges the *decorum* in her which he would once have found the least attractive of qualities in any young woman: **Henry Crawford had too much sense not to feel the worth of good principles in a wife, though he was too little accustomed to serious reflection to know them by their proper name; but when he talked of her having such a steadiness and** regularity of conduct, such a high notion of honour, and such an observance of decorum as might warrant any man in the fullest dependence on her faith and integrity, he expressed what was inspired by the knowledge of her being well-principled and religious.

Of all the heroines, pious, timid Fanny is most consistently praised for the related virtues of *propriety* and *decorum*. When Henry first begins to show an interest in her, **Fanny's reception of it was so proper and modest** that her uncle sees nothing to displease him; and speaking later of Henry's more marked attentions, he assures her, **'You always received them very properly'**. Dismayed to find herself the principal lady in company at the Grants' dinner party, she submits to the distinction **as her own propriety of mind directed.**

Although the two words are sometimes virtually interchangeable, *decorum* relates mainly to correctness of conduct; *propriety* denotes that which is fitting, appropriate and motivated by good taste or good sense across a broad field of human concern. Wherever choices have to be made, be they moral, social or aesthetic, they can be made *properly* or *improperly*. Because they have such a wide application, *propriety and impropriety, proper and improper, properly and improperly* are among the most frequently encountered terms in Jane Austen's writing. This implies a constant tone of judgement, not only on the part of the author, but one character on another.

Emma is surprised to find that Mr Martin's marriage proposal to Harriet, contained in a letter, **expressed good sense, warm attachment, liberality, propriety, even delicacy of feeling.** Speaking of Mrs Weston's manners, she assures the infuriating Mrs Elton that **their propriety, simplicity and elegance would make them the safest model for any young woman.** Henry Tilney is described, semi-humorously, by his sister as thinking in **'the utmost propriety of diction'**. Fanny Price is commended by her uncle for **the neatness and propriety of her dress.** Marooned at Portsmouth, **the abode of noise, disorder and impropriety,** and longing to be at Mansfield again, Fanny reflects that **in her uncle's house there would have been a consideration of times and seasons, a regulation of subject, a propriety, an attention towards everybody.** Elinor Dashwood assures her sister that Edward Ferrars, though no artist himself, when looking at pictures possesses **'an innate propriety and simplicity** of taste'. Written composition, manners, diction, dress, household arrangements, aesthetic taste – all can be characterized by *propriety* – by making good choices from the options available, which is what all Jane Austen's worthy characters do (or learn to do).

Others know how to use *propriety* to mask their true natures, especially when they happen to be well-educated, avaricious men of the world. At the beginning of *Sense and Sensibility*, we are told of the 'rather cold hearted, and rather selfish' John Dashwood that **he was, in general, well-respected; for he conducted himself with propriety in the discharge of his ordinary duties.** In this case, it is the public generally who are taken in, but elsewhere even the more discerning characters are misled by appearances: Mr Elliot, who turns out to be the villain of *Persuasion*, being 'hollow and black' according to Mrs Smith, the woman he has defrauded – Mr Elliot impresses Anne on his first appearance **by the readiness and propriety of his apologies;** and Lady Russell has finally to acknowledge **that because Mr Elliot's manners had precisely pleased her in their propriety and correctness, their general politeness and suavity, she had been too quick in receiving them as the certain result of the most correct opinions and well-regulated mind.**

Some characters know theoretically what is right and proper according to the rules of their society, but have to contend with their baser instincts. Maria Bertram struggles to conceal hers when the sight of Julia on the barouche box with Henry Crawford, laughing and talking, **was a perpetual source of irritation which her own sense of propriety could but just smooth over.** ('**Maria has such a strict sense of propriety**', her aunt assures Mrs Rushworth, '**so much of that true delicacy which one seldom meets with nowadays**' – having no insight into the disposition of the niece who had been brought up under her eye.) Elizabeth Elliot's struggles are less effective. Knowing that she should ask the Musgroves to dine with them in Bath, but unwilling to let them see the reduction in servants and style that a dinner would betray, **it was a struggle between propriety and vanity; but vanity got the better,** and no dinner invitation is issued.

Characters criticize one another for lack of propriety – sometimes directly, sometimes to a third person. '**Are you lost to every feeling of propriety and delicacy?**' demands Lady Catherine of Elizabeth Bennet, while Darcy, in the letter with which he attempts to rebut Elizabeth's accusations of the night before – his ill-phrased marriage proposal – explains his reasons for separating Bingley from Jane: '**the situation of your mother's family, though objectionable, was nothing in comparison of that total want of propriety so frequently, so almost uniformly betrayed by herself, by your three younger sisters, and occasionally even by your father**'. Readers of *Pride and Prejudice* sometimes follow Lady Catherine's lead in supposing that it is the difference in social status between Darcy and Elizabeth that he is first so snobbishly aware of, and over which love eventually triumphs; but it is in fact the *behaviour* of much of the Bennet family that he scorns, not their lack of wealth or rank – and Elizabeth, who feels much the same about her relations' faults, comes to acknowledge that the substance of his objections is true, though their expression was not very kind. As she gazes on Darcy's portrait at Pemberley, she **thought of his regard with a deeper sentiment of gratitude than it had ever raised before; she remembered its warmth, and softened its impropriety of expression.**

Later she has to defend him against her father's misconceptions: '**Indeed, he has no improper pride**'. That is, the pride remaining in Darcy – he has conquered his former excess – is *proper*, is seemly, in one of his rank and character as an upright and honourable gentleman.

In talking through the discovery that Frank Churchill and Jane Fairfax have been for months secretly engaged, Mrs Weston speaks of '**the impropriety of his conduct**', at which Emma exclaims, '**Impropriety! Oh! Mrs Weston, it is too calm a censure. Much, much beyond impropriety**', although she does not offer a more appropriate or stronger word. Soon enough Emma is reflecting on her own mounting faults, her **abominable suspicions of an improper attachment to Mr Dixon** on Jane's part; **how improperly she had been acting by Harriet!** and how on Box Hill, in relation to Miss Bates, **her own behaviour had been so very improper!**

'**I do not censure her opinions, but there certainly is impropriety in making them public**', Edmund tells Fanny of Mary. If the author appears to risk Edmund seeming holier-than-thou for criticizing the behavioural shortcomings of someone he otherwise loves, this is not the first time she has taken such a gamble. Elinor Dashwood does the same, though in her case the offending person is a beloved sister: 'Her systems have all the unfortunate tendency of setting propriety at naught', Elinor says of Marianne to Colonel Brandon. The elder sister frequently tries to reason with the younger on this subject. Elinor did once or twice venture to suggest the propriety of some self-command in witnessing her open show of affection to Willoughby; and when Marianne accepts the gift of a horse from her admirer, Elinor ventured to doubt the propriety of her receiving such a present from a man so little, or at least so lately known to them. Marianne's warm response is that 'I should hold myself guilty of greater impropriety in accepting a horse from my brother, than from Willoughby.' The next occasion for remonstrance occurs when Marianne travels in an open carriage alone with Willoughby to Allenham, and Elinor sees fit to tell her that 'the pleasantness of an employment does not always evince its propriety'. Marianne asserts that 'if there had been any real impropriety in what I did, I should have been sensible of it at the time, for we always know when we are acting wrong', and when Elinor points out that at the very least, she has exposed herself to impertinent remarks, Marianne comes back with 'If the impertinent remarks of Mrs Jennings are to be the proof of impropriety in conduct, we are all offending every moment of our lives.'

For many readers, Marianne's 'heart' trumps Elinor's 'head' here, even though the elder sister is seen to be right in the long run. Had Marianne's romance developed into an honourable engagement and happy marriage, it could be argued, Elinor's warnings would have seemed mean-spirited. (Acceptable from a mother, maybe – but not from a nineteen-year-old sister.) But in offering a valuable gift to a girl to whom he has not openly pledged himself, and in taking her alone in his carriage, Willoughby is in fact showing a lack of care for Marianne's reputation that no honourable gentleman would risk – a lack of *propriety* according to the rules of his society. In slighting too easily the forms of worldly propriety, he displayed a want of caution which Elinor could not approve. This romance *cannot* turn out well, and Elinor is right to be uneasy almost from its beginning. And at its end, her condemnation of Willoughby's heartless response to Marianne's affectionate, confiding notes, did not blind her to the impropriety of their having been written at all.

Proper as an adjective usually feels less strict than does *propriety* as a noun. When Willoughby gives **every assurance of his admiring Pope no more than is proper** this can be glossed as 'no more than is fitting' – according to Marianne's beliefs, of course. The word is used throughout the novels in many equally lightweight contexts, for example in the description of the Musgrove girls adding knick-knacks to give the parlour at Uppercross **the proper air of confusion** – the fashionable air.

'**We are not really so much brother and sister as to make it at all improper**', Emma says teasingly when inviting Mr Knightley to dance with her. She is proud of **having given Harriet's fancy a proper direction** in matters of the heart, and observing Frank Churchill's attention to his stepmother, is satisfied that **nothing could be more proper or pleasing than his whole manner to her.** Mr Knightley, meanwhile, not being privy to Emma's secret thoughts, **had seen only proper attention and pleasing behaviour** in her treatment of Jane Fairfax, newly arrived in Highbury. Later, when Jane rejects the reformed Emma's attempts to be of service to her, **it mortified her that she was given so little credit for proper feeling, or esteemed so little worthy as a friend; but she had the consolation of knowing that her intentions were good, and of being able to say to herself, that could Mr Knightley have been privy to all her attempts of assisting Jane Fairfax, could he even have seen into her heart, he would not, on this occasion, have found anything to reprove.**

Anne Elliot requires no reproof from anybody, always ready as she is to enter sympathetically into the feelings of others. **Anne said what was proper** in response to her sister's whining greeting – she lightly acknowledges and then cheerfully turns the subject. When Henrietta Musgrove confides in her, Anne **said all that was reasonable and proper on the business**, leaving Henrietta well satisfied. Carrying a much more powerful impact is what Anne overhears Captain Wentworth saying at Lyme, in discussing who should stay behind to attend to the injured Louisa, '**No-one so proper, so capable as Anne!**' She is, indeed, almost overpowered by this proof of his confidence in her judgement.

In Bath, Elizabeth Elliot wastes time in saying **the proper nothings**, mere empty civilities. The word *proper*, used with heavy irony, characterizes the whole of Maria Bertram's relation with Mr

Rushworth, until the dreadful *impropriety* with which it finishes. The couple get engaged **after dancing with each other at a proper number of balls** and (despite Maria's deepening contempt) when they eventually marry it is with **a very proper wedding** – the right clothes and the right show of emotion on the part of the onlookers. Both courtship and marriage are empty shams, but satisfy society's demands for appearances.

Properest is the rather awkward superlative form of the word occasionally used by Jane Austen. '**You, who have not a mother's feelings, are a great deal the properest person**', says Mary Musgrove, when Anne offers to stay at home with her sick child. Captain Wentworth, discussing Louisa's engagement to Captain Benwick, says to Anne, '**When you had the presence of mind to suggest that Benwick would be the properest person to fetch a surgeon, you could have little idea of his being eventually one of those most concerned in her recovery.**' Dreading the occasional show of impatience by Mr John Knightley in dealings with her father, Emma comforts herself: **the beginning, however, of every visit displayed none but the properest feelings, and this being of necessity so short might be hoped to pass away in unsullied cordiality.** Catherine Morland, accused by Isabella of encouraging her brother, begs her to '**make him understand what I mean, in the properest way**'.

Improper is a strong term of disapproval used by several older women in the novels. Lady Russell thinks Anne's engagement at nineteen **a wrong thing: indiscreet, improper.** Lady Catherine de Bourgh pronounces, '**I cannot bear the idea of two young women travelling post by themselves. It is highly improper.**' Mrs Norris **could not but consider it as absolutely unnecessary, and even improper, that Fanny should have a regular lady's horse of her own in the style of her cousins.** Even Lady Bertram, in between more important concerns, makes use of the word. '**Do not act anything improper, my dear**', said Lady Bertram. '**Sir Thomas would not like it. Fanny, ring the bell; I must have my dinner.**' And Fanny herself – an old woman before her time, some would say (or a Victorian matriarch in the making) – finds the female parts in *Lovers' Vows* **totally improper for home representation – the situation of one, the language of the other, so unfit to be expressed by any woman of modesty.**

But in this proto-Victorian novel in which censure of other people is so prevalent, let it not be forgotten that, for a period, Henry Crawford does try to live up to what is required of him. Not only is Sir Thomas impressed by the way his proposals for Fanny have been made: **so well, so openly, so liberally, so properly;** Henry himself asks Fanny, seeing her shake her head at something he says, '**Did you think me speaking improperly? – lightly, irreverently on the subject? Only tell me if I was. Only tell me if I was wrong. I want to be set right. Nay, nay I entreat you.**' and in Portsmouth he kindly gives Fanny time to recover from the shock of seeing him, devoting himself entirely to her mother, **addressing her and attending to her with the utmost politeness and propriety, at the same time with a degree of friendliness – of interest at least – which was making his manner perfect;** so that by the end of the day, Fanny has to admit **she thought him altogether improved since she had seen him; he was much more gentle, obliging and attentive to other people's feelings than he had ever been at Mansfield; she had never seen him so near being agreeable; his behaviour to her father could not offend, and there was something particularly kind and proper in the notice he took of Susan.**

We applaud Jane Austen for showing us a flawed man morally improving, struggling, growing, reaching for better things – even if he ultimately fails.

17

A Nice Distinction

ENRY TILNEY, WHOSE cleverness and verbal playfulness mirror Jane Austen's own (though as a man, he allows himself to pontificate where a woman might hesitate to do so) gives the naïve and admiring Catherine Morland a lesson in the true – or at least, the original – meaning of the word *nice*. In his 1755 dictionary, Dr Johnson had given the word only definitions of fastidiousness, neatness and precision. Yet by 1769 it is first recorded being used as a general, bland term of approval. Thirty years later, when Jane Austen wrote the first version of *Northanger Abbey*, it had become an unthinking part of many people's vocabulary – especially young people. 'But now really', Catherine asks, 'do not you think *Udolpho* the nicest book in the world?' Henry won't let her get away with that: 'The nicest – by which I suppose you mean the neatest. That must depend on the binding.'

Miss Tilney steps in to excuse Henry's impertinence: 'He is forever finding fault with me, for some incorrectness of language, and now he is taking the same liberty with you. The word 'nicest' as you used it, did not suit him.'

'I am sure', cried Catherine, 'I did not mean to say anything wrong; but it *is* a nice book, and why should I not call it so?'

'Very true', said Henry, 'and this is a very nice day, and we are taking a very nice walk, and you are two very nice young ladies. Oh! It is a very nice word indeed! It does for everything. Originally perhaps it was applied only to express neatness, propriety, delicacy, or refinement – people were nice in their dress, in their sentiments, or their choice. But now every commendation on every subject is comprised in that one word.'

'While, in fact', cried his sister, 'it ought only to be applied to you, without any commendation at all. You are more nice than wise. Come, Miss Morland, let us leave him to meditate over our faults in the utmost propriety of diction, while we praise *Udolpho* in whatever terms we like best.'

How clever Miss Tilney is in thus turning the tables on her brother, all done with perfect good humour (we can imagine him laughing), and how good-natured she is in taking upon herself Catherine's unwitting sins of speech, to spare her any mortification. Catherine has already offended in this way before, without drawing her author's condemnation, when in the early chapters she assures Mrs Allen that her headdress has not been damaged but **'looks very nice'**, and when she exclaims, as rain threatens to derail her plans, **'It was such a nice-looking morning'**. Luckily, by the time Henry challenges her, Catherine is already so much inclined to think him wonderful that he cannot weary her with his pedantry, and from his conversation her mind receives ideas that have never come her way before. Her parents are well-educated and sensible, but fine discrimination between words is not one of their mental endowments. But Catherine is a quick learner, and never offends by misusing the word *nice* after Henry's explanation on Beechen Cliff. One day, perhaps, when she has learnt to think like him, Catherine will be able to spar with Henry on his own terms, as his sister does. And we can be sure that their children will never get away with any sloppiness of speech.

As we might expect, Jane Austen herself enjoys using the words *nice* and *nicety* with their proper meaning, that is, to express nuances of fastidiousness, discernment and delicacy. These are qualities which the best of her characters possess, so the term is important to her. Fanny Price, unable to stomach the food at her parents' Portsmouth home, **was nice only from natural delicacy**, in contrast to Mr Crawford's being brought up to luxury and indulgence at the table. Natural delicacy is a good quality for a heroine to possess; habits of luxury, though leading to the same squeamishness, are bad.

Delicate could certainly be the synonym for *nice* in this passage from *Sense and Sensibility* (that is, delicately aware of other people's feelings): **It was several days before Willoughby's name was mentioned** before Marianne by any of her family; Sir John and Mrs Jennings, indeed, were not so nice; their witticisms added pain to many a painful hour. A little later, Elinor could not suppose that Sir John would be more nice in proclaiming his suspicions of her regard for Edward, than he had been in respect to Marianne. Sir John and Mrs Jennings would be more polite if they were more *nice*.

In *Persuasion*, the summing up tells us that: There is a quickness of perception in some, a nicety in the discernment of character, a natural penetration, in short, which no experience in others can equal, and Lady Russell had been less gifted in this part of understanding than her young friend. Lady Russell has prided herself on being well-judging – but she is not intuitive. Even less discerning than Lady Russell is the obtuse Mrs Rushworth, so that when Mrs Norris admired the nice discernment of character which could so well distinguish merit in her son's choice of Maria Bertram for his bride, our faith in all four of them – Rushworth mother and son, Mrs Norris and Maria – is underwhelming.

Henry Crawford is much more aware of human cross-currents, and knows exactly how to manipulate people. 'It requires great powers, great nicety, to give her playfulness and simplicity without extravagance', he says when trying to flatter Julia Bertram into accepting the less desirable role of Amelia in *Lovers' Vows*, adding, 'it requires a delicacy of feeling ... a gentlewoman – a Julia Bertram'.

'Choosy', 'fastidious' 'exacting' and 'delicate' can each be cited as synonyms for *nice*. 'We must not be so nice', Tom Bertram urges as one play after another is rejected for performance at Mansfield Park. He does not mean that the group must not be so polite or so kind to one another; he means, and is understood to mean, that they must not be so choosy. And when Maria echoes the phrase defensively in countering Edmund's criticism of the play eventually chosen, she means not only 'choosy' but 'fastidious': 'If we are so very nice', she says, 'we shall never act anything'.

'We must not be nice, and ask for all the virtues into the bargain', Emma says of the prospect of Frank Churchill's arrival – well-bred and agreeable as he is rumoured to be, that will be sufficient, in Emma's view, to make a sensation in Highbury. She knows it would be unreasonable to ask for more. When arrangements for the ball at the Crown are being discussed, foundering on where best to serve refreshments, Mr Weston takes up Frank's suggestion of inviting Miss Bates to give her opinion: '**I do not know a properer person for showing us how to do away difficulties. Fetch Miss Bates. We are growing a little too nice. She is a standing lesson in how to be happy.**' As with the would-be actors at Mansfield Park, being too *nice* leads to indecision and dissatisfaction with all the options.

More positively, Emma uses the term in connection with Harriet's marriage prospects, asserting that she need not accept the first proposal that comes her way since '**a girl with such loveliness as Harriet, had a certainty of being admired and sought after, of having the power of choosing among many, consequently a claim to be nice**'. That is, in rather cruder language, Harriet's beauty is likely to bring her many suitors, from whom she will be able to pick and choose, where a plainer woman will have to put up with what she can get (like Charlotte Lucas).

'**Good company requires only birth, education and manners, and with regard to education is not very nice**', says Mr Elliot, toning down Anne's high-minded definition of what good company entails – in her view, clever, well-informed people, who have a great deal of conversation. To read *nice* in its present meaning into this sentence would puzzle or confuse the modern reader – how can education have connotations that are not very agreeable, not very pleasant? But translate *nice* as 'exacting', and Mr Elliot's slightly cynical meaning becomes abundantly clear. Less clear is whether Anne – and the reader – are meant to be reassured, impressed or distressed by his man-of-the-world opinions.

'Fastidious' is often the implication when the word is used in matters of the heart: '**You and Miss Crawford have made me too nice**', Edmund says to Fanny, telling her that he has been spoilt for common female society. The same meaning applies in Captain Wentworth's exchange with his sister:

'**Anybody between fifteen and thirty may have me for the asking. A little beauty, a few smiles, and a few compliments to the navy, and I am a lost man. Should not this be enough for a sailor, who has had no society among women to make him nice?**'

He said it, she knew, to be contradicted. His bright proud eye spoke the conviction that he was nice.

Similarly, to explain Anne Elliot's failure to fall in love with anybody else after the breach with Captain Wentworth, the author cites **the nice tone of her mind, the fastidiousness of her taste.** And when Anne herself is considering whether Mr Elliot might be planning to court her sister Elizabeth in Bath, **most earnestly did she wish that he might not be too nice, or too observant, if Elizabeth were his object.** Anne, who seems charitably to wish the match for Elizabeth's sake, fears that if Mr Elliot looks too closely into Elizabeth's character, he will not proceed. That Anne should entertain even the mildest desire for Mr Elliot to marry in ignorance of his wife's temper and understanding, is not explained, Anne having no reason at this juncture of the plot to wish him ill. It is one of the many small inconsistencies in *Persuasion* that the author may have eliminated had her health allowed for a thorough-going revision.

These are the shades of meaning when the word is applied to the abilities or conduct of people; in other contexts, *nice* usually indicates 'well-ordered' or 'well-chosen' (like Henry Tilney's book-bindings). The Harvilles' small rented home at Lyme is notable for its **ingenious contrivances and nice arrangements.** William Price somewhat optimistically observes to Fanny, '**we seem to want some of your nice ways and orderliness at my father's. The house is always in confusion. You will set things going in a better way, I am sure. You will tell my mother how it all ought to be.**' Mrs Gardiner, in writing to Elizabeth about '**a low phaeton, with a nice little pair of ponies**', must intend the ponies to be as elegant as the carriage, and well-chosen to accompany it. Also well-ordered, and what we might call fit for purpose (being dry underfoot) are the **nice sheltered path** where Elizabeth Bennet walks at Rosings, and the **nice pavements** of Bath which Mary Musgrove laments while she is obliged to remain in the muddy winter countryside.

Just as Mary speaks only to air her grievances, so Mr Woodhouse mentions only what affects him personally, neither of them being capable of taking a more objective view. In speaking of their new acquaintance Mrs Elton, whose high opinion of herself he takes on trust and whose vulgarity has entirely escaped him, he has only one criticism to offer: 'She speaks a little too quick. A little quickness of voice there is which rather hurts the ear. But I believe I am nice; I do not like strange voices'.

In making this claim for himself, Mr Woodhouse may be calling for sympathy, but he is not exactly boasting. Neither is Edward Ferrars, when he says ruefully that 'unfortunately my own nicety, and the nicety of my friends, have made me what I am, an idle, helpless being. We never could agree in our choice of profession.' It is clear from what immediately follows that Edward is being perfectly sincere and not indulging in what Mr Darcy would call an indirect boast. But certain pretentious people think it reflects well on them to put in a claim to be *nice*. Thus Mrs Elton boasts that her sister Selina has quite a horror of sleeping at an inn, and 'I believe I have caught a little of her nicety. She always travels with her own sheets'. And in discussion with Jane Fairfax, who expresses indifference as to the degree of wealth and elegance of any family who might employ her as governess, Mrs Elton will not let her know her own business best: 'I know you, I know you; you would take up with anything; but I shall be a little more nice.' Mrs Clay, too, playing the game of self-advancement with some subtlety, manages to convince Elizabeth Elliot that upon the subject of marriage her sentiments 'are particularly nice, and that she reprobates all inequality of condition and rank more strongly than most people'.

The novels contain two other forms of the word *nice*: firstly an alternative noun; for if *nicety* can apply only to human character, something else is needed for inanimate objects, and that is *niceness*. When Edmund makes his gift to Fanny, she opens the parcel to find in all the niceness of jeweller's packing, a plain gold chain.

Secondly the adverb, used most properly when Edmund tells Fanny that 'You look very nicely indeed', which gives the modern reader a slight jolt, as we would say 'you look very nice'. In a less rigorous way, the adverb is frequently used by and of the more lightweight characters: Harriet Smith exclaims after listening to Emma, 'How nicely you talk! I love to hear you'; and asks no more of life than to be in company nicely dressed herself, and seeing others nicely dressed. The only commendation that Emma can vouchsafe on Mrs Elton's appearance in Highbury is 'Very nicely dressed indeed; a remarkably elegant gown', bland remarks that will do for common consumption. Lady Bertram is introduced to us as spending her days **sitting, nicely dressed, on a sofa**. Mr Woodhouse recommends his neighbours should treat their gift of pork by '**making it into steaks, nicely fried, as ours are fried**', and Lydia Bennet, having made too many purchases so that her boxes crowd out her sisters on their journey home, exclaims '**How nicely we are crammed in!**'

Jane Austen is not above using the word *nice* itself in its less precise sense. Several of the more vulgar characters in *Pride and Prejudice* employ this usage: Lydia with her '**Is this not nice? Is this not an agreeable surprise?**' of a meal at an inn; Mrs Philips with her promise of **a nice comfortable noisy game of lottery tickets, and a little bit of hot supper afterwards**; and Mrs Bennet suggesting '**a nice long walk**' for people she happens to want out of the way.

We are not too much surprised to find the undiscerning Mrs Grant saying, '**Henry, you shall marry the youngest Miss Bertram, a nice, handsome, good-humoured, accomplished girl, who will make you very happy**'. It is more surprising, however, to hear Emma Woodhouse, with her command of language, speaking of the hind-quarter of Hartfield pork that she has just sent round to the Bates household: '**there will be the leg to be salted, you know, which is so very nice**'. But Emma *is* talking to her childish father, so perhaps she can be excused nursery expressions. Most surprising of all, perhaps, the narrator introduces Emma's younger niece as **a nice little girl about eight months old, who was now making her first visit to Hartfield, and very happy to be danced about in her aunt's arms**. No doubt baby Emma is neat, clean and fragrant; yet *nice* here suggests something more, a smiling, happy little addition to the Knightley family. It is a charming scene; but Henry Tilney would surely reprove his author for her choice of adjective.

Whereas when Admiral Croft says of the two Miss Musgroves, '**And very nice young ladies they both are; I hardly know one from another**', such is Jane Austen's skill in choosing exactly the right phrase, that the nothing-meaning commendation seems apt not only for the speaker, good-humoured and undiscriminating as he is, but for those pleasant but unremarkable young women about whom he speaks.

As has been demonstrated throughout this book, Jane Austen's use of language often differs from our own in subtle ways, sometimes by a shift in meaning, sometimes by endowing abstract terms with greater or lesser weight of approval or censure than they carry today. A brief look at some other of her favourite words concludes the present study.

While *nice* was losing its precise meaning to become a general word of commendation, the adjective *pretty* was undergoing something of a reverse movement, from the wide-ranging to the specific. Today, we use it in purely visual terms. So do both the narrator of Jane Austen's novels and her younger characters. Harriet Smith is called by the narrator **a very pretty girl** and many other young women are so described – none more frequently and consistently than Mary Crawford. On first introduction, we are told that Mary's lively dark eyes and clear brown complexion amount to a **general prettiness**; Edmund's falling under her spell is partly accounted for by her being **pretty, lively, with a harp as elegant as herself,** while Tom Bertram, who is not in love with her, describes her as 'a sweet, pretty, elegant, lively girl', and his sisters, confident in their own attractions, complacently allow her to be **a sweet pretty girl, while they were the finest young women in the country.**

The Miss Bertrams are in fact **decidedly handsome.** It is a word which suits self-confident and comfortably circumstanced young ladies who have grown up with every luxury at their command and 'very little to distress or vex' them. Elizabeth Elliot, at twenty-nine, has taken good care of herself, and is **still the handsome Miss Elliot she had begun to be thirteen years ago.** The first adjective the narrator applies to the prosperous and pampered Emma Woodhouse is *handsome* – it is the third word of the novel; but Mr Knightley, significantly, chooses a different, perhaps an unconsciously more demeaning, term. 'I **shall not attempt to deny Emma's being pretty**', he says somewhat grudgingly to Mrs Weston, when he would prefer to speak of Emma's moral faults than her appearance. Mrs Weston knows he is being demeaning. Her reply is indignant. '**Pretty! Say beautiful rather.**'

The word *pretty* is also applied to the appearance of houses: Catherine Morland with some naïvety exclaims that the drawing room at Woodston Parsonage is 'the prettiest room in the world'. Uppercross Cottage, in *Persuasion*, has been improved for the young squire's habitation and now catches the traveller's eye **with its veranda, French windows and other prettinesses.** Just as feminine prettiness is distinguished from handsomeness or beauty as being perhaps more immediately charming but also more transitory, so Uppercross Cottage may be more visually appealing to the casual viewer than the more considerable aspect of the unmodernized, unfashionable aspect of the Great House.

But older speakers in Jane Austen use **pretty** in a much more diffused way, to indicate general approval of arrangements or behaviour that has nothing to do with aesthetics. It is a favourite word of Mr Woodhouse. Eight years after the event, he is still pleased with Isabella's having given his own name to her first son Henry: '**very pretty of her**' he thinks it. Harriet Smith, Jane Fairfax, Mrs Elton and even the maidservant Hannah are all commended by him at one time or another as **pretty, pretty-spoken** or **pretty-behaved.** Nor is it only women of whom he thus speaks. Mr Elton is, in his eyes, '**a very pretty young man to be sure**', and Frank's letter on the marriage of his father to Miss Taylor is '**an exceeding good, pretty letter**'.

Similarly, Mrs Bennet calls the nieces of Mrs Long '**very pretty behaved girls, and not at all handsome**'; Mrs Morland considers Henry and Elinor Tilney '**very pretty kind of young people**'; and Mrs Jennings uses the word again and again as she reads an insincere letter written by Lucy Steele: '**how prettily she writes!... That sentence is very prettily turned.... It is as pretty a letter as ever I saw.**' Neither she nor Mr Woodhouse is referring to the visual aspect of the handwriting. In all these examples, it is the habit of good, appropriate or correct behaviour that is being commended in the younger generation by the older.

Like *nice, pretty* and even *elegant, amiable* is an adjective that had, by Jane Austen's time, become too commonplace as a term of approval to mean very much at all (and has since lost all currency). Many of her characters use *amiable* to mean little more than mildly pleasing. It is a word forever in the mouth of the undiscriminating Mr Collins, from begging Mr Bennet's leave to apologize **for injuring your amiable**

daughters by the entail, to his assertion that his own neighbourhood contains **many amiable young women**, his fawning description of Elizabeth's **loveliness and amiable qualifications**, and all his eventual self-satisfied talk of his **amiable Charlotte.**

The narrator herself has fun with the hackneyed nature of the word at the beginning of *Northanger Abbey*, when she tells us that her heroine has reached the age of seventeen **without having seen one amiable youth who could call forth her sensibility.** However, when Jane Austen describes Marianne Dashwood as **generous, amiable, interesting**, she is speaking with no tongue in cheek. The narrator wants us to know that Marianne really is loveable, as well as *interesting* – that is, capable of engaging our feelings on her behalf.

Marianne herself chooses her words with care, avoiding language that is 'worn and hackneyed out of all sense and meaning', so that when she uses the word *amiable*, she means something by it. '**Edward is very amiable, and I love him tenderly**', she declares, even while criticizing his eyes, his figure, his lack of taste for drawing and his unanimated style of reading aloud. Though his deficiencies strike her so forcibly, she can still say with perfect honesty (for Marianne is never insincere), '**I have the highest opinion in the world of his goodness and sense. I think him everything that is worthy and amiable.**'

Even in *Pride and Prejudice*, the word is not always used as loosely as it is by Mr Collins. Elizabeth herself, defending Mr Darcy against her father's charge of being proud and unpleasant, says feelingly, '**Indeed he has no improper pride. He is perfectly amiable. You do not know what he really is.**' To Darcy himself, referring to her own initial incivility towards him, she jests, '**had you not been really amiable, you would have hated me for it**'. *Amiable* is not an epithet we would immediately associate with Mr Darcy yet, after Elizabeth's eyes are open to his merits, it recurs often in her thoughts of him: respecting his courtesy towards the Gardiners, and his treatment of his servants and tenants. '**In what an amiable light does this place him!**' is the turning point in her assessment, made on hearing the testimony of his housekeeper.

Mr Knightley, famously, defines the word *amiable* as showing delicacy towards the feelings of other people – one of his own most admirable characteristics – but this is only part of the story. Indeed, the generally reliable Mr Knightley is here so taken up with directing his scorn towards what he sees as Frank Churchill's failings that he focuses on only one aspect of the word, the proper meaning of which is loveable, worthy of being loved. Delicacy towards the feelings of other people is a necessary but not sufficient quality of *amiability*.

The *amiable* character manifests itself in a myriad ways – Jane Austen never repeats exactly the same mixture – but *complaisance, obligingness* and *sweetness* may be components. *Complaisance* is an interesting word, not to be confused with *complacency*, which denotes quiet satisfaction or contentment, though without the smugness it suggests today: when Frank Churchill talks of 'home' to mean Highbury, it **made his father look on him with fresh complacency.** Mr Darcy, trying to assess whether Jane Bennet was in love with his friend, and not above a little wishful thinking, considers she must be indifferent to Bingley: **'there was a constant complacency in her air and manner, not often united with great sensibility'.** Jane Bennet is – often as the result of some effort – uniformly cheerful and serene, and does not wear her heart on her sleeve; but no one could call her smug.

Complaisance is a more positive virtue, meaning as it does an unselfish readiness to comply with others' wishes. When Mrs Jennings conveys the Dashwood sisters to London as her guests, **they were three days on their journey, and Marianne's behaviour as they travelled was a happy specimen of what her future complaisance and companionableness to Mrs Jennings might be expected to be. She sat in silence almost the whole way ... except when any object of picturesque beauty within their view drew from her an exclamation of delight exclusively addressed to her sister.** This is the most sustained and unprovoked rudeness of which any heroine is guilty – far ruder than Emma's momentary lapse on Box Hill – and Mrs Jennings, admittedly somewhat obtuse, is all the more saintly for not resenting it. Her kindness to Marianne in London is untinctured by any resentment.

Another heroine finding herself to be a travelling companion is more justified in *her* lack of *complaisance*. Tricked into taking a second drive with John Thorpe, and finding his company more and more objectionable, Catherine Morland's **complaisance was no longer what it had been in their former airing,** when her good nature had induced her to listen submissively and reply pleasantly to his various boasts and lies. And Emma, too, has to be shut up in a carriage with an unpleasant man, experiencing all his ill-judged pretensions, before she realizes that her former behaviour to Mr Elton **had been so complaisant and obliging, so full of courtesy and attention** as might have misled him into thinking himself the object of romantic interest on her part.

During the casting of *Lovers' Vows*, as Tom Bertram urges Julia to take the part of Cottager's Wife – which she finds insulting – Henry Crawford, in whose interest it is to keep Julia sweet, protests: '**It will be impossible to make anything of it fit for your sister, and we must not suffer her good nature to be imposed on.... She must not be left to her own complaisance.**' This is sheer flattery. Julia, of course, is possessed of no such innate good nature as Catherine Morland, despite having manners **carefully formed to general civility and obligingness** – like her sister. Neither Julia nor Maria is capable of unselfishness, though they are sometimes forced into the outward show of it, as when Julia cannot, without a violation of the rules of polite behaviour, get away from tiresome Mrs Rushworth at Sotherton. Neither sister will willingly oblige others if it runs counter to their own desires. They **had no idea of carrying their obliging manners to the sacrifice of any real pleasure.** Maria especially, in her deportment towards her fiancé Mr Rushworth, **showed rather conscious superiority than any solicitude to oblige him.** She does not care enough about him even to simulate the *appearance* of being obliging. She *does* care what Henry thinks about her. When both the Miss Bertrams are anxious to secure the barouche-box seat next to him for the journey to Sotherton, they meditate **how best, and with the most appearance of obliging the others, to secure it.**

Mary Crawford seems better endowed in this respect. Reunited with her harp, **she played with the greatest obligingness.** Invited to join the Miss Bertrams in a glee, **she tripped off to the instrument, leaving Edmund looking after her in an ecstasy of admiration of all her many virtues, from her obliging manners down to her light and graceful tread....** 'How well she walks, and how readily she falls in with the inclination of others, joining them the moment she is asked.' Although stunned by her message, conveyed by Henry, that she is ready to act any part in any play they might choose, with the ingenuity of love Edmund manages **to dwell more on the obliging, accommodating purport of the message than on anything else.**

Her brother, too, as his courtship of Fanny progresses, improves in this respect. In Portsmouth, Fanny observes **he was much more gentle, obliging and attentive to other people's feelings than he had ever been.** Fanny as observer and judge is more reliable than Edmund; if she feels this, despite herself, we can believe that it is true – even if the change is not lasting. The irony in *Mansfield Park* is that it is Fanny who is happy to oblige most people most of the time, but who finds herself being seriously disobliging twice: once when participation in the theatricals violates her sense of what is due to her uncle; and again, in a matter of incomparably greater import for her whole future happiness, when her rejection of Henry Crawford's proposal of marriage renders her liable to the charge of ingratitude from that uncle – to whom she owes almost everything – himself. Fanny is called upon to show more faith in the dictates of her own conscience, and greater resistance to the wishes of family members, than any other heroine, indeed any other character, in the six novels. As Fanny finds, to be obliging in small matters is relatively easy; to refuse to be obliging when integrity is at stake may be the greater trial and bring the greater anguish.

Fanny's obstinacy – or her steadfastness, according to one's point of view – is all the more surprising to those around her because of her normal *sweetness* of manner. **The gentleness, modesty and sweetness of her character were warmly expatiated on** by Henry Crawford, **that sweetness which makes so essential a part of every woman's worth in the judgement of man, that though he sometimes loves where it is not, he can never believe it absent.** Here both the narrator and Henry – two intelligent minds – seem to endow *sweetness* with more than the easy appeal of cuteness – that appeal possessed by babies and furry animals – which the word might conjure for us today. Certainly the modern connotations with cloyingness are wholly lacking. *Sweetness* in its more serious moral sense means reluctance to take offence or to cause hurt to other people; readiness to be contented with life as it comes, to fall in with the wishes of other people, and to be of pleasant, accommodating and unselfish manners. (Of course, the word was often used lightly and with little but superficial meaning, like some of the other words in this section. It was praise easily given to call a girl *sweet* or *sweet-tempered* and many characters describe one another this way, sometimes in deliberate flattery, sometimes mindlessly.) However, Emma offers a good definition of the true quality in her enumeration of Harriet's attractions. Having first praised Harriet's looks, she adds: '**Her good nature, too, is not so very slight a claim, comprehending, as it does, real, thorough sweetness of temper and manner, a very humble opinion of herself, and a great readiness to be pleased with other people.**' That Emma may be overestimating Harriet's character is beside the point; with her excellent powers of articulation (sometimes exceeding her powers of judgement), Emma here expresses the proper meaning of *sweetness*.

Despite Emma's occasional doubts to the contrary, when she is in a self-critical mood, 'tenderness of heart' – as exemplified by Mr Woodhouse, Isabella and Harriet – does not trump 'genius and intelligence' or 'clearness of head'. To be fully worthy of the reader's interest and approval, a character must possess good nature *and* intelligence, and it is one of Jane Austen's skills that she can persuade us of the superior intelligence of her heroines, heroes and, in each novel, just a few others.

Human intellect comes in many forms, and Jane Austen chooses from a spectrum of words to describe it. Among the specific mental endowments accredited to her characters are *cleverness, understanding, abilities, talents* and *powers*.

Comparing the friends Darcy and Bingley, Jane Austen tells us: **in understanding Darcy was the superior. Bingley was by no means deficient, but Darcy was clever.** In fact, Bingley's understanding never fails him, if he can be excused the modesty which too readily accepts Darcy's assertion that Jane Bennet has no deep feelings for him. It is Darcy himself, for all his cleverness, who cannot see himself as others see him, and who nearly loses the perfect wife as a consequence of his error. Amusingly, *clever* people are often short of basic common sense or understanding. Emma Woodhouse, too, is described as *clever* in the first sentence of her eponymous novel: **handsome, clever and rich;** and it is true that we delight in her quickness of mind compared with most of those around her – yet she too goes spectacularly wrong because she is, as we might say, like Darcy, too clever for her own good.

Abilities is perhaps the most general term for intellectual capacity. Lady Russell, for example, is **a woman rather of sound than quick abilities.** In this she somewhat resembles Sir Thomas Bertram. But as a man, he merits a more specific term. When Edmund Bertram expresses the wish that his father and Mary Crawford might get better acquainted, he chooses his words instinctively but well. '**He would enjoy her liveliness – and she has talents to value his powers**', he says to Fanny. *Talents* suits the quick and multi-faceted nature of Mary's mind, while the more solid, deliberating mental processes of Sir Thomas are well expressed by *powers*. If we try transposing the two terms, we soon see that it would not work.

A person may possess intellectual or social *powers*. Robert Ferrars, who prides himself on the kind of social ease that his brother Edward so manifestly lacks, boasts, '**We are not all born, you know, with the same powers – the same address.**' Fanny Price is not so wholly immune to Henry as she intends: **she felt his powers; he was entertaining, and his manners so improved.** Edmund thinks that **with such powers,** Henry must succeed in winning Fanny eventually. Henry himself has declared that an engaged woman, such as Maria Bertram, may '**exert all her powers of pleasing without suspicion**'. The word may also apply to a specific field of endeavour: Tom Bertram justifies his theatre as an opportunity for the young people to '**exercise our powers in something new**'.

The opposite is the case with the word *talents*, which did not then imply a special, limited aptitude, as today. It was not only a general but a neutral term: often commendable, but with its suggestion of being 'quick on the uptake' holding dangers. Those who possess the quality may be disposed to impatience with others and pride in themselves. As children, the Miss Bertrams are possessed of **promising talents and early information** but are entirely deficient in self-knowledge, generosity and humility. Mr Bennet warns Elizabeth that a woman of '**your lively talents**' would risk her happiness and even her respectability in a (mentally) unequal marriage. Elizabeth herself prefers to think of her mental endowments as *abilities*, and acknowledges her error of judgement with the exclamation 'I, **who have valued myself on my abilities!**' While clearly seeing her father's peculiarities, she credits him with **abilities which Mr Darcy himself need not disdain.** By the end of the book, Elizabeth can relax, knowing her father and husband are able to converse as two equally intelligent men, of neither of whom she need feel ashamed.

Not so with *Mrs* Bennet, who is *not* transformed into **a sensible, amiable, well-informed woman** by the happy events in her family. She begins the book as **a woman of mean understanding** and ends it still **invariably silly.** *Silly*, not *stupid*, is the antonym of *clever* or *sensible*. In Jane Austen's time, *stupid* retained its original meaning of 'in a stupor'; half-asleep, stupefied by the dullness of the occasion or the limitations of the mind; alternatively, of being the cause of stupefaction: as may be a book, a party, a person or even the weather. The latter is what Catherine Morland means by the **stupid pamphlets** which General Tilney *says* he stays up to read – for would not they send him to sleep? Mr Palmer, confined indoors with nothing to do, declares '**Sir John is as stupid as the weather**', for not having a billiard room in the house. After Frank Churchill has left Highbury, Emma Woodhouse examines her own '**sensation of listlessness, weariness, stupidity, this disinclination to sit down and employ myself, this feeling of everything's being dull and insipid about the house!**' She does not mean she has suddenly lost her intelligence; rather that her usual high spirits have been momentarily dulled. Anne Elliot wearies of the **elegant stupidity** of the parties favoured by her father and sister and even Elizabeth Bennet's cynical remark, as she is about to set off for Kent, that '**stupid men are the only ones worth knowing after all**', refers rather to the stupefaction than the silliness of Mr Collins's company, though these defects may certainly be thought of as closely intertwined.

Dull-witted, unresponsive, half-asleep (her usual state, in fact) is what Lady Bertram means when she says, '**Fanny, you must do something to keep me awake. Fetch the cards. I feel so very stupid.**' The point is that on this occasion even she is aware of an extraordinary degree of *ennui* pervading the whole house, after the excitements of the ball the previous night. Henry Tilney, too, builds on the meaning of unresponsive and slow-witted when he says, in reply to Catherine's naive assumption that gentlemen are too clever to read novels: '**The person, be it gentleman or lady, who has not pleasure in a good novel, must be intolerably stupid.**'

This study of the abstract concepts in Jane Austen's vocabulary ends, as it began, with *Northanger Abbey*, her novel most concerned with the proper use of language. On this subject, the author finds a mouthpiece in Henry Tilney. By abusing their detractors, Henry reinforces what his narrator has already claimed for novels in general: that they, more than any other literary productions, are **work in which the greatest powers of the mind are displayed, in which the most thorough knowledge of human nature, the happiest delineation of its varieties, the liveliest effusions of wit and humour are conveyed to the world in the best chosen language.** This may not apply to every novel in the world, but it certainly applies to Jane Austen's.

Select Bibliography

Austen, Jane, *The Novels of Jane Austen* edited by R.W. Chapman (Oxford University Press, 1967) including Chapman, R.W. 'Miss Austen's English' in Volume 1, *Sense and Sensibility.*

Austen, Jane, *The Cambridge Edition of the Works of Jane Austen* edited by Janet Todd *et al* (Cambridge University Press, 2005) including Mandal, Anthony, 'Language' in Volume 9, *Jane Austen in Context.*

Austen, Jane, *Jane Austen's Letters* edited by Deirdre Le Faye (Oxford University Press, 1995).

Austen-Leigh, J.E. *et al*, *A Memoir of Jane Austen and other Family Recollections,* edited by Kathryn Sutherland (Oxford University Press, 2002).

Bradbrook, Frank W., *Jane Austen and her Predecessors* (Cambridge University Press, 1966).

Collins, Irene, *Jane Austen, the Parson's Daughter* (Hambledon Press, 1998).

Crabb, George, *English Synonymes* (Harper & Brothers, 1917, revised edition).

Hardy, Barbara, *A Reading of Jane Austen* (The Athlone Press, 1979).

Harman, Claire, *Jane's Fame* (Canongate Books, 2009).

Johnson, Samuel, *A Dictionary of the English Language* (1755).

Knox-Shaw, Peter, *Jane Austen and the Enlightenment* (Cambridge University Press, 2004).

Lascelles, Mary, *Jane Austen and her Art* (Oxford University Press, 1939).

Lewis, C.S., *Studies in Words* (Cambridge University Press, 1960).

Liddell, Robert, *The Novels of Jane Austen* (Longmans, 1963).

Lodge, David, *Language of Fiction* (Routledge and Kegan Paul, 1966).

Oxford English Dictionary (Oxford University Press).

Phillips, K.C., *Jane Austen's English* (Andre Deutsch, 1970).

Piozzi, Hester Lynch, *British Synonymy* (P. Byrne, 1794).

Southam, B.C., *Jane Austen's Literary Manuscripts* (Oxford University Press, 1954).

Stokes, Myra, *The Language of Jane Austen* (Macmillan, 1991).

Tandon, Bharat, *Jane Austen and the Morality of Conversation*, (Anthem Press, 2003).

Tave, Stuart M., *Some Words of Jane Austen* (University of Chicago Press, 1973).

Tomalin, Claire, *Jane Austen: a Life* (Viking, 1997).